# ENGAGING PRIMITIVE ANXIETIES OF THE EMERGING SELF

# ENGAGING PRIMITIVE ANXIETIES OF THE EMERGING SELF

## The Legacy of Frances Tustin

edited by

*Howard B. Levine*
*and David G. Power*

Routledge
Taylor & Francis Group
LONDON AND NEW YORK

First published 2017 by Karnac Books Ltd.

2 Park Square, Milton Park, Abingdon, Oxfordshire OX14 4RN
52 Vanderbilt Avenue, New York, NY 10017

*Routledge is an imprint of the Taylor & Francis Group, an informa business*

First issued in hardback 2019



British Library Cataloguing in Publication Data

A C.I.P. for this book is available from the British Library

ISBN 978-1-78220-297-4 (pbk)
ISBN 978-0-367-32434-6 (pbk)

Edited, designed and produced by The Studio Publishing Services Ltd
www.publishingservicesuk.co.uk
email: studio@publishingservicesuk.co.uk

*CONTENTS*

## *ABOUT THE EDITORS AND CONTRIBUTORS*

**Vincenzo Bonaminio**, PhD, is a training and supervising analyst and full member of the Italian Psychoanalytic Society, Adjunct Professor at "Sapienza", University of Rome, Director of the "Winnicott-Centro", Rome, Director of the *i*W Winnicott Institute, a Training Course in Child and Adolescent Psychoanalytic Psychotherapy and in private psychoanalytic practice (adult and child) in Rome. He is on the European Editorial Board of the *International Journal of Psychoanalysis* and has been Vice-President and Chair of the Programme Committee of the European Psychoanalytic Federation (EPF). He is Co-Editor of *Richard e Piggle* and the psychoanalytic series of books entitled "Psicoanalisi Contemporanea". In 2001, he was awarded the Fifth International Frances Tustin Memorial Prize and Lecture and in 2009, the Thirteenth International Frances Tustin Memorial Prize and Lecture. He has published extensively and presented papers in Italian and English at many national and international psychoanalytic congresses and is the author of the book *Nas margens de mundos infinitos . . .": A presença do analista e do analisando no espaço transicional em uma perspectiva contemporânea do pensamento de Winnicott* (Rio de Janeiro, Brazil, 2010).

**Paulo Duarte Guimarães Filho** is a training, supervising, child and adult analyst of the Brazilian Psychoanalytic Society of São Paulo, where he organized and was the Chair of the Study and Research Group of Pervasive Developmental Disorders. He has been interested in clinical and neurobiological aspects of autistic spectrum disorders and epistemological issues in psychoanalysis, having written several papers on these topics. He also participated in the Committee of Conceptual Research and in the New Initiative Funding Committee of IPA. Recently, he has studied links between psychoanalysis and Peirce's philosophy, writing papers about Peirce and Bion and Peirce and Winnicott.

**Joshua Durban** is a training and supervising child and adult psychoanalyst and teacher at the Israeli Psychoanalytic Society and Institute, Jerusalem, and a faculty member of Sackler School of Medicine, Tel-Aviv University, The Psychotherapy Program. He works in private psychoanalytic practice in Tel-Aviv with ASD and psychotic children and adults. He is the founder of the Israeli Psychoanalytic Inter-Disciplinary Forum for the study of ASD.

**Judy K. Eekhoff** is an IPA certified training and supervising psychoanalyst and a licensed child psychologist. She has a private practice in Seattle, Washington, where she also teaches, writes, and consults. She is a full faculty member of Northwestern Psychoanalytic Society & Institute, of the Seattle Psychoanalytic Society and Institute, and of COR Northwest Family Development Center. Dr Eekhoff is on the editorial board of the *American Journal of Psychoanalysis*.

**Ofra Eshel** is a faculty member, and training and supervising analyst of the Israel Psychoanalytic Society and a member of the International Psychoanalytical Association (IPA); co-founder, former coordinator, and faculty member of the Program of Psychoanalytic Psychotherapy for Advanced Psychotherapists at the Israel Psychoanalytic Society, and of the Israel Winnicott Center, and she is on the advisory board of the International Winnicott Association (IWA); founder and head of the post-graduate track "Independent Psychoanalysis: Radical Breakthroughs" (2016) at the advanced studies of the Program of Psychotherapy, Sackler Faculty of Medicine, Tel-Aviv University. She is the book review editor of *Sihot-Dialogue, Israel Journal of Psychotherapy*.

Her papers were published in psychoanalytic journals and presented at national and international conferences. She was a visiting scholar at the Psychoanalytic Institute of North California (PINC, San Francisco, in 2013), received the Leonard J. Comess Fund grant at the New Center for Psychoanalysis (NCP, Los Angeles, 2011), the David Hammond grant at the Massachusetts Institute for Psychoanalysis (MIP, Boston, 2016), and awarded the 2013 Frances Tustin Memorial Prize. She was featured in 2012 in *Globes* (Israel's financial newspaper and magazine) as the sixteenth of the fifty most influential women in Israel. She is in private practice in Tel-Aviv, Israel.

**Celia Fix Korbivcher** is a training, and supervising analyst and child analyst from the Brazilian Psychoanalytic Society of São Paulo. Dr Korbivcher has published several papers in Brazilian and international journals, including the *International Journal of Psychoanalysis*. She has authored a book, *Autistic Transformations. Bion´s Theory and Autistic Phenomena*, published in Portuguese in 2010 by Imago Ed. and in English in 2013 by Karnac. In 2004, she received the First International Parthenope Thalamo Bion Prize and, in 2005, the Ninth Frances Tustin Memorial Prize.

**Howard B. Levine**, a former member of the Board of Directors of the IPA, is on the faculty at the Psychoanalytic Institute of New England East (PINE), the editorial Board of the *International Journal of Psychoanalysis* and *Psychoanalytic Inquiry*, and in private practice in Brookline, MA. He is a member of the Contemporary Freudian Society, the Newport Psychoanalytic Institute, and a founding member of the Group for the Study of Psychoanalytic Process (GSPP) and the Boston Group for Psychoanalytic Studies (BGPS). He has authored numerous articles, book chapters, and reviews on psychoanalytic process and technique, intersubjectivity, the treatment of primitive personality disorders, and the consequences and treatment of early trauma and childhood sexual abuse. He is the editor of *Adult Analysis and Childhood Sexual Abuse* (Analytic Press, 1990); co-editor (with Lawrence Brown) of *Growth and Turbulence in the Container/Contained* (Routledge, 2013); (with Gail Reed and Dominique Scarfone) of *Unrepresented States and the Construction of Meaning* (Karnac, 2013); (with Gail Reed) *Responses to Freud's Screen Memories Paper* (Karnac, 2014); (with Giuseppe Civitarese) *The W. R. Bion Tradition* (Karnac, 2015); (with

Jose Junqueira de Mattos and Gisele Brito) *Bion in Brazil* (Karnac, forthcoming).

**Riccardo Lombardi** is a training and supervising analyst of the Italian Psychoanalytic Society (SPI) and the author of several papers on the body–mind relation, time, psychosis, and other severe mental disturbances, which have been published in the leading psychoanalytic journals. He has a full-time private practice in Rome. He is the author of the book *Formless Infinity. Clinical Explorations of Matte Blanco and Bion* (London, Routledge, 2014).

**Bernd Nissen** is a psychoanalyst and training analyst in the DPV (IPA) in Berlin and editor of several books, among other subjects, on hypochondria (2003), autistoid phenomena (2006), emerging of mental elements (2009), and processes of transformations (2012). He has published many contributions on pathological organisations, autistoid dynamics, hypochondria, perversion, and theory of science, among other topics. He is also Co-editor of the *Jahrbuch der Psychoanalyse.*

**Anna Oliva De Cesarei** is a training and supervising analyst at the Italian Psychoanalytic Society and an expert in child and adolescent psychoanalysis. She lives and works in Brescia, in North Italy and has published many papers about precocious trauma and problems connected to the sense of existence and about the difficulty in structuring a psychic scene. In 2010, she published the book, *Searching for the Thread of Life. Primitive Identifications and Narcissistic Structure of the Character.*

**Lía Pistiner de Cortiñas** is a training analyst and full member of the Argentine Psychoanalytical Society (SAP) and fellow of the International Psychoanalytical Association (IPA). She is the author of many books and papers, including *The Aesthetic Dimension of the Mind, Variations on a Theme of Bion* (London, Karnac, 2009); *On Mental Growth, Bion's Ideas that Transform the Psychoanalytic Clinical Practice* (Buenos Aires, 2011, Ed. Biebel (to be published in English by Karnac)); "Science and fiction in the psychoanalytical field", a chapter in *Bion Today,* edited by C. Mawson, (London, Karnac); *Autismo. Una Perspectiva Psicoanalitica* (Buenos Aires, 2015); "Transcending the caesura: the road towards insight"; a paper in *Building on Bion:*

*Branches* (London, Jessica Kingsley, 2003); a contributor to the Bion section of *The Edinburgh International Encyclopedia of Psychoanalysis* (Edinburgh: Edinburgh University Press, 2007).

**David G. Power** is a founding member of the Boston Group for Psychoanalytic Studies and Past President, supervisory and teaching analyst at the Massachusetts Institute for Psychoanalysis. He maintains a private practice in psychoanalysis, psychotherapy, and supervision in Cambridge, Massachusetts.

**Annie Reiner** is a senior faculty member and training analyst at the Psychoanalytic Center of California (PCC) in Los Angeles. Her work was profoundly influenced by the ideas of Wilfred Bion, with whom she studied briefly in the 1970s. Her writings appear in numerous journals and anthologies, and she is editor of a new book called, *Of Things Invisible To Mortal Sight: A Celebration of the Work of James S. Grotstein* (Karnac, 2016). The most recent book of her own work is *Bion and Being: Passion and the Creative Mind* (Karnac, 2012), which examines Bion's concept of O in its philosophical and theological aspects, as well as through the artistic works of poets and authors. Dr Reiner is also an accomplished poet, playwright, and painter, with four books of poems, a book of short stories, and six children's books, which she also illustrated. She practices and supervises in Beverly Hills, California.

**Alina Schellekes** is a clinical psychologist and a training and supervising psychoanalyst of the Israeli Psychoanalytic Society. She teaches and supervises at the Israeli Psychoanalytic Society and at the Tel-Aviv University Program of Psychotherapy, where she is the founder and head of the Primitive Mental States track. In 2006, she received Honorary Mention in the Phyllis Meadow Award in New York for excellence in psychoanalytical writing. In November 2008, she received in Los Angeles the Twelfth Tustin International Prize for her paper: "The dread of falling and dissolving". She is a senior clinical psychologist at Brill Mental Health Center, Tel Aviv and in private clinical practice in Qiryat Ono, Israel. Her main topic of interest, both in her teaching and in her publications, is the study of primitive mental states.

**David Simpson** is a training and supervising psychoanalyst at the British Psychoanalytic Association, and a Fellow of the British Psychoanalytic Society. He is an honorary consultant psychiatrist at the Tavistock Clinic London where he was Director of Child and Adolescent Psychiatric Training and honorary senior lecturer at University College Medical School, and was co-chair of the Autism Workshop and Learning Disabilities Service. His interests include the childhood roots of adult difficulties and intergenerational transmission.

# Introduction

*David G. Power*

Non-neurotic states of mind and the mental processes that characterize them are of great interest for contemporary psychoanalysis. Weakened capacities to represent one's mental life, difficulties with symbolization, reliance on evacuation, erasure, and foreclosure, as well as other direct forms of discharge to manage psychic distress, and activation of annihilatory levels of anxiety, all present the practicing analyst with significant challenges in creating an analytic process, managing and maintaining an analytic frame, and dealing with the countertransference. Patients who present with these difficulties place great demands on the analyst to be a lively, engaging presence, to be flexible and spontaneous, to trust in and rely on reverie, despite profound challenges to the analyst's own representational capacities, and to be willing to employ these capacities in the service of assisting patients' efforts to "weave psychic patches" in response to holes or tears in the psyche. The task nowadays is often one of helping to fill in psychic voids, where representation of experience is absent or weak, and less often one of simply uncovering repressed, conflictually laden, but symbolically represented, content (Levine, et al., 2013; Mitrani, 1995; Roussillon, 2011).

These difficulties, both conceptual and technical, are especially highlighted in psychoanalytic work with patients who demonstrate a variety of autistic disturbances, whether they are formally diagnosed as autistic, or on the Asperger's spectrum, or described as manifesting autistic states or barriers (Klein, 1980, Tustin, 1986). Although the differences between these various types of clinical presentations may be vast, important similiarities arise from the fact that, for each, endogenous autosensuousness (Tustin, 1992, p. 18) dominates mental life to an extent that mental development is endangered by the limit that sensory life places on the growth of subjectivity. Said slightly differently, in all these disorders, sensory life becomes an obstacle to, rather than a springboard for, emotional growth and psychological development.

The chapters in this volume represent some of the latest attempts to push psychoanalytic thinking into areas far from its original Freudian origins, continuing lines of exploration into the earliest beginnings of psychic life, of the relationship between the sensory world and the psychic, of pre-object mental life, and of the birth of symbolic capacities in the infant–mother dyad. These continuing psychoanalytic explorations now give us a thoroughly convincing picture of the deeply intersubjective nature of the human psyche and the necessity of an engaged, "other mind" to incubate and nurture the growth of the infant's mental development. Without this engagement, unconscious in many respects, what Williams (2007) described as the achievement of establishing a mind is threatened and hampered, leaving the developing person vulnerable to ". . . what is essentially a reflexive existence" (p. 408).

Strangely, recognition of the unique contribution that a psychoanalytic approach has to offer for the understanding of what are now termed "autistic spectrum disorders" (ASD) has steadily eroded in recent years, despite the burgeoning sophistication of analytic thinking about the etiology and treatment of these disorders. This erosion is perhaps especially noticeable in the USA, where psychoanalytic approaches to the treatment of patients presenting with various biologically based disorders have also suffered a similar fate. But, as several contributors to this volume note, the erroneous dismissal of psychoanalytic treatment with respect to autistic spectrum disorders is also evident internationally. (See, for instance, comments by Bonaminio and Duarte, this volume.) At the same time, many writers have noted the increasing incidence of persons diagnosed with ASD. While the reasons for this increase are unclear and still being debated, the burgeoning number of these patients places inexorable demands on our field for more sophisticated, thoughtful, and effective treatments aimed not simply at behavioral change and social integration (important as these goals are, particularly at the more extreme end of the spectrum), but at fostering and promoting growth in the patient's internal, psychic worlds and overall personality functioning. These latter challenges are ones that a distinctly psychoanalytic understanding, and the treatment approaches that arise from it, are uniquely capable of meeting.

As the present volume illustrates, psychoanalytic approaches add richness and depth when approaching patients with these puzzling and demanding clinical presentations and often, especially in the more complicated cases and where these disorders are manifest in childhood, are supported by, collaborate with, and interdigitate with a variety of other treatments. Within these integrated frameworks of treatment, the essential contribution of psychoanalytic interventions is toward the growth of the mind, the capacity for representation and symbolic thought, and the development of that complex mental and emotional framework that we recognize as characterizing personhood, announced by the presence of a true subjectivity that can be expressed in words, feelings, and thoughts, as well as the capacity to enter into emotionally involved relationships with others (see also Duarte's discussion of the social brain, this volume). Frances Tustin, a true pioneer in applying psychoanalytic thinking to childhood autism and what she later termed "psychogenic autism and autistic barriers in non autistic adults", stated our task this way:

> The essential quality of any method used for psychotic children should be to help them towards humanness. For most of the time, they feel that they are God's animals or things. The ordinariness of being a human being is not available to them. (quoted in Grotstein, 1997, p. 269)

The chapters in this volume were all inspired by the groundbreaking work and creative contributions of Tustin, a clinician with an astounding capacity to enter into the often closed and sensory dominated world of autistic children. Tustin emerged from her clinical forays with fresh, revealing insights into what might otherwise appear to be perplexing and meaningless behaviors and her insights have fostered a body of increasingly sophisticated elaborations by others of her original work.[1]

Trained in the Kleinian tradition in England and analyzed for many years by Wilfred Bion, Tustin's work can be seen as an extension of these traditions (Kleinian and Bionian), furthering and developing their interest in how a capacity to symbolize develops, how structures necessary for "thinking thoughts" come into being, and in the important role of phantasy in the overall development and maintenance of the psyche. Furthermore, her work on autism and autistic defenses can be understood as continuing the interest of others, especially Bion, on the relationship between the object's absence, the capacity to recognize and tolerate this absence, and the eventual development of thought born from the capacity to discriminate real gratification from hallucination.

Many of Tustin's most important contributions belong to a line of investigations originating with Esther Bick and which also includes the work of Donald Meltzer and his colleagues. Although strongly influenced by Klein and Bion, Tustin differed with them in crucial ways, as did Bick and Meltzer. In particular, Bick, Meltzer, and Tustin did not believe that recognition of the object's separateness, and its availability as a container to be projected into, was present for the infant from birth. In their view, projective identification was not initially possible for the infant because there was no innate conception of internal space. Through their investigations, they conceptualized a stage prior to the paranoid–schizoid that had to be successfully traversed in order for the processes of splitting and projective identification to be possible. At this very early stage, container–contained functions are not yet available.

Bick's observational studies of early infants and their caregivers gave rise to several concepts which are foundational to the psychoanalytic understanding of autism and autistic barriers. She pointed to the importance for the infant of skin-to-skin contact, conceptualizing that the infant is subject to states of feeling held together by skin contact with the mother or states of falling apart when this contact is missing.[2] Both states are passively experienced, since the infant feels no sense of inherent agency in its own cohesion. Bick (1968) wrote,

> . . . in its most primitive form the parts of the personality are felt to have no binding force amongst themselves and must therefore be held together in a way that is experienced by them passively, by the skin functioning as a boundary. (p. 484)

These states of feeling held together are accompanied by feelings of security, calmness, and safety, while the states of falling apart give rise to terrifying states of annihilatory anxiety, fears of spilling endlessly into space, and dissolution (in her contribution, Korbivcher describes these unintegrated states and their clinical presentations and offers us a careful analysis of how these states manifest in analytic work, their impact on the analyst, and their relationship both to Tustin's concept of autistic objects and to Bion's theory of transformations). In Bick's view, the actual external object is crucial to the infant's psychological safety since there is, as yet, no capacity to fill its absence through hallucinatory solutions. The first object of introjection at this stage is the skin-to-skin contact, experienced and introjected in its function as a containing boundary. In this early period, the physical and the psychological are conceptualized as indistinguishable (one is reminded here of Freud's dictum "The ego is first and foremost a bodily ego"), and the self and other are indistinguishable as well (in fact, these terms lose their meaning at this level of experience). We can notice in Bick's description this direct equivalence between the physical and the psychological, the material and the immaterial, inner and outer reality, self and other.

The successful introjection of this primary object and its capacity to provide boundedness lays the early groundwork, the nascent framework, for a capacity for containment of experience. What was passively experienced can, through introjection of the object's function, become an active capacity. We can immediately appreciate the intersubjective nature of this process, its dependence on careful attunement of the carer with the infant, and its primary importance for beginning the process of what Bion would describe as the capacity to think thoughts. What we think of as the capacities to represent experience and to symbolize find their early roots here, and these capacities flourish and grow, or fail and wither, depending on the vicissitudes of these early interchanges and their introjection.

Along with boundedness, still felt passively and as a combined somatic–psychic experience, there evolves a beginning sense of space divided by the membrane initially made possible by skin-to-skin contact, giving rise now to what Bick called a psychic skin.

The introjection of this primary object as a containing function allows there now to be, psychologically, a skin enfolding the psyche, and, thus, for a beginning sense of space that can hold things. This is a primary, foundational experience and is an achievement that has to be worked for and accomplished by the infant–carer dyad. With a beginning sense of internal and external space now available to the infant, the capacity to take in other objects and their functions, the mental processes of ingestion, digestion, and evacuation, and the ability to communicate to and affect another through projective identification are all increasingly possible.

But what happens if this process goes awry? In the absence of introjecting the boundaried/containing function of the primary object, Bick believed the infant searched for a substitute by which it could attempt to hold itself together (whether we see this as a defense against annihilatory anxieties or as an attempt to grow and move forward is debatable. Compare, for instance, the papers by Durban and Lombardi in this volume). There is great ingenuity evident in the forms these substitutes can take, ranging from muscular tightening and rigidity to overdevelopment of ideational capacities, but, despite their ingenious diversity, they share in common a quality of pseudo independence and compensation. Bick labeled them secondary skin formations, a term meant to highlight the fact that, regardless of the objective nature of this compensatory activity, its central subjective function was sensory–binding.

The processes Bick observed, and the problems stemming from their having gone awry, were further developed by Meltzer and his colleagues (Meltzer et al., 1975) in their study of autistic children. Spatiality becomes a crucial limiting factor in their view. Without a sense of interiority, their own or the object's, identificatory processes remain at a level analogous to early skin-to-skin contact. Rather than evolving cycles of projective and introjective identification that would serve to push forward development of a mental apparatus and capacities for psychic representation, adhesive identification prevails. Where autistic processes dominate, projection into a contained space (Bion's container–contained) is not available either for defensive or developmental reasons, and adhesive maneuvers hold sway. Various manifestations of sticking onto the surface of the object prevail, and, in their more obvious forms, can be readily observed (see Pistiner's case of Mariela, this volume). Other more subtle forms of adhesive identification can be quite difficult to recognize, especially in those patients who present with autistic barriers but whose functioning otherwise displays a wider range of capacity for symbolization. In these latter cases, the analyst's countertransference and evolving subjective experience of the patient are the surest source for their recognition. An example of this challenge and of its resolution through recourse to the analyst's experience can be seen in Eekhoff's lengthy case discussion.

In Tustin's understanding, the infant fated to become autistic is exposed prematurely[3] to recognition of the mother as a physically separate object and because this recognition is experienced as developmentally premature (from the standpoint of the infant's experience) it is felt as a violent rupture of the physical intactness of the infant itself, opening a hole through which the infant's existence can pour out never-endingly. Tustin's image for this process, again from the infant's perspective, was that the removal of the nipple tore off with it the infant's mouth. That is to say, the shock of prematurely recognizing physical separateness (metaphorically, the removal of the nipple from the mouth and the physical space between infant and mother created by this action) is experienced by the infant somato-psychically (a physical tearing of the nascent self through which existence spills out). Part of the traumatic impact of this experience stems from what is *not* experienced—the infant fails to subjectively appropriate possession of an orifice with which it can, increasingly under its own control, regulate movements into and out of itself in congress with the object world. Without this sense of voluntary closing and opening, but with a sense of traumatic injury instead, psychic emergency measures ensue aimed at plugging this "black hole". It is the objects and actions clung to and repeated as emergency measures and attempts at repair that Tustin called "autistic objects" and "autistic shapes". Both terms denote a turning toward sensory experience as a means of blocking the wound and providing a seal to protect the endangered self. Along with attempting to plug the black hole, these sensory preoccupations psychically obliterate the awareness of separateness and, in this way, they substitute for object relatedness rather than promote it. Thus, unlike transitional objects, autistic objects and autistic shapes do not facilitate a path toward object relations, but instead block or even erase this path. Said more simply, in Tustin's view, the autistic object or shape substitutes for the object rather than fostering its gradual and tolerable recognition as separate, thus derailing the development of true object relatedness that would follow on from this evolving recognition. With respect to the object's absence, in these states, faith in the object withers and hopes for its return vanish.

The process described by Tustin subverts the development of thought, representational capacities, and symbolization because it short-circuits the ability to recognize and tolerate the absence of the object and the frustration that accompanies this absence. There is no representation of an absent other, not even a hallucinated other, and, consequently, no mental evolution toward a capacity for bearing absence via recourse to phantasy and thought. In Winnicott's terms, there is no transitional space within which objects can be found/created. As others have pointed out, this short-circuiting of the processes for thinking leads to a flattened psychic spatiality, a spatiality that tends toward the two dimensional and away from the growth of an internal space in which phantasy and thought can gestate. There is an atrophy of identificatory processes such that adhesive pseudo-relatedness dominates and mimicry and various forms of adopting physical/sensory aspects of the other are prominent.[4] Durban, in this volume, offers us a lengthy case example of this process, which he terms mantling and which he sees as especially obstructive in the phase of treatment during which there is forward analytic movement and the patient is beginning to emerge from her autistic shell. For Durban, this process, the opposite of the dismantling[5] processes described by Meltzer and colleagues (1975) is an avoidant and defensive maneuver by the patient aimed at warding off the anxiety generated by forward development. Durban illustrates how a psychoanalytically sensitive, careful, but still actively interpretative stance can gradually interrupt this defensive maneuver and support a resumption of forward movement and lessen the need for clinging to autistic defenses.

Lombardi, also in this volume, offers a quite different view of this same process for us to consider. Reviewing several of Tustin's published clinical accounts, Lombardi sees the patient's effort to mimic or drape himself with attributes of the analyst as part of the emerging process itself, rather than as a defensive reaction to it. Stressing the developmentally forward trajectory of this mimicry rather than its defensive purpose, Lombardi draws our attention to:

> . . . the child's creative effort in attempting to construct a realistic corporeal reference (with hair, ear, nose, etc.) so as to approach a first conscious perception of the existence of his own body, within whose limits he might be able to recognize himself. (p. 103)

For Lombardi, the patient is striving to reverse a severe dissociation between mind and body, a dissociation that limits the capacity to develop the mind further. This striving is toward greater integration between mind and body rather than defensively aimed at blocking out the other. For Lombardi the demand on the analyst is for recognition of these nascent attempts to recognize and, thereby, begin to appropriate the personal, sensorial reality of the body.

Similar issues are raised in Eekhoff's contribution. Discussing her treatment of an adult patient who showed evidence of autistic-like enclaves, Eekhoff comments on the need to recognize and interpret, albeit with analytic sensitivity, her patient's use of mimicry and twinning so as to separate out defensive repetition from the nascent emergence of vitality and genuine expressions of aliveness. In Eekhoff's work, we see recognition of the potential of forward movement inherent in mimicry, similar to Lombardi's perspective. She suggests we view these movements as steps toward taking in the analyst as a first psychic "center of gravity", crucial and necessary steps given the absence of any sense of internal containment that can serve to hold the patient together. As such, they serve a positive function while offering the ever present danger of becoming an avoidance and impasse in the treatment.

In Eekhoff, Schellekes, and Eshel, we see highly skilled and sensitive clinicians working with Tustin's ideas and concepts in ways that extend and elaborate them for wider clinical use. Tustin (1986) herself was comfortable with this "rippling out" of her ideas to include the not formally autistic patient. These wider applications were given impetus by S. Klein's work as well (Klein, 1980). So, we see Eekhoff applying these ideas to work with patients who could be thought of as on the narcissistic or schizoid spectrum, while Schellekes uses Tustin's formulations to enrich our understanding of certain hypochondriacal presentations.

Likewise, De Cesarei describes her careful work with a patient who is on what she terms the "narcissism–autism bipolarity", a concept she employs to describe patients in whom a "dissociated, undifferentiated autistically encapsulated structure is overlaid by a more 'normal' looking pseudo-neurotic layer of functioning". Nissen applies Tustin's thinking to what he calls "autistoid organizations", severe states in patients who are not constitutionally autistic but in whom he observes an "absence of projective identification because the hope of a containing object has been abandoned". In Reiner's discussion of Beckett and his relationship to Bion, we find a thoughtful contemplation on the simultaneously destructive, and yet also creative, outcome of early failures in containment by the object. In discussing Beckett's life and work, we hear an analyst–writer's meditation on both the pain and suffering that arose from Beckett's experience of autistic phenomena in himself as well as his genius in attempting to represent the experiences they give rise to in his characters. All of these writers show the richness and fertility offered by expanding Tustin's original creative insights to understand clinical situations that, on first appearance, might seem unrelated to the problems of autism.

Yet, our efforts to extend these discoveries into newer and newer areas raise questions we must seriously consider. How far can we take these concepts from the original source of their discovery? What are the limits beyond which these concepts lose their original meaningfulness and, when we reach those limits, do we need to consider a more fundamental redefinition and reconceptualization of their meaning?

Eshel, for instance, gives us a lengthy clinical example in which she demonstrates the usefulness of Winnicott's (1963) ideas as presented in "Fear of breakdown" and subsequently illustrated by his wife Clare Winnicott (1980). Eshel draws inspiration from Tustin's (as well as Grotstein's) concept of "black holes" but takes care to redefine the term. In her beautifully rendered clinical exposition, she redefines the term "black hole" as

> an interpersonal phenomenon regarding less disturbed individuals, whose interpersonal and intersubjective psychic space is dominated by a central object which is experienced essentially as a black hole. Thus, they are either gripped by its enormous, compelling pull, or are petrified in their interpersonal psychic space out of fear of being pulled over its edge. My usage of this term differs from Tustin's and Grotstein's formulations of the black hole, which describe the nature of internal mental space in primitive mental disorders resulting from an infantile catastrophe of very early separateness from the primal mother. Unlike these authors, I apply the astrophysical black hole metaphorically to an interpersonal phenomenon. I use it to illustrate the nature of the fundamental experience of emotional closeness, love, and intimate relationships of individuals, who otherwise generally

> function in their social and professional life. This black hole experience in the interpersonal psychic space is caused mainly by the impact of a psychically "dead" parent, particularly the impact of the psychically "dead mother" (Andre Green's 1986 concept) and her deadening world of blank bereavement, depression and deadness on her child. (p. 45)

What are the implications of extending the black hole concept in this fashion? What began with Tustin as a description of subjectively perceived, traumatically induced bodily damage (the mouth torn away with the nipple) becomes now an interpersonal and intersubjective phenomenon. The experience Eshel is describing seems much further along the continuum of object recognition and so it now includes a much more object related dimension, most especially the presence of an absence, an object akin to, as Eshel tells us, the "dead mother" in Green's (1986) work. Eshel is quite explicit in her redefinition of the concept as referring to an interpersonal and intersubjective experience of the object rather than as a description of internal mental space. Eshel's black hole seems to be the presence of an absence, albeit a traumatically experienced one presumably accompanied by phantasy. If so, we can see that the black hole concept has come a long way from its origin as a description characterizing the experience of an early infant who perceives himself damaged by loss of a body part in proximity with an object not yet sufficiently recognized as a physically separate other. Recall that this latter, original description described an experience that prevented the development of internal space, phantasy, and object relatedness. The absence of part of the self has become the absence of a presence, or the presence of an absence.

Of related interest is Eshel's use of Winnicott in describing the requirements placed on the analysis and the analyst in dealing with these early traumatic situations. Winnicott features prominently in a number of this volume's chapters, an interesting fact given that Tustin discovered Winnicott's work relatively late in the development of her own ideas.[6] According to Spensley (1995), she felt there was great harmony between their views, and clearly many of our contributors also find in Winnicott a set of ideas compatible with Tustin's contributions.

In Eshel's work we have an eloquent example of Winnicott's view that the early trauma has to be revived, re-experienced (perhaps more accurately said as "experienced for the first time") and lived through in the presence of an analyst who survives (she would add that the analyst's at-one-ment with this experience of reliving is crucial, a process she terms "withnessing"). This perspective rests heavily on the insistent working in the patient of an effort to re-experience the original trauma in the present so as to master it (integrate it into a now competent enough ego) and thereby relegate it to the past (allowing for a traumatic past to be established and experienced as separate from the present). As she notes, citing Hernandez (1998), this perspective of Winnicott's is a creative re-working of Freud's idea that a repressed memory acts to regain consciousness. In Eshel's perspective (and Winnicott's) this press toward consciousness occurs in the presence of an object, and, in fact, occurs because of the object's "compelling pull" (p. 45). Is this not a long way from a black hole that needs to be plugged via recourse to non-human, non-symbolic (i.e., autistic) objects in order that the trauma suffered by the premature recognition of separateness from the object be prevented? Are we seeing again here the tension noted earlier between autistic phenomena seen as primarily defensive and avoidant or seen as faltering steps toward developmental repair of early trauma? Does this use of the term "black hole" suggest that phantasy plays a prominent role psychically in these conditions?

The issue of phantasy and the use of autistic defences is a complex and controversial one. Grotstein took up this issue in a paper at the first Frances Tustin Memorial conference (Grotstein, 1997). In his view, Tustin moved too far away from Klein's view on the fundamental role of phantasy in structuring all mental life, even the mental life of the autistic patients Tustin was working to understand. Where Tustin saw a "black hole", a void, and absence of representation, Grotstein saw a phantasy of a "black hole", and a set of related phantasies about the two dimensional nature of the object. For Grotstein, the important contributions of Bick, Meltzer, and Tustin lay in their explication of phantasy life characterizing the earliest stages of primitive mental life, the earliest stages of Klein's paranoid–schizoid stage, rather than in their argument for a separate stage of mental life prior to the paranoid–schizoid. In this early paranoid–schizoid stage, he argued, the object can still be recognized, is three dimensional, and projective mechanisms are employed. To account for the observations of phenomena such as adhesive identification, he suggests that this early stage is characterized by a dual track in which the infant experiences the object as both separate and not separate.

> By dual track, I infer that the infant is born with a simultaneous experience of separateness from the very beginning and continuing on one track and experiences continuing primary identification on another track. Thus, in the autistic stage of adhesive identification, the infant is experimenting with his/her capacity to de-differentiate back into autistic sanctuary (back into track one) and, therefore, appear to be autistic *vis-à-vis* the object, and, at the same time, is developing confidence in his/her skin's capacity to delineate his/her relationship with the external world (Grotstein, 1980, pp. 503–504).[7]

In his contribution to this volume, Simpson revisits questions about the relationship between autistic states, autistic mechanisms, and unconscious phantasy life, as well as the relationship between autistic phenomena and the paranoid–schizoid stage of psychic development. In his view, autistic states defend against unconscious phantasy and imply a profound inhibition in curiosity about the object (an object recognizably separate from birth). Simpson argues that autistic states should be seen as one manifestation of the more general phenomena of psychic retreats.

The increasing recognition that the infant has some capacity to recognize the object as separate from the beginning (Stern, 1985), the development of the concept of psychological autism (Tustin, 1993), and the application of Tustin's ideas to understand clinical situations clearly outside of the Asperger's spectrum, require us to deal with aspects of mental functioning in which phantasy is both present and also lacking, and in which symbolic capacities and their absence co-exist and interact in complicated and challenging ways. A number of the clinical examples described in this volume show how phantasy life and its absence can seem to run parallel to each other, or how represented and symbolically meaningful fantasy life can become infused with a heightened preoccupation with physical sensation, thus blurring the distinction between what is potentially interpretable by the analyst and what is essentially a turning away from the symbolic toward a sensation based and, hence, unrepresented mode of experience devoid of interpretable meaning. This interweaving of phantasy and non-phantasy, of symbolized and non-symbolized, makes for difficult clinical moments in which the analyst might discover in himself a misleading tendency to attribute more meaning to content than is ultimately warranted. What can appear to be meaningful might instead be the camouflaged presence of a sensory dominated area of mental life. As several writers here discover, and recount for us, the most reliable recourse in these situations is often a return to one's own immediate experience.

The psychoanalytic study of autism, and the light it sheds on the clinical phenomena variously termed autistic barriers, autistic enclaves, autistic encapsulations, or autistoid organizations, continues to fulfill its promise of relevance for the clinical understanding of a wide range of primitive mental states.

Of this relevance, Li Causi wrote:

> Dismantling, employment of mindlessness, impairment of temporal and spatial concepts are observable in ordinary and ill people alike. These formulations are invaluable in thinking about highly disturbed patients, omnipotent and destructive, where the concepts of narcissistic organization, minute splitting mechanisms, interpretation of attacks on the objects do not seem to describe fully, or usefully, their experience. Basic mental functions have been attacked, or lost, or perhaps never developed (Li Causi, 2010, p. 82)

If we take seriously Bion's idea that life is made meaningful by a process of psychic appropriation of experience through dreaming, then employing our psychoanalytic instruments to understand those states of mind where sensation invades the "theatre for generating meaning" (Meltzer, 2009) holds hope for understanding not only those sensation dominated states themselves, but any mental state in which representation and symbolization are threatened.

## *Notes*

1. See particularly in this regard, the work of Anne Alvarez, Judith Mitrani, and Maria Rhode.
2. The importance of skin-to-skin contact in the early development of ego functions has been further elaborated by Anzieu (1989).
3. The extent to which this recognition is premature is determined by both constitutional hyperreactivity and environmental factors.
4. See Power (2016) for a particularly detailed clinical case in which this occurs with the analyst's voice.

5. Dismantling refers to a passive falling into mindlessness brought about by suspending attention and allowing the senses to be dispersed and unintegrated. A passive letting go of any holding together of the senses, dismantling works against the organized, complex and multifaceted appreciation of an object.
6. Most probably, this was an artifact of the British training model at that time.
7. See also Roussillon (2011), who argues that the opening of a gap between the relationship to the object and the use of the object allows for "The subjective appropriation of the work of symbolization . . . [and] will enable the secret of symbolization to be gradually revealed" (p. 182).

## *References*


Anzieu, D. (1989). *The Skin Ego*. New Haven, CT: Yale University Press.

Bick, E. (1968). The experience of the skin in early object-relations. *International Journal of Psychoanalysis, 49*: 484–486.

Green, A. (1986). The dead mother. In: *On Private Madness* (pp. 142–173). London: Hogarth Press.

Grotstein, J. S. (1980). A proposed revision of the psychoanalytic concept of primitive mental states: an introduction to a new psychoanalytic metapsychology. *Contemporary Psychoanalysis, 16*: 479–546.

Grotstein, J. S. (1997). One pilgrim's progress: notes on Frances Tustin's contributions to the psychoanalytic conception of autism. In: T. Mitrani & J. L. Mitrani (Eds.), *Encounters with Autistic States: A Memorial Tribute to Frances Tustin* (pp. 257–290). Northvale, NJ: Jason Aronson.

Hernandez, M. (1998). Winnicott's "Fear of breakdown": on and beyond trauma. *Diacritics, 28*: 134–143.

Klein, S. (1980). Autistic phenomena in neurotic patients. *International Journal of Psychoanalysis, 61*(3): 395–401.

Levine, H. B., Reed, G. S., & Scarfone, D. (2013). *Unrepresented Mental States and the Construction of Meaning: Clinical and Theoretical Contributions*. London: Karnac.

Li Causi, R. (2010). Dimensionality, adhesive identification, splitting. In: M. Harris (Ed.), *A Meltzer Reader: Selections from the Writings of Donald Meltzer* (pp. 81–82). London: Karnac.

Meltzer, D. (2009). *Dream-Life: A Re-Examination of the Psychoanalytic Theory and Technique*. London: Karnac.

Meltzer, D., Bremner, J., Hoxter, S., Weddell, D., & Wittenberg, I. (1975). *Explorations in Autism*. London: Karnac.

Mitrani, J. L. (1995). Toward an understanding of unmentalized experience. *Psychoanalytic Quarterly*, *64*: 68–112.
Power, D. (2016). The use of the analyst as autistic shape. *International Journal of Psychoanalysis*, *97*: 975–998.
Roussillon, R. (2011). *Primitive Agony and Symbolization*. London: Karnac.
Spensley, S. (1995). *Frances Tustin: Makers of Modern Psychotherapy*. New York: Routledge.
Stern, D. (1985). *The Interpersonal World of the Infant*. New York: Basic Books.
Tustin, F. (1986). *Autistic Barriers in Neurotic Patients*. New Haven, CT: Yale University Press.
Tustin, F. (1992). *Autistic States in Children* (revised edn). London: Routledge.
Tustin, F. (1993). On psychogenic autism. *Psychoanalytic Inquiry*, *13*: 34–41.
Williams, P. (2007). The body and the mind (including of the analyst) in the treatment of a psychotic state: some reflections. *Psychoanalytic Dialogues*, *17*(3): 401–409.
Winnicott, C. (1980). Fear of breakdown: a clinical example. *International Journal of Psychoanalysis*, *61*: 351–357.
Winnicott, D. W. (1963). Fear of breakdown. In: G. Kohon (Ed.), *The British School of Psychoanalysis. The Independent Tradition* (pp. 173–182). London: Free Association Books, 1986. Reprinted in: C. Winnicott, R. Shepherd, & M. Davis (Eds.), *Psycho-analytic Explorations* (pp. 87–95). Cambridge, MA: Harvard University Press, 1989.

*CHAPTER ONE*

# Finding a center of gravity via proximity with the analyst

*Judy K. Eekhoff*

> "I have created a shell out of assessment and the stories I make from it. It is what holds me, what gives me a center of gravity. When you expose me, I feel flayed open and back to a place where no one exists, not me, not you . . . nothing. You cannot possibly know what that feels like—reality comes in and nothing is there"
>
> (An analytic patient)

## *Center of gravity*

Psychoanalytic technique has changed. Some of this change involves learning to work with increasingly more and more difficult to reach patients (Joseph, 1989). British object relations clinicians working with autistic and post autistic states such as Tustin (1972, 1987), Meltzer (1975a,b), Bion (1967, 1987), Mitrani (1992, 1998, 2001, 2011), and Alvarez (1992, 2012) following Freud and Klein, have greatly influenced this shift. They, along with others, shifted psychoanalytic technique away from a one-person exploration of repressed states towards a two-person exploration of evolving internal and external relationships. The analytic task is no longer limited to being an observer who interprets. Instead, the analyst has become a participant observer who engages. Transference and countertransference have taken on new meanings as a result and are used differently than once was true. When working with autistic or post autistic states, this change is particularly relevant. The analyst's countertransference becomes a guide.

Primordial states of suspension require different responses from the analyst than other more developed states of mind. A patient "in suspension" is difficult to engage. In order for there to be any kind of engagement, the analyst may allow herself to become an extension of the patient. More accurately, she becomes aware of how she is being used in this primordial sense. Just as an autistic child borrows the body of the analyst, using her hand to pick up a toy, so do emerging adult patients "borrow" via mimicry aspects of the analyst in order to have an experience of existence. In this way, they exist outside of themselves, in the space and substance of others, finding their centers of gravity in whomever they are with. If the analyst does not notice this, the work will come to an impasse as even their speech reflects the way in which they use borrowed symbols to communicate.

In working with neurotic patients who have autistic barriers, it is easy to focus on their neurosis and not the autistic mechanisms that underlie them. Without an analyst or another person to recognize the somatic and concrete nature of these autistic barriers, these patients will be caught in a cycle of mimicry, imitation, obsession, and somatization that seems unchangeable. They will be stuck to their bright minds and adhered to obsessive attempts at perfection. Their autistic barriers foreclose recognition of the other, so they cling to the analyst sensually while being relatively unaware of their own or their analyst's psychic existence. In clinging sensually, they are lost to the emotional connection that makes learning from experience possible.

Boundary confusions enable these patients to identify and become whomever they are with at a cost to their own capacity for identification. Tustin (1972, 1980, 1987) calls this process of fusing with whoever they are with entanglement. Gaddini (1969) explores the imitation with which they create themselves. Eekhoff (2011, 2013) examines the value these mimicries serve upon emergence. Living in a forever now, without a sense of life and a future, these psychically dead patients are protected from the awareness of their own mortality. Time and space are not relevant. When the patient begins to use the analyst as something other than an extension of herself, time begins, space opens up, and death becomes inevitable. One must be alive in order to die.

Emergence from fusion with everything and everyone makes these patients painfully aware of having been lost in space and suspended in time. This suspension makes all experience of equal weight, without gravity to enable foregrounding and backgrounding aspects of experience. Such equalizing of experiences renders decision making difficult, if not impossible. All details are equally important so how can one choose? Emergence involves the classification and subordination of information, so as to create differing values or weight for each experience. Emergence, where awareness is heightened, is terrifying, disorganizing, and shame provoking. It might include severe psychosomatic life-threatening illness or psychotic states. Emergent states, when emotion is unleashed and separateness is encountered, are states of terror, horror, and rage, which *the analyst will feel first*. Emergent states feel intolerable.

The proximity of the analyst does not help to mediate these states initially. The proximity, of which the patient has been unaware, places the analyst in a helpless and vulnerable position of being witness to the ongoing psychic annihilation without being able to have an impact on it. Being witness is not exactly what happens, for the analyst is personally affected by her experience of observing the patient. Instead of projecting into the analyst, the patient, via massive projection outside of the analyst, spills, falls, dissolves, or floats into infinite psychic space. The patient disperses. Nothing seems to hold the patient together. The analyst can only observe, without being able to reach or gather, hold or contain the patient. This helpless vulnerability and willingness to be personally impacted begins to affect the patient. The patient's own observer notices the existence and proximity of another. To see and observe is to be alive.

Being proximate to someone who has suspended growth and development via the extreme methods of dismantling sensory perceptions so as to interfere not only with symbolic processing but with emotional relationship is also narcissistically wounding. Initially, the experience for the analyst is one of disbelief and then of horror. The analyst must persevere and survive not being used or related to (Winnicott, 1969) in order to get to know the unique and individual essence of the patient. In getting to know the patient, the analyst will learn things about herself she would rather not know.

Surviving as a person and as an analyst is particularly difficult when working with such primordial states in our patients. To analyze a patient who does not seem to be psychically present seems impossible. To be treated as if one does not exist is deeply troubling. Equally troubling is to experience the absent patient. What appears absent in the patient is a subjective sense of self that includes a center that would hold emotional experience and make meaning of it. The missing center, in phantasy, has been projected out into the universe in search of a container and has found none. Without the sense of a containing other, there can be no introjection of an internal containing function. There is no center of gravity.

Without internal containment, these patients have phantasies of falling, spilling, dissolving, or evaporating. These states of flowing-over-at-oneness (Tustin, 1972, 1981, 1987) where the patient projects everything that might have been inside out into infinite space resemble, but are not the same as, Freud's description of primary narcissism. Patients often describe themselves as being a sieve or having an empty core. The empty hole is contained within a shell created from concrete sensory experiences that have been "dismantled" and re-configured as something else. The analyst's proximity enables her to gather these dispersed bits. Meltzer (1975b) has called this "gathering the transference."

Patients who are difficult to reach struggle with overwhelming sensual experience that interferes with their introjective processes. Equivalency replaces identification as a primitive method of relationship (Tustin, 1987, p. 127). Equivalency clouds the mind, much as fog surrounds and blurs objects, wiping out differentiations that mark opportunities for identification. Equivalency distorts the senses, turning the perceptual body into an obstacle that distorts and interferes with development. Equivalency places the center of gravity outside the body instead of inside. An internal center of gravity anchors the subjective perceptual experience in a reality that informs, teaches, and facilitates identifications, which accumulate and form a sense of identity. Bion (1962, p. 8) calls this process alpha function.

Although focused on sensate experiences, these patients demonstrate very little awareness of being in their bodies. Without being in their bodies, they have no ongoing sense of being (Winnicott) or existing as a solid person. Without this sense of solidity, they have no center to hold them to the ground so as to have a "floor for experience" (Eaton, 2015). They psychically exist in space or in the bodies of those around them, without recognizing the other as being important or even present. In an analysis, they exist in the analyst even while they appear to not be in relationship or to benefit from transference interpretations. Existence in the analyst occurs with a primordial sensory experience of adhesive equivalency and could more accurately be described as existing on the analyst or as the analyst.

What appears to be emotional awareness of another person is a visual acuity about appearances, an auditory sensitivity that recognizes every tone, timbre, and rhythm of the analyst's voice, and a tactile awareness that distracts from an accumulated storehouse of experience. Since these patients are often bright, they are able to use their observations for a parody of relationship. When these observations are put together into stories, it might appear that the patient is attuned and in relationship with others. This is a mirage.

These emergent sensory states are an elaboration of the tactile world of autistic states (Meltzer, 1975b; Tustin, 1987). They are not yet connected to the imaginary world of symbol formation, of individuation, and of separateness from their internal and external objects. They are not relational except in the most primordial sense. Bion gives us a way to think about these sensory states of emergence when he writes about beta elements. He writes (1962, p. 8),

> If there are only beta-elements, which cannot be made unconscious, there can be no repression, suppression, or learning. This creates the impression that the patient is incapable of discrimination. He cannot be unaware of any single sensory stimulus: yet such hypersensitivity is not contact with reality.

Evacuation of beta elements occurs with emergence. In a pure autistic state, the sensory can be pleasurable and self-protective (Meltzer, 1975a). As projection of the sensory begins, the internal and external objects become confused. The analyst's reverie and alpha function are used to bring reality to the relationship and the accompanying turbulence is extreme.

Many, but not all, of the patients I have seen clinically who suffer from what appears to be post autistic states have suffered a premature separation from their mothers at birth either through medical necessity or through their mother's suffering of severe postpartum depression or psychosis. They could also have had a genetic vulnerability, but I am unable to know this. These patients have recovered from what seems to have been their infantile psychogenic autism and are able to lead productive professional lives. However, they continue to suffer from post autistic states that severely inhibit their relational abilities.

I believe that a therapeutic alliance begins with proximity that invokes somatic and sensory associations within the analyst. The analyst must notice and identify with these sensory experiences so as to find the patient. Once found, these identifications evoke or call forth the patient (Alvarez, 2012). These identifications are vitalizing. Initially, it might appear that the analyst is identifying something foreign to the patient and using identification to fantasize or dream into being a person who is not there. It might also appear that, in introjectively identifying with the patient, I am no longer following Bion's admonition to use no memory, no desire, and no understanding (1970, pp. 41–54), which, according to De Bianchedi (1991), would also imply no identification.

On the contrary, I believe that such identification comes from an evolution in the analyst of the non-represented experience of the hour and enables me as an analyst to deepen my reverie and my receptivity and make a connection with my difficult to reach patient. In deepening my receptivity, I am left in the world of my imagination and illusions of connection, since these patients are under-developed relationally. This identification reflects the degree to which I, as the analyst, am dependent upon my patient. It is related to Bion's (1970, p. 28) idea of at-one-ment and its evolution.

The psychic proximity of the analyst, which is manifested physically and emotionally, consciously and unconsciously, enables her to communicate via her body and her emotions, first with herself, then with her patient. Her eyes, voice, and facial expressions demonstrate the impact of the patient upon her. In this way, the analyst's introjective identification communicates openness and receptivity as well as a presence that calls forth the lost soul (Alvarez, 2012; Scarfone, 2015). Calling forth or going in and getting the patient eventually includes putting into language the experience of introjective identification (Ferenczi, 1952). Introjective identification is the vehicle for becoming a center of gravity.

Since, without substance, there is no reliable shape, no inside or outside, there also is no phantasy of the inside of an object. Attachment to the surface of the other is evidence for existence while interest in mental processes is minimal. It then becomes necessary for the analyst to find within herself identifications that link with the patient. It requires a simultaneous experience of self and other such as is found in integration of the paranoid–schizoid and depressive positions.

In this sense, the analyst becomes the center of gravity for the patient, enabling a floor for experience to develop. Emerging patients have their center of gravity in the space outside themselves and in the analyst. It is as if their experience of their skin (Bick, 1968, 1986) or their skin ego (Anzieu, 1985) cannot hold them together. These patients experience themselves as non-solid and so cannot count on themselves to "be there". Even when they have a sense of themselves, they seemingly have no means of gathering themselves together or in experiencing how these aspects of themselves relate to each other. It is as if their very molecules lack cohesion and disperse. All aspects of themselves have equal weight, making decision making difficult.

Their center of gravity is found in space, not in substance. Until they become more solid in phantasy, they cannot have an internal psychic center of gravity to stabilize them and to allow them to have a foreground and a background of experience. Equilibrium is not possible without a sense of solidity. Being embodied with an internal center of gravity makes having a floor for experience possible. A floor for experience helps build a subjective sense of self and other.

I want to introduce a patient who taught me this. Since working with her, I have been able to recognize these somatic defenses in other patients and understand that their seeming lack of anxiety, affective expression, and valued relationships are side effects of a deeper process of a suspended existence that must be understood if a therapeutic alliance is to be formed.

Let me tell you about Kay and, more specifically, since I have written about her before (Eekhoff, 2010, 2011), of her emergence.

## *Kay*

I worked with Kay for many years, first as a once a week therapy patient, later in analysis. Initially, she came to see me because she said something was missing in her. Reportedly, everything she did she carefully thought about and planned. As a result, she was a successful professional with a graduate degree, intelligent and competent. Her husband was successful and "good". She was "politically correct", with two children and a beautifully decorated home and garden. She was a soft-spoken, gentle, well-groomed woman who read all the best books. She had a large social network, entertained regularly, had hobbies, and no one knew "she preferred to be alone". She had the life she had because she wanted to appear normal. She reported feeling nothing for her husband or her children. When she went to the cinema, she saw a lot of people loving and having all kinds of emotions. She reportedly did not have those. She came to me because she believed she did not know how to love.

Kay was initially a good storyteller, describing her observations in such a way as to amuse and entertain me. Her vocabulary was extensive and contained many words about emotion. I was not moved by them, in spite of their difficult content. Her stories seemed flat to me. Soon I realized that her words were borrowed, not embodied. Her stories were meaningless and interpreting them as if they were symbolic was an error. The same was true about her dreams, which were plentiful. At times, I doubted that she knew the difference between storytelling, dreaming, and hallucinating. Nothing seemed to have meaning except as it enhanced her image.

I alone was dissatisfied with the therapy. She felt she was a good patient and I was a good therapist. She told me she got a lot out of her work with me. She had an amazing tolerance for silence, speaking only if she thought I was uncomfortable. When she began using the couch, she could be silent for whole sessions, unable to read my posture and facial expressions, and did not mind. Later, she described that time as "agreeable, with me floating a foot above your couch". I remember it as her lying there, as if in a coffin, unmoving, hands crossed upon her chest, seemingly not even breathing.

She was extremely compliant, precise about details, observant about every change in what I wore, how I looked, the content of my office. These changes did not bother her; they were just noticed. In fact, looking back, nothing seemed to bother her. She was primarily indifferent to most things, which made her appear calm and unruffled, in spite of her obsessive preoccupation with appearances. I came to understand that this indifference represented the way in which all experience was of equal weight to her and did not last beyond the moment.

She cared a lot about appearing normal and so her cooking, her decorating, her dress and make-up were perfect. Details were all equally important to her. She reported that when she went to restaurants, she never knew what to order and so always ordered what someone else did. I believe this was because the perceived equivalency of her choices made decision making impossible. She received accolades for her work, but felt she was fooling others by "copying the good workers and stealing everybody else's ideas".

When I was with her, I did not recognize myself. That is, I could not feel any emotions, other than a very mild curiosity. I found this disturbing. I was often overly busy in my mind and came to recognize this cognitive busyness as a defense against something I did not begin to know. I felt no projective identification and initially could find little with which to connect with her. I really could not imagine why she kept coming or what I gave her. We were the same age, yet she seemed ageless. Through the years, I aged; she did not. She maintained her youthful body, her clear expressionless eyes, her smooth and unlined face and her unruffled mien no matter what happened to her.

Until her emergence from her sensate cocoon, she was unruffled by any life event or by anything I said or did. I simply could not reach her. No one did. Transference interpretations were met with some variation of, "If you say so." I first recognized her as emerging when I began to recognize bits and pieces of myself in her—gestures, phrases, and tones of speech. As she emerged somewhat more, she became quite dramatic, but again she was not "in" her drama. She was merely being a better actress than when I met her. I had given her more sophisticated material for mimicry. During this stage, I began to find myself more and more in her. This was extremely disturbing. I felt crazy and disoriented. When I attempted to interpret, she would agree and change, once again becoming whom she perceived I wanted. Today, I might think of this as my introjective identification with her very weak projective identifications.

In spite of this, she was a wonderful teacher for me. Once she learned that I was not interested in her stories about others, she began to describe herself. Her observational capacities meant that she could describe states with a detail I had not heard before. Although she did not seem to embody what she told me about herself, I learned that her descriptions were accurate. She did not have much of a contact barrier between inside and outside. Primary process material was presented as reality. Once named, it was gone forever unless I remembered and brought it back. The Freudian concept of repression did not seem to apply to her mental process of forgetting. She could not repress that which had never been thought. I had difficulty believing she could say something without thinking it.

After the fact, I came to think of these "lost experiences" as sensory rather than mental and, therefore, unable to be remembered. They were unrepresented (Levine et al., 2013) in spite of having been spoken. Perhaps these descriptions were of events that Scarfone would call re-presentations. They taught me much about her. I learned of her states of dissolving, falling forever, of floating in space, and of indifference to her experience or the experiences of others. She simply did not get upset about anything. In retrospect, this might also have been due to the fact that time was an immediate experience for her. Once past, the event was no more.

As her descriptions evolved, I became increasingly disturbed. I had never imagined such a barren internal world or such an artificial, superficial, unconnected life. It was not that she had an empty mind. Her mind was full to the brim, spilling with the details of her life, her observations, what she saw and read. She was extremely sensitive. She reported to me that the hardest thing about therapy, and then analysis, was that she had to speak first. She was usually silent and comfortable in the company of others, including her family. She spoke after figuring out what others thought and fed back to them some version of themselves.

As she emerged, I experienced immense rage, cruelty, and horror. I feared I could not help her. I feared I was making a terrible mistake and driving her crazy. I was flooded with corrosive doubt. Eventually, I felt terror I had never known before, terror that she would kill me, her children, and herself. I had been fooled by her stories in spite of not believing them or seemingly being moved by them. I had been perplexed by her dreaming as I did not think she symbolized, but borrowed symbols (Meltzer, 1975b). Could she be having borrowed dreams? None of her thoughts seemed to begin inside of her. Instead, everything she presented to me, from her movements, gestures, clothes, make-up and jewelry, stories, thoughts, and behaviour, were evoked by outside stimuli which she claimed as her own, just as she claimed and became me.

Whereas initially she created a perfect match with me, as she emerged, she demanded that I match her perfectly. Since this was impossible for me to do, I failed her again and again. She began to judge me harshly for my failures. At times, I sat still, barely breathing out of my attempt to reach her. Much as a mother often matches the breathing of her nursing infant, I found myself breathing with her. My failures were very frustrating for her, as they meant I was not perfect. They also meant that we were not equivalent. We were not identical, or even the same.

As she emerged, many illnesses occurred. I feared her health would deteriorate so she would die. A lung collapsed and required two surgeries. I wondered about the breathing in the office. Her back "went out"; her skin broke out into rashes, hives, and pimples. There were days when she could not get out of bed except to come to my office. Other days she sat in her rocking chair, rocking, and wondered how the days could pass so fast. Still she never missed a session. I felt that what I interpreted did no good at all. Again I wondered why she kept coming, perhaps unconsciously hoping she would stop. Just as she was going to many expert doctors for help with her ailments, I began to find consultants to help me find her. I felt comforted by whatever they said about her.

It was also about this time that her posture on the couch began to change. Rather than lying as a corpse in a coffin, hands crossed upon her chest, she began to move her hands. I soon learned to interpret these hand movements. For example, while telling me a dream, she would gesture, then stop, leaving her hand suspended in the air. The story of her dream would continue, but I came to recognize these suspensions as post autistic states of sensory dismantling (Meltzer, 1975b, p. 8). They were aspects of an obsessional attention that pushed all awareness of me away. At the time, I thought she was dissociating while still talking. Today, I would not call those states dissociation, although she was separating or disassociating her mind and her sensations. I would call them suspensions.

She would also put her hands together and move them apart in idiosyncratic gestures of union and separation. She would latch on to the thumb of her right hand and pull on it with her left, sometimes causing me to cringe in sympathy with the pain it might cause. She did not seem to feel pain. At other times, she would pinch her left hand with her right, telling me it made her feel present with me.

Again, I would cringe, although one day when she pinched herself, I had an image of a nursing baby pinching her mother's breast.

In the hour, I would interpret the moments when I felt I was not there in her experience. I marked, just by naming, the moments she psychically disappeared and was gone. These were two distinct states that felt very different. It seemed there was room in the session for only one of us at a time. We seemed to take turns. I described this to her. At first, she did not know what I was talking about. This experience was horrific to me. As I watched her "disappear" herself or me, I despaired of reaching her. I felt helpless and guilty for not helping. When I could no longer explain or describe, I used what Alvarez (2012, p. 12) has since called a vitalizing level of interpretation where I created the meaning. I feared that I was again making it up, giving her more material to mimic. Yet, I intuited I had to try to go in and get her (Eekhoff, 2015).

When I failed to be one with her and she could not find a perfect fit with me, she began to disintegrate. The first time I noticed this, it came after I had moved office space. Afterwards, I realized that she had attached sensually, not to me, but to my previous office. The move deeply affected her. As a result, she could not use her senses to attach to me. This was very different from the earlier suspensions. She was not angry with me but began to hallucinate. First, she entered my consulting room convinced that we had just met in the street. She wondered why I did not say hello, and how I got back so quickly since I was walking the opposite direction. Another time she thought I was attempting to strangle her. She leapt screaming from the couch, "Don't kill me," putting her hands to her neck to remove what she perceived to be my hands strangling her. Later, she thought someone else was in the room threatening me. When she sat up, she said, "It must be me."

This began, slowly over months, a presentation in the transference of her anger and disappointment in me. She was projecting. I celebrated this change silently. I felt she was beginning to experience herself and me as having an inside. The analysis began to feel like the analysis of a borderline woman, who alternated between clinging and claustrophobic fear of me. It was a very tumultuous time with door slamming, forgetting sessions, coming late, and veiled threats about killing me or herself. Once, she turned at the door of my consulting room and said, "If I ever come here when it is not my time, please do not let me in."

Still these states would alternate with the previous states of entanglement and fusion. When I spoke, she would cringe. When I was silent, she would weep silently. If I moved too fast, she would dissociate. These dissociations were experienced differently than the previous states of suspension. I was able to again mark these and later interpret them. Differentiating post autistic states from borderline states was not easy. I had to observe and "feel" her carefully. I had to listen to her replies to my interpretations and determine if she were mimicking or taking in whole, identifying or copying, integrating or incorporating. It was slow, painstaking work. I continually felt inadequate and despairing.

Worse still, as her psychic deadness changed and she came alive, the suffering I had previously felt was experienced in both of us. She was suffering, too. I could barely tolerate her suffering. I felt so cruel, so sadistic. I doubted psychoanalysis and myself. I wondered if she were not better off psychically dead and whether I should have encouraged her to end. She began physically to age and arrived at one session with her hair dyed a bright red. I was horrified. I began to want to get rid of her. Her concrete focusing on every minutia in life decreased, but there were no illusions to soften the edges of her experience.

These countertransference feelings were difficult and useful. I was able to use them for what felt more and more like analytic interpretations. The work progressed. The transitional space between us opened so there was more ambivalence and less black and white thinking. Her world began to take on color. Her sadness and grief were profound. Three times she set an end date and each time would cycle through all the previous levels of our work together; however, she was not grieving. I attempted to stay open to her leaving without completing the analysis.

The grief for me was great. I did not feel she was finished. Some of this was my own, for I had come to value her and her persistence in being what she called "a real woman". In spite of trying to work without memory and desire, I felt hope for her. Faith in the process returned to me. The faith and hope were also hers. There was separation between us at times. There were two people in the room. Two people in the room meant two centers of gravity. This meant that the center of gravity in the session could be the unknown, not the concrete details of her life.

I was no longer afraid that she would kill herself or me. We had more ability to collaborate and not just take turns. She had a center of gravity within her that made it possible to have a floor for her experience. Her experience with me was accumulating. She had attached to me, not as equivalent to her, but as a separate person. She felt dependent upon me, and this was interpretable, just as her indifference to me had been. As the indifference lessened, she began to be able to give different experiences differing values. She could make decisions. Her lack of grief could also be interpreted and so, as each date of proposed termination approached, it was changed.

Changing a termination date is not something I typically do and yet, letting her go and letting her stay seemed extremely important. We circled around each other, orbiting, with a gravitational pull that kept us separate and attached, separate and connected, not lost in space. Eventually, she began to feel and express gratitude. With gratitude, came grief over how she had treated me. She was appalled at how indifferent she had been to me, then superior to me, then dismissing of me, and so on through murderous rage, unspeakable terror of me, and finally horror as she stepped aside to observe herself behaving as she did. She was sorry for her threats and intimidations as well as for her clinging refusal to leave and let others have what she had.

She set a fourth date for termination. This time, as the months passed and the date approached, she grieved. She remembered the good times with me and reclaimed good times from her childhood. She grieved the premature loss of her innocence and re-indexed her life experiences in such a way as to give them meaning. Whereas, when she came to therapy, she believed she had been terribly abused as a child and unable to remember it, she now came to believe those fantasies were part of her resentment for not being believed about hallucinations she had had as a child. She had emerged from indifferent states in childhood.

She recalled her meanness and cruelty to her mother and children at school with sadness and shame. At the same time, she developed compassion for herself and humility. When finally she left me, both of us acknowledged that neither of us was perfect. There would always be more work to do. We could have done it better and faster and with more grace. However, our work together had been good enough. She was able to laugh and make fun of herself and me. She was able to miss me and still leave. She knew how to love.

## *Conclusion*

Psychoanalytic proximity includes, but is not limited to, the physical and emotional presence of the analyst in relation to the patient. Psychoanalytic proximity includes an analytic capacity to experience and name primordial states of being in such a way as to resonate with an unrepresented, yet present, emotional and sensate state of the patient. Such proximity involves courage to speak the unspeakable and faith in the animate enlivening capacity of human relationship. Whereas it includes being with the patient "without memory or desire", I believe it simultaneously involves a state of reverie that includes an understanding of knowing when to be absolutely still and open and when to "go in and get" the emerging patient. This reverie includes the analyst's introjective identification of the unformed and unrepresented potential for existing as a live and relational human being.

Emerging from autistic encapsulation is a painful and terrifying experience. Primitive anxieties, such as mimicry, psychic equivalency, suspension, and dismantling, which are simultaneously defenses against the reality of separateness, have previously functioned to protect the person from unbearable states of mind. These anxieties are simultaneously not defenses, but normal aspects of all development. With increased capacities for bearing pain, defenses against an awareness of existence are minimized. Tustin reminds us that treating these difficult to reach patients will take us to places where no normal person would wish to go. Although these primitive anxieties are always available for all of us, they are increasingly less necessary protections against the reality of separation as projective and introjective identifications develop.

Accompanying and analyzing these emerging patients begins with patient and analyst proximity. Proximity is a spatial and temporal condition that challenges the delusions of flowing-over-at-oneness. Subjectively, proximity is a perceptual sensate experience, not an emotional or cognitive experience. It is not a traditional transference relationship, but is relational. Psychoanalytic proximity is more emotional and empathic than sensate, yet the sensate is informative. Awareness of a live other's physical proximity is seemingly absent in autistic children. My experience with patients like Kay is that emotional awareness of the other comes and goes depending upon the stressors in life and in the moment of the analytic encounter. To be aware of proximity is to be aware of separateness. Such awareness is also, at times, lacking in neurotic patients who have an empty core and are difficult to reach.

Some neurotic patients experience states of mind in which they do not exist. Without a sense of existing there can be no awareness of the proximity of the analyst. For the analyst, being in the now without memory or desire is particularly difficult when the now of the patient is a delusional state of non-existence of both self and other. The analyst might, therefore, confuse clinging and adhesive second skin phenomenon for connection. The patient's flowing-over-at-oneness as a defense against the awareness of separateness creates a force field that evokes these primordial symbiotic processes in the analyst. This twinning experience enables the analyst to introjectively identify with the patient and to be emotionally proximate with her. Twinning experiences, although often nearly unbearable for the analyst, are more tolerable for the patient.

Proximity enables the analyst to introjectively identify with the patient. This introjection creates a space between the unmentalized aspects of the patient and the analyst, facilitating space for identification that enables mentalization and the emergence of the other as an object available for internalization by the patient. About such a state of being, Green (1973) says

> All that can be said of this metaphorical moment which suspends the inquiring function is that it can only be expressed in terms of being. Yet no knowledge arises from it, because it is itself the point at which knowledge can start. (p. 116)

Facilitating emergence means the analyst becomes a center of gravity, which provides a gathering point for the condensation and distillation of the lost self. To do this, she must allow herself to become an extension of the patient and to speak as if they were one. The patient's attachment becomes very concrete—a matter of proximity, of physical contact, not emotional intimacy. Proximity assures a sensate experience of surface-to-surface oneness, almost as if the two were one, but not quite. Meanwhile, the analyst is in multiple states at once, lending herself, suspending her own ego functions while using her reverie to invoke projections from the patient, with which she can introjectively identify. Once this happens, she has available within her the data with which to formulate a thought and to speak. I believe this is what Alvarez means by vitalizing interpretations.

In working deeply in a long-term analysis or with patients suffering on the autistic continuum, the analyst must become the unformed "I" of the patient in order for the patient to find his or her own subjective experience. This is not a cognitive task. We are back to the very essence of existence or being and engaged in a process of becoming. The analyst and the patient fuse so much as to lose the self-experience. This is new territory within psychoanalysis that Freud did not explore, but Tustin, Bion, Meltzer, Mitrani, Alvarez, and their followers have.

Emergence is difficult for both the patient and the analyst. The intensity of primitive states of horror, terror, and rage and the psychotic and autistic defenses against them create corrosive doubts about the value of our work. Patients suffer tremendously as they emerge. Analysts do, too. I will end with a quote from the patient I quoted at the beginning of this chapter. She said, "Before feeling gravity, you have to have a sense of existing. There is no gravity without existence. There is no sharing without having."

## *References*


Alvarez, A. (1992). *Live Company: Psychoanalytic Psychotherapy with Autistic, Borderline, Deprived, and Abused Children*. London: Routledge.

Alvarez, A. (2012). *The Thinking Heart: Three Levels of Psychoanalytic Therapy with Disturbed Children*. London: Routledge.

Anzieu, D. (1985). *The Skin Ego*. New Haven, CT: Yale University Press, 1989.

Bick, E. (1968). The experience of skin in early object relations. *International Journal of Psychoanalysis, 49*: 484–486.

Bick, E. (1986). Further considerations on the function of the skin in early object relations. *British Journal of Psychotherapy, 2*: 292–299.

Bion, W. R. (1962). *Learning from Experience*. London: Heinemann [reprinted London: Karnac, 1984].

Bion, W. R. (1967). *Second Thoughts: Selected Papers on Psychoanalysis*. New York: Jason Aronson.

Bion, W. R. (1970). *Attention and Interpretation*. London: Tavistock.

Bion, W. R. (1987). Making the best of a bad job. In: *Clinical Seminars and Four Papers* (pp. 247–257). Abingdon: Fleetwood Press.

De Bianchedi, E. T. (1991). Psychic change: the 'becoming' of an inquiry.

*International Journal of Psychoanalysis, 72*: 6–15.
Eaton, J. (2015). Building a floor for experience: a model for thinking about children's experience. In: N. Tracey (Ed.), *Transgenerational Trauma and the Aboriginal Preschool Child: Healing Through Intervention* (pp. 43–70). New York: Rowman and Littlefield.
Eekhoff, J. K. (2010). Between body and mind: transforming physical experience into psychic development in the clinical situation. Paper presented to Vancouver Psychoanalytic Society, Vancouver, BC, Canada.
Eekhoff, J. K. (2011). The value of pathological mimicry. Paper presented to Northwestern Psychoanalytic Society, Seattle, Washington.
Eekhoff, J. K. (2013). Infantile trauma, therapeutic impasses, and recovery. *American Journal of Psychoanalysis, 73*: 353–369.
Eekhoff, J. K. (2015). The silent transference: clinical reflections on Ferenczi, Klein, and Bion. *Canadian Journal of Psychoanalysis, 23*(1): 57–73.
Ferenczi, S. (1952). Introjection and transference. In: *First Contributions to Psychoanalysis*, E. Jones (Trans.) (pp. 35–93). New York: Brunner/Mazel.
Gaddini, E. (1969). On imitation. *International Journal of Psychoanalysis, 50*: 275–484.
Green, A. (1973). On negative capability—a critical review of W. R. Bion's Attention and Interpretation. *International Journal of Psychoanalysis, 54*: 115–119.
Levine, H. B., Reed, G. S., & Scarfone, D. (Eds.) (2013). *Unrepresented States and the Construction of Meaning: Clinical and Theoretical Contributions*. London: Karnac.
Meltzer, D. (1975a). Adhesive identification. *Contemporary Psychoanalysis, 11*: 289–310.
Meltzer, D. (1975b). *Explorations in Autism: A Psychoanalytic Study*. New York: Karnac.
Mitrani, J. L. (1992). On the survival function of autistic manoeuvres in adult patients. *International Journal of Psycho-Analysis, 73*: 549–559.
Mitrani, J. L. (1998). Unbearable ecstasy, reverence and awe, and the perpetuation of an "aesthetic conflict". *Psychoanalytic Quarterly, 67*: 102–127.
Mitrani, J. L. (2001). *Ordinary People and Extra-ordinary Protections*. Philadelphia, PA: Brunner-Routledge.
Mitrani, J. L. (2011). Trying to enter the long black branches: some technical extensions of the work of Frances Tustin for the analysis of autistic states in adults. *International Journal of Psychoanalysis, 92*: 1–22.
Scarfone, D. (2015). *The Unpast: The Actual Unconscious*. New York: The

Unconscious in Translation.
Tustin, F. (1972). *Autism and Childhood Psychosis.* London: Hogarth Press.
Tustin, F. (1980). Autistic objects. *International Review of Psycho-analysis, 7*: 27–40.
Tustin, F. (1981). *Autistic States in Children.* Boston, MA: Routledge & Kegan Paul.
Tustin, F. (1987). *Autistic Barriers in Neurotic Patients.* New Haven, CT: Yale University Press.
Winnicott, D. W. (1969). The use of an object. *International Journal of Psycho-analysis, 50*: 711–716.

CHAPTER TWO

# Daydreaming and hypochondria: when daydreaming goes wrong and hypochondria becomes an autistic retreat

*Alina Schellekes*

> "Since there was nothing at all I was certain of, since I needed to be provided at every instant with a new confirmation of my existence, nothing was in my very own, undoubted, sole possession . . . naturally I became unsure even [of] the thing nearest to me, my own body . . . I scarcely dared to move, certainly not to exercise, I remained weakly, I was amazed by everything I could still command as by miracle, for instance, my good digestion; that sufficed to lose it, and now the way was open to every sort of hypochondria"
>
> (Kafka, 1953[1919])

This short extract from Kafka's letter to his father is most evocative of the experience of loss of contact with one's body and of the ensuing need to achieve control over one's physical existence, through incessant awareness to body's manifestations and to any real or imagined physical dysfunction. Kafka's long standing mental investment in keeping the body safe culminated in a very special achievement: it is claimed (Drucker, 2002) that Kafka received the gold medal of the American Safety Society in 1912, because of his outstanding contributions to workplace safety, and in particular the invention of the modern safety helmet, commonly called a hard hat. Because of his innovation, substantially fewer steel workers were killed in industrial accidents. Ironically enough, his invention protected many people's heads, that body organ which Kafka himself could still use even when his body "remained rather short and weak" (Kafka, 1949).

In a letter to Ferenczi written in 1912, Freud mentioned that he had "always felt the obscurity in the question of hypochondria to be a disgraceful gap in our work" (Jones, 1955, p. 453). One hundred years later, we are not in a much better position, since it seems that the ambiguity and uncertainty inherent in the hypochondriac mode of being contaminate the study surrounding it (Lang, 2007). I think that this state is due to much confusion that exists regarding a clear-cut classification of hypochondria, which stems from the fact that it is both a feature in many psychiatric conditions and an entity in itself. Due to this confusion, many of the psychoanalytic writings on this topic (Bronstein, 2011; Meltzer, 1964; Rosenfeld, 1984) have attempted, with partial results, to make clearer distinctions between hypochondria, somatic delusion, psychosomatic states, and hysteria. For my present focus, I would limit myself only to a few remarks regarding this theoretical debate.

The main clinical distinction between hypochondria and psychosomatic states is that in the former a flooding and intense anxiety regarding the body is frequently present, while in the latter, such anxiety is usually absent. Moreover, the psychosomatic's mode of being has been extensively described as suppressing affect to such an extent that his affective life has been described as being alexithymic (Sifneos, 1973) or "concrete/operational" (Marty & de M'Uzan, 1963), terms used by the American and French schools, respectively, to describe the poverty of affect and fantasy. Since the hypochondriac's flooding, but unsymbolized, anxiety is so prevalent, hypochondria has been historically (Freud, 1893) classified as one of the types of actual neurosis, a term used by Freud to include intense physical and emotional states, such as neurasthenia, anxiety neurosis, and hypochondria. All these states are characterized by a high level of excitation that has not been processed and transformed into digestible mentation (Mitrani, 1995), as opposed to hysteria, which is considered to be the prototype of the neurotic symptom that embodies dense symbolism, in spite of its physical appearance. Put in simple and phenomenological words, the hypochondriac is flooded by body related anxiety, while the hysteric presents a physical symptom, rich with symbolic connotations, but accompanied by relative emotional indifference.

Although this debate is fascinating, it is much beyond the scope of this chapter, since my present interest is to focus on hypochondriac anxiety *per se* and its relation to excessive daydreaming. When I speak of anxiety in this context, I try to limit myself to conditions in which hypochondria neither achieves the status of a delusion, nor is it part of an organic disease, whether psychosomatic or not, but is, nevertheless, extremely disabling of one's ability to live physically and emotionally. Even in otherwise relatively well functioning personalities, the hypochondriac involvement with the body might become so extensive that, at its extremity, it can induce autistic-like withdrawals into a world of hypertrophied attention to one's sensations, where daydreaming disease and deterioration and the ensuing flooding anxiety become densely intermingled, creating a very painful and detached existence.

When working with hypochondriac patients, one of the striking clinical features is the extensive mental elaboration and detailed imagination about any possible harm to, or disease in, one's body, or, by proxy, in one's close relatives. One excessively indulges in self-observation and overvalues one's perception of the body, both of which are accompanied by the conviction of being ill and by disintegrating anxiety (Stolorow, 1979), that is not part of a somatic condition (Nissen, 2000). The hypochondriac imagines how every little sign of physical distress and every minor symptom will lead to catastrophic and lethal consequences. Many times, as I have seen with several patients, the imagined scenario includes almost a trance-like state of mind, in which the hypochondriac gets carried away into an elaborate fantasy of how he (or a very close person) will be diagnosed as gravely sick, how his organs will deteriorate, how days and nights will be spent in pain and anguish while undergoing medical treatments and prolonged hospitalizations, how lonely and frightful such states will be experienced. These daydreamed narratives, when employed excessively, acquire autistic features, as the hypochondriac sinks into a world governed by sensations, getting more and more detached from his surroundings and wailing/lamenting his miserable imagined existence that will befall him. Although flooding anxiety is often present, in my experience this type of daydreaming disease-related scenarios acquires many times an oneiric quality in which a visible contradiction exists between the frightening content of the hypochondriac fantasy and the affect and tone of voice that accompany the verbalization of the fantasy. In these instances, while imagining the expected somatic catastrophe, the melody of speech and the affect expressed are not always anxiety laden, but sometimes convey a sense of being carried away into a land of dreaming, full of masochistic painful stimulation. It is important to note that the essence of the hereby described daydream fantasy is not always accompanied by death anxiety proper (though, apparently, one would suspect that, since most imagined diseases are terminal), but, rather, by a rich imagery of the state of being ill, of suffering, of the body being invaded by malady, pain, and medical intrusive practices.[1] The masochistic component is evident in this imagery,[2] as the hypochondriac is both terrorized by his conviction of being ill and, at the same time, fascinated by, and immersed in, his bodily sensations; he is both anxious about all medical interventions and, simultaneously, solicits medical care and procedures for any vague or specific complaint (Barsky & Klerman, 1983). Thus, I propose that the hypochondriac ideation is a mixture of layers, some in which masochistic symbol-laden fantasies prevail and some in which the very sinking into and imagining physical sensations becomes a sort of "autistic shape" that lacks symbolic activity, thus creating an autistic sensations-related enclave.

This state of excessive detachment from reality, which is part of the hypochondriac ideation, has ancient roots in the history of the individual. Before proceeding to additional theoretical aspects, I would like to relate briefly to a clinical case that portrays some of the main points of my present discussion.

## *Iris*

My relation with Iris has been a very long one with multiple and complex facets. For the purpose of this chapter, I focus only on a few relevant issues that are pertinent to the topic of hypochondria and daydreaming, leaving aside many nuances that are part of Iris's rich personality and of our deep emotional relation over many meaningful years, that could potentially enrich our understanding of her, but all this is beyond my present scope. Iris, a professionally successful writer in her thirties, married with three children, contacted me when her eldest son was a few months old, due to terrible hypochondriac anxieties related to her small baby. She was devastated whenever the baby had any sign of physical distress and more so when he had any clear physical symptoms. Both of these were instantly experienced by Iris as grave symptoms heralding an incipient terminal disease or other physical catastrophes. In subsequent years, two more babies were born and, with all three children, she experienced the same degree of hypochondriac crises that would make her sink for days and nights into abyssal anxiety, while constructing elaborate daydreams about the imagined physical sensations and catastrophe that would befall herself and her children. These daydreams included rich details of future scenarios in which her children would become gravely ill, would suffer immensely both physically and emotionally, would undergo painful medical procedures, and would slowly deteriorate until the inevitable end. The imagination was less concerned with the danger of losing the child or with death *per se*, but much more with all the devitalizing bodily sensations and states that would precede death. Alternately, Iris would react to her own physical real or imagined symptoms with similar anxiety, the main content of which was rich imagining of sensations and symptoms and of how her children would become orphans, how much they would suffer; she would calculate various ages at which being an orphan might be more bearable and less devastating, hoping that she would have the chance to live until that age so that her children would not prematurely experience such a terrible loss.

In parallel to the extensive preoccupation with the diseased body, it soon struck me that this hypochondriac layer masked a very special relation to her live body, from which she seemed completely disconnected. Her physical appearance gave the impression that she had no interest in the way she looked. She was not physically neglected, but it seemed that her body was in a sort of suspended state, not really being experienced, except through possible disease. She showed little interest or pleasure in sex, would hardly pay any attention to clothes, to her haircut, and generally to having any pleasure from her body. Sometimes, I had the feeling that she lived in a sort of emotional blindness to her live body that I would call *a negative hypochondriasis*, so as to emphasize the lack of emotional investment in the details of the living and healthy body and the lack of experiencing her body as alive and full of vitality. This dual relation to her body became more and more striking, as it seemed to mirror a very deep and old schism in her emotional existence that gradually unfolded in analysis. On the one hand, she functioned relatively well in everything that her life required, though most of the time she was tired and lacking energy; on the other hand, she lived in a sort of daydreaming existence, slightly disconnected from the reality of her life, only superficially being involved with her significant others. She maintained few social relations, as her emotional energy was deeply involved either in this fantasying existence or in dealing with her extensive hypochondriac anxieties.

During our sessions, a very special presence of Iris began to preoccupy me. She was devoted to the analytic process, always came to the sessions, talked, brought quite rich material, but there was on many occasions some lack of focus, as if she was not totally present, as if some disconnection from reality kept her in a semi-dreamy state. Sometimes, she would slightly lose connection with time issues, or she would not notice any changes in my clinic that were noticed and reacted to by most of my patients, and on occasion she gave the feeling that my presence was a very important background, but that she was not really in contact with me on a deeper level. Moreover, for years she continued to be ambivalent towards me, as if never really knowing whether she was in the right place, many times fantasizing that this or that other analyst would certainly be a better place to be. She would openly and frequently describe how excited she felt when she imagined herself with another analyst, whom she came to know or heard about, but she never really considered leaving her analysis.

The daydreaming of better places, better families, better analysts alternated in the sessions with the description of her hypochondriac anxieties which attacked her frequently. Gradually, I became aware that, in spite of the terrifying content of her anxieties, often there was a daydreaming quality in the way she described them, as if she had been taken away into a world of fantasy, which she would not avoid. Her tone of voice also frequently became like a dreamy melody, speaking or slightly singing the imagined catastrophes, as if she also found some known, but unthought, gratification in the hypochondriac scenarios. At times, as if caught by some contagious disease, I found myself struggling with a sort of daydreaming state, in which I was slightly losing contact with Iris, bordering on the sensation one has in hypnogogic states. The most striking feature of these states of mine was that I became both aware of, and observed, my daydreaming, while simultaneously I could barely prevent its sharp intensity. It is important, in this context, to emphasize that such a state has little to do with free association, as the feeling is of being taken away and losing contact with both external *and* internal reality.

I have detailed these non-verbal, transferential intricacies as they became a tunnel through which we could gradually approach experientially some of the historic roots of Iris's emotional development. From a very early age, Iris experienced her parents as living in their own slightly disconnected world, being simultaneously loving towards her and narcissistically and sexually immersed with each other. It seems that her parents had been unaware of the impact and implications that their stormy involvement with each other, and considerable disconnection from real matters, had for Iris's fragile existence and developmental needs. Iris learned to disconnect herself from her internal reality and from what was experienced as a very invasive and flooding presence of her parents, which was far beyond her abilities to digest and understand.[3] Although such presence had evident exciting qualities, it simultaneously became a haunting presence. It seems that Iris developed all sorts of techniques to shut out her sensory channels so as to become disconnected both from her parents' flooding presence and from her own internal scene. During these times, she oscillated between excitation, anxiety, and confusion, all eventually culminating in her need to silence her own senses and to become immersed in a state of disconnection from her body. She gradually developed her fantasying abilities, which offered her a daydreaming envelope that protected her from unbearable realities.

While growing up, she became exposed to many separations and peregrinations that created much instability in her life and which, again, were beyond her abilities to contain. Due to her precocious ego development, whose damaging effects have been thoroughly described by many (Klein, 1930; Mitrani, 2007; Winnicott, 1962) and due to her high intelligence and wealth of abilities, she could adapt well enough, but she developed more and more strategies of disconnection: she would thoroughly engage in daydreaming, fantasying better parents and homes; she would deny frustrating or traumatic experiences, creating idealizing scenarios, or would eventually retreat into her own body, sinking into a world of hypersensitive reactivity to sensations, a sort of autistic shell of auto-sensuality (Tustin, 1990) that ultimately flooded her with hypochondriac anxiety. Thus, her exaggerated daydreaming and disconnecting abilities, which had been established early in her life, became both the carrier of her longstanding anxiety and the means to deny it through projection into the body. Simultaneously, in my understanding, through developing the hypochondriac anxieties and through daydreaming catastrophic scenarios, she maintained a very faithful relation with her early objects: she was both invaded by unbearable anxiety (as she had been since a very early age) in the form of experiencing her body as under attack by a terminal disease, and, at the same time, she maintained her disconnected emotional existence through daydreaming of both a catastrophic nature, such as in hypochondriac scenarios, and an idealized fantasized future, such as when daydreaming of better husbands or better analysts. In addition, I would say that the hypochondriac anxiety also connected her with her formerly denied/suspended body, even if in a distorted way, and to longings for being taken care of (Granek, 1989). Moreover, her hypersensitivity to any physical sign became, in my view, a mimicry of a displaced-unto-the-body longing for attentive care.

As is evident in Iris's case, the early experiences of many hypochondriac patients are, in my view, frequently colored by an object presence which was experienced as either too exciting or too invasive (or a mixture of both), whether in terms of its inconsistency or in terms of flooding the infant with stimuli which were beyond his containing and processing abilities.[4] The parent's ability to help the small child in processing and representing the many sensations he experiences, of whose importance Tustin talks so extensively (Tustin, 1981, 1990), is, thus, hindered, leaving the child in what she called "an agony of consciousness" due to premature or traumatic emotional separation from the object. Even when the object's presence seems quite devoted, its invasive quality is confusing and overwhelming as it usually lacks any boundaries, so that, for a child's mind, such an object presence is experienced as frightening and threatening his separate sense of self (Arlow & Brenner, 1969; Nissen, 2000; Skogstad, 2013; Williams, 2004). In such a state of invasion, the normal process of projecting one's unbearable sensations into the object is almost impossible, since the parent's ability to employ his alpha function is rather deficient and the omega function (the reversal of the alpha function: the parental object projecting his emotional needs into the child), which Williams (1997) speaks about, becomes the dominant one. When one is overwhelmed by internal unbearable and indigestible states of mind and by external confusing and flooding experiences, one develops various emotional tactics, as we all know, but the one I wish to emphasize here, as I tried to illustrate through Iris's case, is the development of a detached, almost dissociative, stance made possible by the construction of a private imaginary world, disconnected from reality and, apparently, from emotional proximity to the invasive object, which Meltzer called a "pseudo-contact barrier of the day dream" (Meltzer, 1983). The infant, thus, learns to disconnect through building imaginary worlds, wherein he finds comfort and illusionary control.

In this context, it is not surprising that frequently this excessive daydreaming quality of which I am talking generates, in later phases of development, fantastic scenarios of idealized places, wonderful persons and relationships, all imagined as blissful, conflict free zones of emotional serenity. These scenarios seem to mask a fantasized regressive oneness with the primary object, a "fantasized reversal of a calamity that has occurred and a restitution of an inner homeostasis that was disturbed years ago where a blissful unity with the all good mother of symbiosis" (Akhtar, 1996, p. 732) and infantile omnipotence would be possible. This fantasized reunion can become an excessive hope that, more often than not, creates heavy demands on real objects to fulfill this reunion. Such a state promotes the quality of keeping reality at a distance, living in the future, while the present becomes a continuous source of masochistic suffering.

One can be mistaken and think of these daydreams as a version of the family romance fantasy, but, in my view, they are of a much more primitive and pervasive nature, as they often become slightly regressive cocoons that enable one to retreat into imagined worlds of better times and better relations. The blissful imagined oneness with an ideal object, that is present in these fantasies, is quite similar to the quality of the timelessness experience (Hägglund, 2001; Levine, 2009; Schellekes, 2010, 2017), in which interpersonal differentiations are blurred, as are any distinctions between time dimensions: past, present, and future. When past experiences are traumatic and thoughts about future raise the potential of re-traumatization by expected frustrations and losses, the timelessness experience enables one to live temporarily in a state wherein time freezes in a sort of illusionary everlasting presence, thus negating the flow of time and the inevitability of losses and death. It is not surprising that many of the patients who tend to negate time dimensions and live in such timeless modalities achieve this through excessive daydreaming, which becomes an efficient primitive method for denying painful reality. I would suggest calling such excessive daydreaming a *daydreaming envelope*, functioning, in many ways, in a similar fashion to the envelopes described by Anzieu (Anzieu, 1989) and Houzel (1990).

In normal development, though fantasizing is a less mature mode of experiencing, expressing and modulating inner experience rather than abstract and symbolic thinking, it is an important and creative means on various levels. To name just a few of these levels, it might help in processing inner and outer experiences (Sugarman, 2008), it aids one in tolerating the object's absence, thus constituting a midpoint in the process of internalization, and it enables one to express ambitions and to anticipate important personal events (Lussheimer, 1954).

However, when fantasizing becomes excessive, it becomes what Winnicott named "fantasying", a dissociated addictive mental activity, keeping one in a state of distractibility and absentmindedness, absorbing much of one's emotional energy, but not necessarily enriching one's ability to think, to dream, and to be actively involved in life or, to put it in Winnicott's humoristic words: "nothing is likely to happen because of the fact that in the dissociated state so much is happening . . . and immediately, except that it does not happen at all" (Winniccott, 1971, p. 26). The omnipotent satisfaction inherent in the daydream thus becomes an additional obstacle to active involvement in life, as most real experiences face one with one's own and with others' limitations.

The above description portrays a situation in which excessive satisfying daydreaming activity might crystallize an effective defense against invasiveness. However, things are more complicated, as one never totally relinquishes one's relation to the object. The repetitive need to stay attached to the object is ever present, even if in disguised form. Thus, when the infant/child's mind is flooded by unbearable excitation or by erratic, painful, emotional experiences, often an "attachment to pain" (Aisenstein & Gibeault, 1991; Valenstein, 1973) develops. Put differently, rather than separating from the painful quality of the object's presence and rather than mourning this separation, in the hypochondriac's development one encounters an adhesive attachment to the painful physical and emotional qualities that had characterized the object's presence. In other words, in my opinion, the imagined pain and suffering that the hypochondriac so extensively fears becomes, through his elaborate attention to physical sensations and imagined scenarios of disease, a sort of psychic retreat (Steiner, 1993) into the body, wherein the imagined pain keeps alive the connection with the frustrating invasive object, who often becomes installed in the fantasy of the sick organ.

Thus, although apparently having been tormented by the object's confusing and invasive presence, one becomes the unconscious director of the hypochondriacal drama in which the object that has never really been mourned and integrated is ever kept alive through self-torment, embodied in the rich imagery of suffering and disease (see also Gutwinski, 1997). This imagery echoes the invasive aspects of the original emotional reality, that reality that had been experienced, but never became mentally assimilated. However, in the hypochondriac's subjective experience, he is the passive victim of the feared diseases that act in this scenario as a threatening concrete and somatic reality. In other words, in my view, the hypochondriac vicariously aims at distancing himself from unbearable emotional states, of both internal and external origin, by frequently developing, early in his development, excessive, disconnecting daydreaming propensities, which, sooner or later, also become the venue for daydreaming somatic catastrophes. Thus, the body and the elaborate preoccupation with his somatic states potentially could have become a screen against the possible intrusion of the object (Aisenstein & Gibeault, 1991).[5] However, the hypochondriac's incessant absorption with his body keeps him forever invaded by anxiety, thus never relinquishing close contact with his invasive anxiety-provoking internal objects, with what was meant to be expelled from the emotional sphere. Moreover, the state of being ill could be viewed as a somatic embodiment of an unconscious search for a particular role responsiveness (Sandler, 1976) on the part of the significant other/therapist. Put differently, the hypochondriac's awareness of every slight change in the functioning of the organs mirrors how he wishes the other would tune into him (Granek, 1989; Rosenman & Handelsman, 1978).

Nevertheless, things are even more complicated, since the early object relations of the hypochondriac were never solely frustrating and painful, but often an admixture of excitement and suffering, so that great confusion becomes the axis of one's experiences. Very relevant here is Rosenfeld's understanding of the genesis of hypochondria, as resulting from confusion related to deficiency in splitting mechanisms (Rosenfeld, 1958, 1964).[6] When such confusion prevails, suffering becomes a source of pleasure while erotic life becomes a source of suffering. Many times the hypochondriac becomes addicted to fantasized suffering, while having difficulties in enjoying his real erotic life. The frustrations experienced in his erotic life become an additional venue of suffering and a potential source for additional detachment and retreat into daydreaming, this time into rich scenarios of sexual arousal and romantic experiences with imaginary partners, who are fantasized as promising to rescue the hypochondriac from his real erotic life, which, more often than not, is kept under control and is maintained as a source of suffering. In other words, one can see how the hypochondriac's confusing link to the object as both exciting, frustrating, and pain inducing is maintained in such a complex and imprisoning matrix of real and imagined relations.

## *Some clinical implications*

The intricate relation between hypochondriac anxiety and excessive daydreaming has, in my view, important implications for our clinical work. Since this relation is part and parcel of the internal object relations matrix that I have attempted to describe, it goes without saying that the main focus in working with the hypochondriac would necessarily relate to this matrix. However, I would like to make a few more emphases that seem important to me for the present discussion.

First, since the hypochondriac keeps such close contact with his body at the expense of his ability to be involved with objects on a deeper and more intimate level, the therapy/analysis should gradually create a protected space wherein one can risk relating without feeling invaded and without needing to disconnect and retreat into hypersensitive listening to the body. If enough of the analytic work goes well enough, both analyst and patient can save each other from the danger of plunging into excessive disconnection that often happens through the daydreaming envelope and other dissociative modes. This dreaminess and preoccupation with the imagined diseased body keeps one away from what is missing on the interpersonal level. In my analytic work with Iris, it took a long time until Iris could risk engaging on a deeper level with me, without needing to distance herself from intimate and deep contact. In parallel, it required substantial work on my part to reclaim myself, sometimes with Iris's help, both conscious and veiled, from what seemed to be a partial sinking into contagious daydreaming.

Second, in parallel to the working through of a richer and deeper involvement with the analyst, great effort is needed so that other relations, present and past, can enfold in a more meaningful and creative way. Frequently, hypochondriac patients have neither internally digested the impact that significant others had on them, nor are they deeply aware of the impact they themselves have on others. Relations are experienced in highly static ways, in which the object has no ability to generate new meanings and new realities, and, consequently, the subject's ability to be involved in dynamic and creative relations has been hindered as well.[7] Since the detached, uninvolved relations are largely connected with an underlying need for a perfect and blissful union with the object, wherein one can feel safe and omnipotent, the core of the analytic work becomes the need both to enable regression to primordial states of mind that have not been experienced enough in the presence of an involved but neither invasive nor detached object, and, nonetheless, to gradually enable the patient to risk being involved in less than ideal emotional relations while mourning the ideal object. Although one can say that this is one of the goals in almost any analysis, I wish to put special emphasis on these dialectics in the present context, because, as said, the hypochondriac's reliance on daydreaming idealized future scenarios is so strong that it disconnects him from the reality of his life, which is not necessarily as bad as is feared.

Third, the hypochondriac anxiety masks a deep-seated denial of death and, by extension, of any limitation. The body is expected to be in a perfect state forever, with no weakness or ailment, as if one can experience absolute somatic security, and, by proxy, absolute emotional stability. These features not only become a main part of the excessive daydreaming activity, but also of the need to live in a timeless modality wherein limits and terminality are denied. This denial becomes a main issue in analysis, where time and limitations are an intrinsic part of the analytic texture. In other words, repeated attention should be paid to the various tactics employed by the hypochondriac in order to deny the flow of time and of aging, whether in life or in analysis. Moreover, since the hypochondriac anxiety is also a way of installing an imagined control over the body, there is great need to consolidate the hypochondriac's ability to tolerate uncertainty and, specifically, to bear a body that does not stand up to his idealized expectations (see also Starčević's (1989) discussion on narcissism and hypochondriasis), all this without experiencing a complete lack of control, agony, and helplessness.

Fourth, if analytic work can progress well enough, it is my understanding that the hypochondriac will gradually substitute his hypersensitive attention to the body with more mature, verbal means, so that his abilities to process emotional experiences will not be channeled into the body, but will become part of his matrix of internal and external relations. This, of course, necessitates a great deal of thinking and verbalizing on the part of the analyst, especially so since the hypochondriac's tendency is to blur and disconnect from his emotional life via hypochondriac anxiety or the daydreaming envelope.

Fifth, as said before, the hypochondriac anxiety and intensified attention to various parts of the body are often a distorted way to be in contact with a body that is not experienced as alive. Thus, the feared pain or disease, in this or that organ, becomes a mapping—the body device through imagined pain. To the extent that the hypochondriac can become more connected to his feelings and to his live body, including, needless to say, his sexuality, there is a great chance that the contact with the body can be experienced as a source of pleasure, rather than as an imagined disease. Consequently, the more the hypochondriac can be in touch with, and contain, the vitality of his body, the less prominent will be the need to use hypochondriac anxiety as the main venue for contact with an otherwise suspended body,[8] a state which I called *negative hypochondria*. In my work with Iris, extensive work had to be carried out so that she could get more and more in touch with her body, with her sexuality, and, gradually, she became more and more alive and full of vitality. Her ability to experience desire and to enjoy sexual relations increased immensely, even if many times her desires were still part of fantasies about idealized and unachievable partners. The more Iris became connected on a deeper level to me and to her body, the less intense and less frequent were her hypochondriac anxieties.

Sixth, although hypochondria was originally considered a "toxic damming up of libido linked to a narcissistic regression" (Freud, 1914c), one can think of unconscious conflictual issues underlying the hypochondriac symptom, such as unconscious beating and torture fantasies, related to denied hostility towards important objects (Broden & Myers, 1981), or to early traumatic auditory primal scene experiences (Niederland, 1958), unconscious fantasies of an internal persecutor playing the function of a concretely repressed superego (Arlow & Brenner, 1969), and displacement of castration anxiety into fears of becoming ill or altered (Fenichel, 1945). It is not my intention to elaborate now on these possible underlying unconscious dynamics, but it is important to note their relevance, since they all raise the idea of the denial of, and inability to deal with, aggression that is so often part of the deflection that the hypochondriac anxiety enables. Consequently, the need to enable the hypochondriac to be exposed to his aggressive parts without fearing either being destroyed or destroying is of great relevance. Needless to say, this might have a great impact on lessening the masochistic attachment to pain that I discussed earlier on.

Seventh, a great deal of tolerance is needed when working with the hypochondriac patient, since his catastrophic anxieties can be of such magnitude as to incur the analyst's need to defend himself from what might sometimes be experienced as a potential physical and emotional deluge. It is my belief that writing this chapter is a vicarious way of maintaining an analytic stance when facing such a deluge, as I have frequently experienced with some of my hypochondriac patients.

Thinking back to Kafka, whose hypochondria was as strong as his creativity, and whose writings have been only partially saved by his close friend, Max Brod, against Kafka's instruction to have them destroyed after his death, I would like to conclude with the lines that Freud quotes in his paper "On narcissism" (Freud, 1914c), from the last stanza of Heine's "Seven Songs of Creation", in which Heine wonders about the act of creation: "Illness was no doubt the final cause of the whole urge to create. By creating, I could recover; by creating, I became healthy". Unfortunately, neither Kafka nor Molière, who died on stage while taking part in his play, *Le Malade Imaginaire* (The Imaginary Invalid), were saved, in the concrete sense, by the act of creation. Maybe they could have been saved from a premature death had they experienced Freud's saying that

> a strong egoism is a protection against falling ill, but in the last resort we must begin to love in order to not fall ill, and we are bound to fall ill if, in consequence of frustration, we are unable to love. (Freud, 1914c, p. 84)

However, that is doubtful, too, since, if love or meaningful relations are not experienced "as their own reward, but as a necessary evil, to be swallowed despite its unpleasant taste, like a spoonful of medicinal tonic" (Lang, 2007), then I doubt to what extent love can have healing propensities. One hundred years after Freud's "On narcissism", I think we are still left with a lot to think about when we live the dramas of our patients who fight their dread of becoming ill and, even more, their dread of being fully alive.

## *Notes*

1. Of course, this rich imagery of illness details can camouflage an underlying extreme death anxiety, which can, thus, be blurred or even denied. Very intense death anxiety is even more unbearable, as it is often considered to be a result of a failure to internalize the containing/protective functions of the object, so that any disturbing or threatening situation becomes the harbinger of the impending death. The extreme fear of death is, thus, equated in the internal grammar with the experience of a collapse of defenses and regression to the total, infantile helplessness when the omnipotent parental figures had been emotionally unavailable (Starčević, 1989)
2. See also Rosenman (1981), who conceives hypochondriacal concerns as manifestations of psychic masochism wherein anxiety is a form of punishment for bad wishes, and Aisenstein and Gibeault (1991) who discuss the role that hypercathexis of pain has in the hypochondriac anxiety.
3. Although it is not clear to what extent we witness here an "objective memory", a retroactively fantasized occurring, or a mixture of both, what is evident is the invasive quality of this emotional entity. See Spero's (1990) extensive discussion on these topics, which is of great relevance here.
4. The invasive object is a term that was introduced by Williams (2004) to describe conditions in which the infantile self becomes amalgamated with sequelae of uncontained projections *and* with the projective activity of the object that leave the infant in a state of emotional

turbulence and confusion, which, in turn, threaten his very sense of self. The individual who has incorporated an invasive object is likely to feel unstable, depleted of personal meaning, and occupied or haunted by unidentifiable bodily perceptions. Complaints of feeling controlled, alienated, possessed, ill, or diseased might accompany these self-states, invasive projections being akin to "psychosomatic missiles" that are expelled or "fired" into the other. If assailed by invasive projective activity, the trauma would be an amalgam of inchoate experiences, the residuum or precipitate of which may correspond to the "foreign body" experience lodged in the unconscious and in the body and which lacks mental representational status. The infant's body is implicated in the trauma in that it carries the status of a primary object to which the infant relates and which can become installed as an internal object, thus bringing one to "invite" invasion as a sort of identification with invasiveness.

Williams also proposed distinguishing between intrusive and invasive objects. Intrusive objects tend to be motivated by a need to occupy or become a feature of the subject for reasons that can include parasitism and sadism. Invasive objects seek primarily to expel unbearable, infantile conflicts using, for the most part, excessive projective mechanisms. Expulsion is compulsive and violent and it does not appear to strive to colonize or become a feature of the subject in the same way, as its aim is to mold a repository for evacuation prior to a retreat to a position of pathological narcissism (Williams, 2004).

5. This is even more relevant in extreme cases, that border somatic delusions, wherein the hypochondriac aims to expel the diseased parts of his body, unto which his unbearable emotional experiences have been deposited (Rosenfeld, 1984).
6. In Rosenfeld's understanding, it is the hypochondriac's mixture of libidinal and aggressive impulses that intensifies confusional anxieties (confusion between self and object, love and aggression, between pleasure and pain), which, in turn, generate excessive splitting mechanisms so as to get rid of the confusional anxieties. These are first projected into the external world to be later on reintrojected, but this reintrojection is experienced as a violent and invasive intrusion that threatens to spread everywhere (Nissen, 2000). The absorption of these projections into the body attempts to diminish the emotional threat by attempting to keep emotional threats out of the mental sphere by displacing them into the body, thus generating the hypochondriac anxiety.

7. I am grateful to Neville Symington for the generative dialogue we had on these matters (Symington, 2014).
8. In this context, it is relevant to consider Ferrari's (2004) and Lombardi's ( 2002, 2010) emphasis that, in analysis with patients disconnected from their body, it is much needed to work on the vertical axis, that is on one's relation to one's body, as opposed to the common emphasis on the horizontal axis, that is, on transference interpretations.

## *References*

Aisenstein, M., & Gibeault, A. (1991). The work of hypochondria—a contribution to the study of the specificity of hypochondria, in particular in relation to hysterical conversion and organic disease. *International Journal of Psychoanalysis, 72*: 669–680.

Akhtar, S. (1996). "Someday . . ." and "If only . . . " fantasies: pathological optimism and inordinate nostalgia as related forms of idealization. *Journal of the American Psychoanalytic Association, 44*: 723–753.

Anzieu, D. (1989). *The Skin Ego*. New Haven, CT: Yale University Press.

Arlow, J. A., & Brenner, C. (1969). The psychopathology of the psychoses: a proposed revision. *International Journal of Psychoanalysis, 50*: 5–14.

Barsky, A. J., & Klerman, G. L. (1983). Overview: hypochondriasis, bodily complaints and somatic styles. *American Journal of Psychiatry, 140*: 273–283.

Broden, A. R., & Myers, W. A. (1981). Hypochondriacal symptoms as derivatives of unconscious fantasies of being beaten or tortured. *Journal of the American Psychoanalytic Association, 29*: 535–557.

Bronstein, C. (2011). On psychosomatics: the search of meaning. *International Journal of Psychoanalysis,* 92: 173–195.

Drucker, P. F. (2002). *Managing in the New Society*. New York: Truman Talley Books.

Fenichel, O. (1945). *The Psychoanalytic Theory of Neurosis*. New York: Norton.

Ferrari, A. B. (2004). *From the Eclipse of the Body to the Dawn of Thought*. London: Free Association Books.

Freud, S. (1893). Draft B from Extracts from the Fliess Papers. *S. E., 1*: 179–184. London: Hogarth.

Freud, S. (1914c). On narcissism. *S. E., 14*: 67–102. London: Hogarth.

Granek, M. (1989). Hypochondriasis, acting out and counteracting out. *British Journal of Medical Psychology, 62*: 257–264.

Gutwinski, J. (1997). Hypochondria versus the relation to the object. *International Journal of Psychoanalysis, 78*: 53–68.
Hägglund, T. (2001). Timelessness as a positive and negative experience. *Scandinavian Psychoanalytic Review, 24*: 83–92.
Houzel, D. (1990). The concept of psychic envelope. In: D. Anzieu (Ed.), *Psychic Envelopes*. London: Karnac.
Jones, E. (1955). *The Life and Work of Sigmund Freud, Volume Two: Years of Maturity 1901–1919*. London: Hogarth Press.
Kafka, F. (1949). *Diaries of Franz Kafka: 1910–1913*, J. Kresh (Trans.). New York: Schocken Books.
Kafka, F. (1953)[1919]. *Letter to His Father*. New York: Schocken Books.
Klein, M. (1930). The importance of symbol-formation in the development of the ego. *International Journal of Psychoanalysis, 11*: 24–39.
Lang, M. (2007). The hypochondriac: bodies in protest from Herman Melville to Toni Morrison. PhD Dissertation in Comparative Literature, Stony Brook University.
Levine, H. B. (2009). Time and timelessness: inscription and representation. *Journal of the American Psychoanalytic Association, 57*: 333–355.
Lombardi, R. (2002). Primitive mental states and the body. *International Journal of Psychoanalysis, 83*: 363–381.
Lombardi, R. (2010). The body emerging from the "neverland" of nothingness. *Psychoanalytic Quarterly, 79*: 879–909.
Lussheimer, P. (1954). On daydreams. *American Journal of Psychoanalysis, 14*: 83–92.
Marty, P., & de M'Uzan, M. (1963). La pensée opératoire [Mechanical functioning]. *Revue Français Psychanalytique, 27*: 345–356.
Meltzer, D. (1964). The differentiation of somatic delusions from hypochondria. *International Journal of Psychoanalysis, 45*: 246–250.
Meltzer, D. (1983). *Dream-Life: A Re-Examination of the Psychoanalytic Theory and Technique*. London: Karnac.
Mitrani, J. L. (1995). Toward an understanding of unmentalized experience. *Psychoanalytic Quarterly, 64*: 68–112.
Mitrani, J. L. (2007). Some technical implications of Klein's concept of 'premature ego development'. *International Journal of Psychoanalysis, 88*: 825–842.
Niederland, W. G. (1958). Early auditory experiences, beating fantasies and primal scene. *Psychoanalytic Study of the Child, 13*: 471–504.
Nissen, B. (2000). Hypochondria. *International Journal of Psychoanalysis, 81*: 651–666.

Rosenfeld, D. (1984). Hypochondrias, somatic delusion and body scheme in psychoanalytic practice. *International Journal of Psychoanalysis, 65*: 377–387.
Rosenfeld, H. (1958). Some observations on the psychopathology of hypochondriacal states. *International Journal of Psychoanalysis, 39*: 121–124.
Rosenfeld, H. (1964). On the psychopathology of narcissism: a clinical approach. *International Journal of Psychoanalysis, 45*: 332–337.
Rosenman, S. (1981). Hypochondriasis and invidiousness. *Journal of the American Academy of Psychoanalytic Dynamic Psychiatry, 9*: 51–70.
Rosenman, S., & Handelsman, I. (1978). Narcissistic vulnerability, hypochondriacal rumination, and invidiousness. *American Journal of Psychoanalysis, 38*: 57–66.
Sandler, J. (1976). Countertransference and role-responsiveness. *International Review of Psycho-Analysis, 3*: 43–47.
Schellekes, A. (2010). When time stood still: thoughts regarding the dimension of time in primitive mental states. In: M. H. Spero (Ed.), *Ma'arag-The Israel Annual of Psychoanalysis, Volume 1* (pp. 281–303). Jerusalem: The Hebrew University Magnes Press.
Schellekes, A. (2017). When time stood still: thoughts on the dimension of time in primitive mental states. *British Journal of Psychotherapy* (in press).
Sifneos, P. E. (1973). The prevalence of 'alexithymic' characteristics in psychosomatic patients. *Psychotherapy and Psychosomatics, 22*(2): 255–262.
Skogstad, W. (2013). Impervious and intrusive: the impenetrable object in transference and countertransference. *International Journal of Psychoanalysis, 94*: 221–238.
Spero, M. H. (1990). Portal aspects of memory overlay in psychoanalysis—an object relations contribution to screen memory phenomena. *Psychoanalytic Study of the Child, 45*: 79–103.
Starcević, V. (1989). Pathological fear of death, panic attacks, and hypochondriasis. *American Journal of Psychoanalysis, 49*: 347–361.
Steiner, J. (1993). *Psychic Retreats: Pathological Organizations in Psychotic, Neurotic and Borderline Patients*. London: The New Library of Psychoanalysis.
Stolorow, R. D. (1979). Defensive and arrested developmental aspects of death anxiety, hypochondriasis and depersonalization. *International Journal of Psychoanalysis, 60*: 201–213.
Sugarman, A. (2008). Fantasizing as process, not fantasy as content: the importance of mental organization. *Psychoanalytic Inquiry, 28*: 169–189.

Symington, N. (2014). Personal communication.
Tustin, F. (1981). *Autistic States in Children*. London: Tavistock/Routledge.
Tustin, F. (1990). *The Protective Shell in Children and Adults*. London: Karnac.
Valenstein, A. F. (1973). On attachment to painful feelings and the negative therapeutic reaction. *Psychoanalytic Study of the Child, 28*: 365–392.
Williams, G. (1997). Reflections on some dynamics of eating disorders: 'no entry' defences and foreign bodies. *International Journal of Psychoanalysis, 78*: 927–941.
Williams, P. (2004). Incorporation of an invasive object. *International Journal of Psychoanalysis, 85*: 1333–1348.
Winnicott, D. W. (1962). The theory of the parent–infant relationship—contributions to discussion. *International Journal of Psychoanalysis, 43*: 256–257.
Winnicott, D. W. (1971). *Playing and Reality*. London: Tavistock.

CHAPTER THREE

# "Black holes" and "fear of breakdown" in the analysis of a fetishistic–masochistic patient

*Ofra Eshel*

Tustin's (1972, 1986, 1990, 1992) and Grotstein's (1986, 1989, 1990a,b,c, 1993) "black holes" and Winnicott's radical late ideas about unthinkable early breakdown and madness (presented in Winnicott's posthumous papers "Fear of breakdown", 1974, 1986, and "Psychology of madness", 1989) describe the catastrophic nature of early infantile traumatizations. Following an introductory review of these concepts, this chapter will explore how they found powerful expression and intersected in the analysis of a severely perverse patient.

Through a detailed clinical illustration of this difficult analysis with a severely fetishistic–masochistic patient, perversion is understood as the pervert's last-ditch attempt to halt the fall into an abyss of core breakdown. Consequently, the cessation of the perverse practices led in analysis to an extreme collapse and a critical struggle for survival within the annihilating depths of core catastrophe, early breakdown, and madness. This is discussed in the light of Tustin's, Grotstein's and Winnicott's ideas, with the addition of Bion's (1965, 1970) late writings on "transformations in O within the analyst" and "Faith in O".

## *A theoretical–clinical context*

### *Black holes*

The term "black hole" has acquired meaning in the fields of astrophysics (Gribbin, 1992; Hawking, 1988, 1993) and psychoanalysis (Akhtar, 2009). "Black holes" in psychoanalysis, as used by Tustin and Grotstein, refer to the nature of early infantile traumatizations and the collapse into nothingness and meaninglessness, which result in primitive mental disturbances. The term "black hole" was first applied clinically by Bion (1970) in reference to the "infantile catastrophe" of the psychotic. Tustin, and later Grotstein, both analysands of Bion, developed and broadened the use of this term, Tustin to autistic children and Grotstein to psychotics and borderlines. Tustin (1972, 1986, 1990, 1992) regards the "black hole" experience as a very significant element in psychogenic autism. She describes having learned about the black hole from her four-year-old autistic patient, John,[1] whom she refers to in all of her books. Tustin views autism as a reaction to a very early trauma of premature bodily separateness from the primal mother, experienced by the infant as an unbearable rupture of the bonding with the mother, as if a part of his body's surface had been ripped away upon the object's absence, leaving a black hole of depression, despair, rage, terror, helplessness, and hopelessness. (In Tustin's view, this elemental type of depression is akin to Bibring's (1953) "primal" depression and Winnicott's (1979) infantile psychotic depression.) Autistic encapsulation and entanglement arise as protective reactions against the "black hole" type of depression, which these children plug with autistic objects or shapes or with confusional objects.

Spensley, in her book on Tustin (1995), considers Tustin's study of "black hole" phenomenology her most important contribution to psychoanalysis.

Grotstein (1986, 1989, 1990a,b,c, 1993), following Tustin's ideas, further developed the "black hole" experience and applied it to adult patients with primitive mental disorders, adding concepts from astrophysics ("singularity" and "event horizon") which emphasize the "awesome force" of the black hole. He regards the black hole phenomenon as the fundamental experience of the psychotic internal mental space of these patients—an endless, bottomless void of primary meaninglessness, nothingness, disorganization, chaos, and nameless dread where the mother used to be and was prematurely ripped away.

Whereas the psychotic patient seems to have already fallen (metaphorically) into the black hole and become devastated by this cataclysmic experience, the borderline patient appears to exist on its borders, continuously experiencing the threat and the pull of falling over its edge into its horrific interior.

Later, I (Eshel, 1998a) expanded the metaphorical application of the astrophysical "black hole" and the event horizon to an interpersonal phenomenon regarding less disturbed individuals, whose interpersonal and intersubjective psychic space is dominated by a central object which is experienced essentially as a black hole. Thus, they are either gripped by its enormous, compelling pull, or are petrified in their interpersonal psychic space out of fear of being pulled over its edge. My usage of this term differs from Tustin's and Grotstein's formulations of the black hole, which describe the nature of internal mental space in primitive mental disorders resulting from an infantile catastrophe of very early separateness from the primal mother. Unlike these authors, I apply the astrophysical black hole metaphorically to an interpersonal phenomenon. I use it to illustrate the nature of the fundamental experience of emotional closeness, love, and intimate relationships of individuals, who otherwise generally function in their social and professional life. This black hole experience in the interpersonal psychic space is caused mainly by the impact of a psychically "dead" parent, particularly the impact of the psychically "dead mother" (Green's 1986 concept) and her deadening world of blank bereavement, depression, and deadness on her child.

## *Fear of breakdown and madness*

Over the last several years, I have been drawn to Winnicott's unique ideas about the unthinkable early breakdown, as presented in his posthumous papers "Fear of breakdown" (thought to have been written around 1963, but published in 1974), and its continuation, "Psychology of madness" (1989[1965]). Winnicott relates to the disastrous impact of being broken down in infancy, at the time when the ego organization is threatened, since "the ego cannot organize against environmental failure in so far as dependence is a living fact" (Winnicott, 1986[1963], p. 174). It is that extreme primitive agony of early breakdown that Winnicott also calls madness X (and Eigen, following him, refers to as agony X, 1999, 2004). This early breakdown is so unthinkable and "indescribably painful" that it cannot be experienced and a new massive defence organization, which the patient displays as an illness syndrome, is organized against it. Consequently, the individual becomes imprisoned in a dissociated, ever-present "unthinkable state of affairs that underlies the defence organization" (p. 174), which has already happened but, since it has not yet been experienced, it cannot get into the past tense, and is feared and compulsively sought after in the future. It is, thus, an ongoing catastrophe, then, now, about to happen—never and forever,[2] an endless impact on one's being. In Winnicott's unique words:

> The breakdown has already happened, near the beginning of the individual's life . . . but . . . this thing of the past has not happened yet because *the patient was not there for it to happen to*. The only way to "remember" in this case is for the patient *to experience this past thing for the first time in the present*, that is to say, in the transference. This past and future thing then becomes a matter of the here and now, and becomes experienced by the patient for the first time (1986[1963], p. 179, my italics)

Winnicott is describing here a profound inner struggle. In those depths of unthinkable agony of early breakdown or madness are buried both the traumatic past and a "*basic urge*" to experience it and, thus, "to be recovered in experience because it cannot be recovered in memory . . . madness that has to be remembered can only be remembered in the reliving of it" (1989[1965], pp. 126, 125, original italics) in treatment. This evokes the dread of breakdown or of the return of the original madness, but also the patient's great need to reach to this original, unthinkable state of breakdown, to risk reliving and experiencing the early agony, this time in treatment, with the analyst. It is to be relived "in reaction to the analyst's failures and mistakes", but, at the same time, and even more importantly, with the analyst's different holding and "auxiliary ego-supporting function", which will make recovery possible. Thus, the crux of the analytic work that this thinking entails, relates to the critical question of whether this reliving of the devastating past has to happen this time in the same unthinkable, unexperienced way, or whether it can happen and be experienced, even though it has not previously been experienced. The strength of Winnicott's words "'breakdown' to describe the unthinkable state of affairs" and "primitive agonies (anxiety is not a strong enough word here)" captures what is so difficult and crucial in the reliving, experiencing, and recovering in treatment of the emotional intensity of early breakdown.

The great clinical significance of Winnicott's ideas on fear of breakdown is powerfully emphasized by Winnicott himself, from the very beginning of his paper:

> My *clinical experiences* have brought me recently to a new understanding, as I believe, of the meaning of fear of breakdown . . . which is new for me and which perhaps is new for others who work in psychotherapy . . . [This study] leads to a restatement of problems *that puzzle us as we fail to do as well clinically as we would wish to do*. (Winnicott, 1986[1963], p. 173, my italics; cf. Ogden, 2014).

Clare Winnicott commented powerfully when the paper was published posthumously, "something surfaced from the *depths of clinical involvement* into conscious grasp and produced *a new orientation to a whole area of clinical practice*" (1974, p. 103, my italics). Later on, Clare Winnicott (1980) also underscores the crucial clinical importance of Winnicott's paper "Fear of breakdown" in her own paper (which I will quote below).

Indeed, Winnicott's vision opens new possibilities of understanding and working analytically with the more deeply disturbed aspects of patients' personalities and experiences. Hernandez, an eminent Peruvian psychoanalyst, writes in this regard,

> Winnicott's notion, in a way, could be considered a radical reworking of one of Freud's last clinical comments—a reworking of vast consequences. Freud (1937[d]) wrote, "Often enough, when a neurotic is led by an anxiety-state to expect the occurrence of some terrible event, he is in fact merely under the influence of a repressed memory (which is seeking to enter consciousness but cannot become conscious) that something which was at that time terrifying did really happen. I believe that we should gain a great deal of valuable knowledge from work of this kind upon psychotics even if it led to no therapeutic success" (p. 268). But for Winnicott (1963) [regarding the more psychotic phenomena], "the original experience of primitive agony cannot get into the past tense unless the ego can first gather it into its own present time experience and into omnipotent control now (assuming the auxiliary ego-supporting function of the mother

> (analyst)" (p. 177). In the analytic process, the patient may stop looking for or to the past event not yet experienced only if s/he gathers the original environmental failure into the area of her/his omnipotence within the transferential experience. (Hernandez, 1998, p. 137)

The emphasis, thus, lies in allowing the unbearable agony to be gradually experienced and lived out with the analyst in the treatment situation.

"All this is very difficult, time-consuming and painful," writes Winnicott, "but alas, there is no end unless the bottom of the trough has been reached, unless *the thing feared has been experienced*" (1986 [1963], p. 178, original italics).

These ideas have acquired great importance for me in my analytic work with more disturbed patients. I first encountered them in a most powerful, experiential way in the analysis that I now describe.

## *Case illustration*

The clinical material presented here is taken from a four-times-a-week analysis of a patient with severe fetishistic–masochistic perversion, which I have described in an earlier theoretical–clinical paper on perversion (Eshel, 2005). I now proceed to later periods in this analysis.

P started analysis when he was in his late thirties. He was referred to me by a psychiatrist who had first treated him with medication. The psychiatrist told me that his severe perversion had intensified over the last few years, to the point of becoming life-threatening. In the year before he came to her, he had approached several sex therapists who were all so alarmed by the severity of his disturbance that they refused to treat him. When he turned to her, she prescribed medication for compulsive disorders, in an attempt to minimize the compulsive nature of his perverse behavior. However, this was unsuccessful and produced harsh physical side-effects, some of which she found rather puzzling. Therefore, she stopped the medication and told him that, in her opinion, psychoanalysis would be the only treatment that might help him, since it is the most profound form of treatment. It should be mentioned that this man had previously never had anything to do with psychology or psychoanalysis, and I do not believe that he had even heard of the word psychoanalysis before. His agreeing to her proposal was, thus, an indication of his despair and hopelessness. After several unsuccessful attempts at finding him a psychoanalyst, she approached me, knowing I take difficult cases. She seemed hesitant to specify the nature and extent of his perverse behavior, lest I too refuse to treat him. However, at the time, I had been crystallizing my thoughts about extending the reach of therapeutic work through the depth and intensity of psychoanalysis, and about analysis as a unique process of becoming—drawing on the powerful notions of "a new opportunity for development" (Winnicott), "a new beginning [in] the basic fault" (Balint), and "an area of faith' (Eigen). Thus, I thought, psychoanalysis should be able to offer a real treatment option for this person's distress, and I agreed to accept him for analysis.

The man telephoned me the next day. During the initial session, he told me that his severe perversion had started as a shoe fetish of licking and kissing shoes "with a woman's feet in them", along with a masochistic element of wanting them to trample on his fingers, a wish which he recalled having had since kindergarten. It escalated over the years into a masochistic fetish as the "shoe turned into a tool of destruction", and in the past few years it had become a particularly severe and violent masochistic perversion. Over the first months of analysis, he gradually presented me with extremely harsh descriptions, told matter-of-factly, of his almost nightly visits to prostitutes, usually a different one each time, to be humiliated and abused by them in increasingly extreme ways with all sorts of instruments of torture. He would lie there naked, sometimes he would wear a mask, masturbating until he ejaculated, and he would leave beaten, trodden upon, wounded, bleeding, and burned by cigarettes that had been extinguished by the shoes grinding them into his naked body, already yearning for the next abuse. He sought treatment because he knew that, in his own words, "If it goes on like this, it will end in hospital—in a serious injury, or in death."

After a few months of analysis, when he realized that I would not throw him out of treatment because of what he told me, he said, "This is the last stop for me. Psychoanalysis. After that—it's the graveyard." Since then he has been clinging to treatment despite some very difficult periods that we have gone through.

In his "ordinary" life, he was a dreary accountant, in a non-sexual marriage with a woman he knew from work, an accountant like himself, whom he told nothing about his perversion. At the end of the first year of analysis he told her the "truth" about himself and his secret life. She found it unbearable, reacted with shock and revulsion, and decided that they should separate. He left the house, hurt, and they were divorced.

I described this analysis in an earlier paper on perversion, up to the cessation of the perverse practices into the third year of analysis (Eshel, 2005). I emphasized the importance of the analyst's abiding "presencing" and interconnection with the perverse patient, thus being with-in and listening to the perversion beyond its pathology, for its survival function and for the profound loneliness and despair it carries. I pointed out the fundamental function of the evolving process of therapeutic regression in Balint's and, especially, Winnicott's terms in the analysis of the perverse patient; that is, to understand it primarily as a situation of need resulting from an early maternal–environmental failure (rather than manipulative acting out), with the ensuing treatment priorities of holding, analytic reliability, and attentiveness to the patient's need states and dependence. Thus, in Winnicottian terms of regression, the analyst's interconnected "presencing" can be seen as enabling the transformation of the patient's withdrawal and massive self-defensive organization—in this context, the perversion—into regression to dependence in treatment, which carries with it a new opportunity for correcting the patient's past experiences and for emotional development (Winnicott, 1989[1964], 1988, 1992[1954]). Before proceeding to the third year of analysis, I shall recount an example from that earlier period of the analysis that epitomizes these qualities of experience, as presented in my 2005 article.

The patient, here in the second year of analysis, arrived at the first session following my holiday break. (The gaps created by the analyst's vacations are most troublesome in these treatments.) As soon as I opened the door, I noticed his swollen face.

He lay on the couch, and after a brief "How are you?" told me quietly and bluntly, in detached detail, that he had gone to a whore that morning, a cheap one who charges only 100 shekels (about $25), a most violent type, who went wild and slapped him and beat him madly, incessantly, for five minutes, and he came very fast and hard, went home, washed up, and came to the session.

For the first time in this analysis I felt great tiredness and disgust, although he had already recounted far more violent and bizarre scenes, perhaps because of this inundating wretched cheapness. I was thinking to myself, what is the point of all the hard work, of this entire analysis, the great investment of money and years. Better go to a whore every day, get beaten up for five minutes, pay 100 shekels, and be done with it.

And I withdrew, fell silent.

Then I noticed that he became very agitated, in sharp contrast to his former quiet and detached manner. As if he had heard my thoughts, he said, "Nothing can be done. I ask you: What? What is there to say? When I'm butchered, I exist. It's like the Alien got inside my belly and stayed there, breaking out every time, and that's it. Nothing left to do. There's no solution. Everything just gets worse. I'm finished. I was born and I'll die this way. I'll be dead before I'm forty."

He sat up, shaken, suddenly looking so withered, shapeless, and pitiful, with his beaten-up, swollen face. I realized he sensed and knew that I had *abandoned* him, left him wounded and lost on the battlefield, and had gone off to save myself. Thus, I returned to this despicable, despairing, and desperate place, his and mine, and said, "You are so desperate because you felt that I'd given up. And when we both give up there's nothing more to hold on to. It's really very despairing, *but we are going on*."

He lay back quietly, tears in his eyes for the first time in analysis (perhaps in his life), and said, "Death can be so cheap. You should lock me up inside the treatment" (2005, pp. 1089–1090).

I now proceed to the third year of analysis.

Towards the end of the third year, after the perverse practices had ceased, analysis was filled with great agitation and confusion, and with massive holding on to the treatment and to me instead of to the perversion. It led to a deeper regression in the analysis. In the sessions, he would speak feverishly, addressing his words to me, frequently calling me by my first name, Ofra—which he had never done previously—in the sessions and also in the telephone messages which he now began leaving on my voice mail. I present some detailed vignettes, using his own words, as I feel that they most closely depict the actual experience, and convey the turbulent nature of the analytic situation at that time.

It was a Monday session—always a particularly difficult session after the weekend break.

He began: "Don't remember a period in my life like this, don't know what's happening to me, mentally and physically exhausted. Don't know what's happening. [Sighed, and remained silent.] My entire old world is collapsing, dissolving, and disappearing, the whole world of evil, and I'm facing a new world, don't know what to do. I don't have the tools to cope with it."

I said: "Tools need time to develop." But my words remained suspended in space.

He went on: "Don't know, don't know what's happening . . . Don't know, Ofra, just don't know what's happening to me, how all at once this thing that I used to fall into has disappeared, where has it gone? All sorts of strange things, don't know, don't know what's happening in my head [put his hands on his forehead]. Don't know, don't know, not anything I know, all sorts of things are flying in the air. Maybe I'm going mad, don't know, it's as if my brain is emptying out, as if things are flying in the air, like in a hurricane, as if something is making things fly out of my brain. In the last few days things are unclear to me, I'm not in control of what's happening to me, it's as if I'm falling apart, the first time in my life, falling apart completely. Don't know what to do, I'm going mad."

I said, "You're not going mad. You're changing, changing a lot."

He said, "I've never had thoughts like these, never in my life. The very element of violence has disappeared. I'm standing at the entrance to a new world, and I don't know how to behave. What to do with my brain and my dick. Don't know what I want from myself. We talked so much, Ofra, and all of a sudden something big collapsed all at once, not gradually. What a huge jolt." He became silent, and lay quietly, as if sleeping, until the end of the session.

After about eight turbulent months, his confusion diminished. "Apparently I have to get used to this new situation, that I'm not so much of a fetishist any more, and I need to calm down a bit," he said. He continued to abstain from his perverse activities. He frequented the cinema, listened to a lot of music, started exercising on the days that he was not in analysis, and began to look for, and date, women through internet dating sites. He called this period "the age of uncertainty", because previously everything had been familiar to him and under his control. He said, "I've never been out with a woman, I've never touched or been touched by a woman. I've never slept with a woman. I'm very scared of it, it's new. It's hard to get out of the gutter." [He said this even though, in fact, he had been married for years. Here, I would like to add that this was a man who could not bear to be touched. In the first year of treatment, when I asked him about his descriptions of the cruel fetishistic–masochistic practices, why the whores had to dig their high heels into him and extinguish their cigarettes on his body with their shoes rather than with their hands, he replied that he could not bear to be touched by a human hand.]

Nonetheless, despite his deep misgivings and fear, he now proceeded from telephone calls to dates, and began meeting an increasing number of women. These meetings were usually for no more than a single evening. In the course of time it became easier for him to meet women; some of these dates were even enjoyable. And still, deep inside, he felt cut off and vulnerable, and an immense inner emptiness was growing and taking hold of him. It seemed that the fetish that had disappeared had left behind a vacuum and profound emptiness.

Was this what he had foreseen when he spoke repeatedly about his perversion during the first year of analysis?

> "It sustains you more than anything else. You won't let anyone or anything take it away from you. If you give it up, it will be unbearable, since there won't be anything else."

Now, in the fourth year, he was saying:

> It's amazing, amazing, how the fetish took over my entire life, and now there's nothing, nothing. Don't know what's going on here. With women it doesn't seem real, I don't really want it. Last night I talked to that woman who approached me, don't know, it seemed pointless like, what, what, for what, suddenly everything seemed pointless, strange, strange . . . Don't know what to do, Ofra, altogether feel completely cut off. Don't know where everything I've fantasized till now is, where everything that filled me all those years has gone . . . Everything hurls me into a world that has no center. I'm so empty inside . . . Feel so unreal, so unable to exist in the world of the living, and mainly, so ill."

He gave himself time until his birthday, which was very close to the end of the fourth year of analysis, to try it out.

> "The transition between worlds is a tremendous jolt. Ilan Ramon[3] didn't survive the transition between worlds. I'm going through a jolt that is just as great. It will end either in death or in a different life."

But after his birthday, throughout the fifth year of analysis, profound despair, unfathomable emptiness, and death seemed to possess him and to have become the only reality—dreadful and absolute. This was a terrible, excruciating year in analysis. He reverted to searching the internet for the most ferocious fetishistic–masochistic websites with "extreme violence and self-destruction". He masturbated to horrendous fantasies, even though he did not revert to actually performing perverse activities. He said

> "It's a kind of total self-destruction, without any brakes, as if I don't have a drop of self-love in me, a drop of compassion, a drop of self-pity, a drop of anything, anything. It's unbelievable, Ofra, unbelievable; only dread, hatred, violence, feelings of inferiority and fear of criticism."

He requested a year's unpaid leave from work, because he could not live with the huge disparity between his internal world and his external "normal, false" painstaking functioning. "I'm normal there, that's what doesn't let me get better. My death is the normal life which I built all those years around the fetish." He lived on his savings, and his entire existence was drawn into the treatment, collapsed into the treatment. He wanted to be "hospitalized in treatment", and to be: to exist, to feel real.

But now it seemed that the defensive shield of the perversion had been totally breached. "Fetishistic energy isn't an energy of life; it's energy that repairs death. It's between life and death—dead–alive, more dead than alive; death-in-life," he said. Indeed, I, too, had written on perversion as an "autotomous" massive splitting defence in the service of psychic survival so that "not all of me shall die".

> [T]he perverse act seizes and clutches, preventing in its corporeality, in its actuality and intensity, a collapse into dread, psychic deadness and total internal annihilation. Perversion is the pervert's last-ditch attempt to halt the fall into the abyss. (Eshel, 2005, pp. 1078–1079)

But now this last-ditch attempt to halt the fall into the abyss had collapsed. Perversion no longer repaired death, no longer secured survival. Throughout this year, death was the very heart of his existence. It was everywhere, all the time, invading every hour with menacing forcefulness.

He came to every session, never late, never asking for any change of time, arriving psychically and physically ill—"the fetish and violence are destroying every bit of goodness in me"—or lifeless, empty, without the strength and will to live. Frequently, he would sleep during the sessions, a still, motionless, and soundless sleep. He would leave me many telephone messages, at least one message a day, and on Wednesdays and weekend breaks, when we did not meet, he would leave several messages. His words in the sessions and in the phone messages were full of despair, harrowing emptiness, and death, and no attempt on my part to understand and interpret had any significance, meaning, or impact. He would say over and over again,

> "I have nothing to say to you, Ofra; I simply have nothing to say to you. Everything is one huge nothing. I'd rather be sucked into a black hole. Everything's a load of bullshit, everything's empty words, it's better to be sucked into the nothingness, Ofra, and finished—to disappear completely. I just don't have any plans, I don't want any plans, anything; just nothing, Ofra, nothing, I have nothing to say. Everything is so pointless, including your words . . . They're so meaningless, there's nothing in them, Ofra, nothing, nothing."

Suddenly, unexpectedly (and perhaps not so unexpectedly) during this period, harsh details of his very early childhood were revealed. Until now, whenever he had asked his mother about his childhood, she had answered, "Everything was fine." But now when he asked, she said, "It was very hard," and told him about the dead baby. It turns out that his mother had had six pregnancies. Two of them ended in miscarriages before the birth of his brother, who was eighteen months older than he; as a result, she was prescribed total bed rest during that pregnancy. She did not work at all during those years, since she was pregnant most of the time, and the pregnancies were difficult. He thought that his father wanted a lot of children. When his mother was pregnant with him, she fell while carrying his brother in her arms, and thought that she was going to miscarry. But he was born, a year and a half after his brother, with a heart defect—PTA, for which he was operated on at the age of seven. In the year after his birth, "when I was very small", his mother did not remember exactly when, she gave birth to another son in her sixth month of pregnancy, and the baby died twelve days later. She remembered only that they had told her something was wrong with it. She did not remember whether she ever saw it, did not remember whether she stayed in the hospital for the twelve days until the infant died. It did not have a name. She did not remember whether they buried it, but somewhere inside his head he remembered that she had once told him that his father and his grandmother (her mother) had taken care of the matter, and buried it. When he was twenty months old, his mother became pregnant with his next brother, who was born when he was two and a half years old, and she almost died in childbirth. I suggested that we were beginning to understand that during those early years his mother had undergone dreadful experiences, misery, suffering, depression, and death. I said that a baby is born into the psyche and body of its mother and comes into being and grows there. And he was born to a mother who became distraught, alive–dead, and his yearning as an infant and small child to attach to, and grow, within her psyche and body had overwhelmed and filled him with her agonized feelings, with depression, death, a dead baby.

At first, it seemed that these words held meaning for him. "I'm a tiny baby that terrible things have happened to," he said. Two and a half years later he would say: "I went mad when I was a baby," but now this emergent understanding very quickly turned into a terrible, lethal attack on my capacity to really meet, take in, and feel the desperation of the fundamental nothingness and death within him. It became something which came from without, illusory, "as if"; too far from that baby and small child overwhelmed by traumatic, annihilating impacts. The more words and the greater the understanding, the wider yawned the gap he felt was between us; there was no real contact with death and dying. He said repeatedly,

> "I'm a dead baby and a perverse adult. All day I've been thinking that I want to die tonight, don't want to get to tomorrow. And that's it. I hope I'll die tonight. Simply feel completely redundant, Ofra, completely redundant. You're so healthy, Ofra, and I'm so sick. There's no point of connection between us. There are big words, and a big illusion, and big lies, but nothing apart from that. After the session with you, I hope I'll go to sleep and won't wake up. Won't wake up."
>
> I said, "Then your body–psyche will decide whether we will be able to go on." And at the end of each session I did not know whether he would survive and come to the next session. There no longer seemed to be even the fragile reminder of his sense of life and hope, only a state of devastating despair.

Analysis was now a meeting place with a terminal object (in Bollas's sense, 1995, p. 76); indeed, a terminal and annihilating[4] object and the despair of his first year of life. Was this his way of making me meet and experience the terminal, annihilating, invasive presence of a depressed, dead–alive m/other in the grip of depression and death, who induced depression and death, and who could not be extricated from death? Or might it be that damage that begins so early cannot be repaired, as he repeated over and over, except in death? To die, and then, perchance, to begin anew?

I was reminded at that point of the last words of Otto Weininger, a brilliant young thinker, imbued with self-hatred, hatred of his Jewish ancestry, and hatred of women. A year after he published his book *Sex and Character* (1903) and converted to Protestantism, at the age of twenty-three, he wrote in his final notes, "An honest man, when he feels that he is irreparably deformed, goes willingly towards death". He wrote this and then killed himself. I was becoming exceedingly worried.

I suggested, for the first time in my clinical work, that he should go back to the psychiatrist who had referred him to me, and get some medication that would afford him temporary relief from this terrible suffering. But he replied angrily and bitterly,

> "How can you say that to me? I thought you were holding the hope, you and psychoanalysis. I don't need anything else to keep my body alive; for that there's the fetish, big time, and familiar for so many years. But I don't exist. I'm not. There's nothing here. I'm dead. That's the fundamental thing—I'm dead."

His words, I felt, cried out the very real ongoing desperation of his being . . .

"In the very ill person there is but little hope of new opportunity" (Winnicott, 1992[1954], p. 281). Inwardly, I struggled to find some hope while faced with this overwhelming, immense desperation. I seized upon Winnicott's later writings on "Fear of breakdown" and "Psychology of madness", which, as I wrote before, are of great importance to me. Winnicott relates to the disastrous impact of being broken down in infancy, when the ego organization is threatened. This early breakdown, or madness, is so unthinkable and "indescribably painful" that it cannot be experienced, and a massive defence organization, which the patient displays as an illness syndrome, is erected against it. In my patient's case, it was the ferocious fetishistic

–masochistic perversion that turned him from a passive victim of unbearable early damage and destruction into an active "doer" of them, over and over again, while beneath it there yawned an abyss of inner death and emptiness.

I reminded myself that, according to Winnicott, in those depths of annihilation and the agony of early breakdown or madness are buried both the traumatic experience and a "basic urge" to experience it and, thus, "to be recovered in experience . . . remembered in the reliving of it" (1989[1965], p. 126) in treatment. This evokes the fear of breakdown or of the return of the original madness, but also the patient's great need to reach to this original, unthinkable state of breakdown, to risk reliving and experiencing the early agony, this time in treatment, with the analyst and his or her different holding and "auxiliary ego-supporting function", which will make recovery possible.

I thought that we were now within this process, touching the core breakdown, madness, and profound devastation. But I was not sure whether he would be able to survive the extreme horror of this breakdown. Can one survive contact with such excruciating breakdown and annihilation? In "Fear of breakdown", Winnicott refers to his patient whose suicide he did not manage to prevent—a patient who wanted to die because of her deep feeling of inner death that had already happened to her psyche in early infancy, although her body continued to live. She killed herself in despair of finding a solution, thus consigning her body to the death that had already happened to the psyche (1986[1963], pp. 179–180).

In the face of these relentless death threats, I tried to extract a promise from him that he would not commit suicide during the next six months.

> I said, "I won't continue the treatment unless you promise not to kill yourself."
>
> He replied, "What, you'll abandon me just like that, after five years like this?"
>
> I said, "You'll always have a place in my thoughts, I'll always care about you, and I'll always think about what's happening to you and how you feel—whether you are alive or dead. And I think that that's the way you'll feel about me. But I won't continue the treatment if you don't promise that you won't kill yourself. There's no point to it if you've already chosen death."

> He said, "And if I promise and don't keep the promise?"
> I said, "I trust your promise."

He did not promise, but he did stop threatening to kill himself. Yet, both in the sessions (he never failed to attend each session) and in the many phone messages that he left me, he wished every night that he would not wake up in the morning. He repeatedly said,

> "I felt sick looking at the internet sites of violence and evil last night. I wished that I wouldn't wake up in the morning. Nothing's happening, I'm completely dead. I've completely despaired of you, of the treatment. Two years without actually engaging in fetishistic activities, and the fetish in my brain is winning, is taking over. And I'm dead, Ofra, simply dead. I'm simply dead. That's it."
>
> I would reply, "These are very troubled words. Thank you for not despairing of sharing these feelings with me."

But I felt that my words were also an attempt to protect myself from the intensity of this violent, repetitive desperation to which I had no answer.

I now come to the point at which something different transpired. It was a Monday session, after the weekend break. At the beginning of the session he said that he was dead. True, for more than two years he had not engaged in any more fetishistic activity, and this month he was not even entering the internet sites, but he was dead. Nothing was happening inside him. Over the weekend he had tried meeting women again, but these meetings did nothing for him. "Nothing's happening. I'm dead, just dead," he said, and fell silent. His words reached deeply within me. Is death really victorious? I no longer tried to extricate us from this state with agreements and promises or with interpretations.

I said, "We've done things. Things have happened. We're trying to do the best we can in this fateful encounter of ours, but we really don't know whether we'll succeed in crossing this huge dead place. It's like sailing on a tiny boat in an ocean of death . . ."

He remained silent, collapsing into a sleep-like state, until the end of the session.

I sat behind him, and Ansky's play *The Dybbuk* came to my mind—how they exorcised the possessing spirit, the dybbuk, from Leah, but then she died. And here, the fetish has gone, but will he live? And I saw a sort of *pieta*—not Michelangelo's well-known, frontal, seated *pieta*, but a figure of a woman walking with a dead body in her arms. I saw her from the side, did not see her face, and she was wandering about. I felt terrible distress, which changed to acceptance, and then I felt sorrow, very quiet, profound, pure sorrow, without words, even to myself. As if this sorrow had become all being. I sat within this immense sorrow, in silence, until the session was over. At the end of the session I woke him up, and he went away, heavily, stooped. Outside, it was dark. Was it the end?

Late that night (more than two hours after he left) he called me, sounding excited. He said,

> "When I left you I wandered around. Eventually I got to the gutter district. I went to the same place where that prostitute had been [a prostitute who three years earlier, after an act of sado-masochistic fetishism, had kissed him and said, 'Why are you like this?']. She wasn't there. There was someone else, someone I think I did fetishistic acts with a long time ago.
>
> "I paid her a reasonably small sum, and she agreed to a kiss and to do it with her hand." [As I mentioned, this was a man who had not been able to bear the touch of a hand, particularly a non-violent touch, and certainly not on his sexual organ.] "She had high heels, but it made no difference, and she had breasts, and a mouth like that. It went very quickly and very smoothly, perhaps too much so. When I finished I trembled terribly, and I burst out laughing. I said, 'Wow, it went so easily.' She didn't understand what I was talking about, or why I was trembling. So that's it, it wasn't like other times, it was nice to get it out like that, it's a shame that I have to pay for it and do it in the gutter. But perhaps it's a stage, I don't know, perhaps it's a stage. I'm still talking to you from the gutter district of Tel-Aviv."
>
> I said, "You sound excited."
>
> "Yes," he replied, "I'm happy, it's so strange."

The next morning he left me a long phone message:

> "I had to tell you how I *feel* this morning. I came home tired last night, and went to sleep. I think that a lot of tiredness had accumulated inside me last night. What happened this morning, there were many times that I wanted very much to come to treatment or to hide there. But this morning I got up, and I don't remember such a real feeling or one so

intense as this feeling. I think the only thing in the world I wanted when I opened my eyes this morning was to come and hide in treatment. Don't know whether it was to hide in you or with you—it's all the same. It's unbelievable how much I wanted to come to you [laughs]. Then I said to myself, it's not so terrifying, in any case it'll be several hours until you get there, and it'll be different then. But that's it, that's it. I wanted to tell you, but I didn't want to disturb you early in the morning. So I waited a couple of hours, telling myself 'She said that I could call.' OK, we'll meet at two."

From that point onwards, although there were other difficult periods, there was a beginning of new movement, and a new sense of aliveness, at first hidden, but gradually becoming more apparent. I think about Winnicott's unforgettable words in "Fear of breakdown": "But, alas, there is no end unless the bottom of the trough has been reached, unless *the thing feared has been experienced*" (1963, p. 178, original italics). And I add, "Unless the bottom of the trough has been reached, *unless the thing feared has been experienced*" in a compassionate holding, within the analyst's "presencing" and interconnecting with the patient's gripping, unbearable agony, devastation, and death. Analyst and patient t(w)ogether there, with-in. For me, it was a very deep moment of being-with-in.

P called the year that followed "a mad race of hope and illusion". Now, suddenly, he no longer masturbated at night to the fetishistic–masochistic fantasy:

"What amazed me was that I had within me some amazing inner strength which I'd never before experienced—I'm sure I'll still pay for it—something which stopped me from performing a fetish. Strange things are really happening. The shoe in the fantasy has disappeared, as if something has blotted it out. I don't know what to say."

He began relationships with two women (he was still afraid of a relationship with only one). He met them, ate with them, listened and talked to them, related to them, entered their houses and their beds. "They are surrogates for learning to live with a woman," he said. The dreadful emptiness gradually faded, but when he tried having sex with them his penis was dead. Yet, although he was extremely embarrassed by these repeated experiences with both women, he refused to imagine a fetish fantasy with them, though he was sure that by doing so he would have had an erection. He repeated over and over, determinedly, "I want different sex. In those moments with them, I felt. I was deeply depressed, I was sad, but I was there. I really was. I existed."

It was also when masturbating that he "bamboozled the automaton" and "created an alternative parallel track". He would now say repeatedly, "We'll live and we'll see." He also began to dream.

One of the two women left him because he refused her suggestion to take Viagra. He met another woman named Doreen, beautiful, and several years older than himself. He felt that "something real is beginning to bud there", and she became his only partner. After three months of "feelings of terror, terror, not simply fear, in bed", his penis began to function. At the session in analysis, exactly two years after the session described above, in which the "bottom" of psychic death had been reached (I was surprised to see that it was on exactly the same date—January 21), he said to me, "I'm waiting for the stage that my search will find myself. As for the tiny boat in the huge ocean, I'm relying on you, and perhaps on myself. It's hard to believe that things change so much." I was surprised to hear that he had retained within himself the memory of the tiny boat in the ocean.

After nine months of the relationship with Doreen, during which he told her about the perverse fetishistic–masochistic world he had been in and she stayed with him, he said to me in our Monday session, after the weekend break,

> "It's seventy-three hours since we met. We've given me a brainwashing. Now I need a heart-washing. I want to learn to love. I want to connect, heart and soul. Inside me, in a sort of bizarre quantum leap, things have been happening that I don't know where they come from and where they're going to, but fuck it, I'm not complaining. Every time I say, wow!, things have been happening, I don't know from where; I also think I'm not trying to destroy them, but even if I did want to destroy them, I doubt whether I would succeed. And all weekend long I've been saying to you, 'Houston, we have a problem.' Once a spacecraft caught fire, and once a spacecraft was saved. I intend to be saved. Just as once I used to say, 'There's nothing inside me and I have nothing,' this time *I want*, this time there *is* inside me, and I *have*. I want to feel more . . . I think that what I'm missing now is love. My brain's racing like mad, my dick is already here, but it's not happening yet in my heart. Still deep-deep-deep-deep, it's not happening yet. Houston, we have a problem here. You have to reply."

And I replied, "Houston hears, Houston's thinking. It's really a distant and dangerous journey, opening up like that and wanting so much to feel."

He said, "All weekend long I said to myself and to you, 'I'm on a journey that began without me, but will end with me.'"

## *"Black hole," breakdown, being-within, and breakthrough*

"I'd rather be sucked into a black hole . . . it's better to be sucked into the nothingness, and finished," said my patient. He said this as the cessation of the perverse practices in the third year of analysis and his subsequent futile attempts to date women in the fourth year led to an extreme collapse into a devouring abyss of core breakdown in the fifth year of analysis. Throughout the entire fifth year we struggled with his descent into all-encompassing devastation, emptiness, psychic death, hopelessness, and violent suicidal despair. A "black hole" of nothingness and death wove together and became the embodiment of a terminal solution, while I mainly tried to ensure survival.

I had already worked with the metaphorical use of the "black hole" and being swept into a black hole of deadness in analysis (Eshel, 1998a). But this time Winnicott's ground-breaking ideas on experiencing the patient's unthinkable, unexperienced breakdown in treatment sustained me, and they became my beacon in this very difficult and dark process. With time, their impact resonated with Clare Winnicott's (1980) strong words, which underscored how crucially important these ideas were to her:

> The moment at which I connected what was happening in the treatment with the theoretical formulation in Winnicott's paper "Fear of breakdown" was for me one of those cumulative experiences when everything adds up and comes together. At that moment I saw the *possibility* of a favourable outcome for my patient. (1980, p. 351, original italics)

Working within this collapse in analysis initially enabled the deep reason for the patient's breakdown in early childhood to unfold. But this knowledge was not transformative. What was needed was the "becoming" of the fundamental possibility that had never been experienced before, of reliving the patient's unbearable deadly breakdown in a "past–present actuality" (Eshel, 2004b); patient-with-analyst within the realness of the breakdown, going through and experiencing the reactivation of the underlying terror and agony that the patient could not experience alone.[5] I describe this as the analyst's "presencing within" and the ensuing deep patient–analyst interconnectedness or "withnessing" in going through the process; *two-in-Oneness* (Eshel, 1998a,b, 2001, 2004a,b, 2005, 2006, 2009, 2010, 2012, 2013a,b).

In keeping with Winnicott's ideas of "fear of breakdown" (1986 [1963]), I would suggest that the advances of the third and fourth year of the analysis "ended in destruction" (p. 178) because there was no reconnecting to the full intensity of the patient's breakdown and annihilation. But these unbearable core states could not be escaped. Hence, all of these menacing, unbearable, and unexperienced feelings were overwhelmingly relived in the treatment over the entire fifth year, in a desperate plea to be experienced, suffered, and transformed. I was there with these feelings, speaking about them and speaking them, listening, thinking, and understanding them, struggling to ensure survival; more and more in the grip of these feelings, but not yet there, in the patient's inmost devastation, not "unless the bottom of the trough ha[d] been reached, unless *the thing feared ha[d] been experienced*" (Winnicott, 1986[1963], p. 178, my italics). I was experiencing the *terror* of breakdown, suicide and death, but not yet death itself until the time that I starkly took them into myself and *was with* the dying child-man, holding the dead body in the arms of my psyche—experiencing, feeling, and then "dreaming" the death (Bion, 1992, p. 216; Eigen, 2001; Grotstein, 2007, 2009; Ogden, 2004). Thus, this desperate attacking plea turned into suffering and profound, immense sorrow within me. It became a wordless, deep psyche-to-psyche interconnectedness or "withnessing", and the death that was taken in and became experienced and suffered for the first time by me-with-him was transformed, and could then become, within him, a different new possibility of being and experiencing.

For me, this way of working has also been profoundly supported in Bion's late writing on the primacy of the analyst's "being" and "becoming" at-one with the patient's unknown and unknowable ultimate emotional reality-O, and a lived, new experience (1970, pp. 26–28). This has lately been elaborated by Grotstein's (2010) and Vermote's (2013) perceptive writings, which underscore the clinical importance of the analyst's "becoming" and "transformations in O within the analyst," and Eigen's (2014) emphasis on analytic work that necessitates "Faith in O" and "Transformation in O". Vermote (2013) has recently formulated an integrative model of psychic functioning for dealing with the unknown. Drawing heavily on Matte-Blanco's and Bion's writings, he distinguishes between three zones, or modes, of psychic functioning with varying degrees of differentiation, different major psychoanalytic models, and different clinical implications for the analyst to describe the scope of psychoanalytic work and the range of possible psychic changes:

1. The mode of reason—oedipal, understanding UC system (Freud, Klein);
2. Transformation in knowledge—container–contained, reverie, dream-work, alpha-function (Bion, Marty, de M'Uzan, Bollas, Botella & Botella, Ogden, Ferro);
3. Transformation in O, when dealing with the most unthought, unknown, undifferentiated zone of psychic functioning (Winnicott, Milner, late Bion, late Lacan). Real, life-giving psychic change occurs at this level of radical, undifferentiated experience between patient and analyst—transformations in O (O from Origin—while the epistemological exploration of the traumatically unthought, in the mode of "transformation in Knowledge or dreamthought," remains at the level of representations. (Thus, the difference between "Transformation in Knowledge" and "Transformation in O" is that T(K) is a thought for something that was not thought yet, and T(O) is a new experience that happens, that can only, in Bion's words, "be 'become', but it cannot be known" (1970, p. 26).

Grotstein, in relating to infantile trauma and chronic resistance, maintains that, unlike the treatment of the healthier personality, the course of treatment of split-off, "castaway patients"

> involves the indivisibility of the transference ↔ countertransference in the analyst's reverie, his or her capacity to "*become*" the patient's anguish and agony. Bion terms this phenomenon "transformations in O within the analyst". (p. 25, original italics)[6]

In this mode of analytic functioning, Bion's enigmatic words acquire their full meaning: "With this [O] the analyst cannot be identified: he must *be* it. . . . at-one-ment with it and evolution . . . that is common to analyst and analysand" (1970, pp. 27, 30, original italics). Bion subsequently offers important guiding words:

> In practice this means *not* that the analyst recalls some relevant memory but that a relevant constellation will *be evoked during the process of at-one-ment with O,* the process denoted by transformation O→K. (1970, p. 33, my italics)

Thus, rather than an epistemological exploration for recovering repressed material (mode 1) and the need for the analyst's reverie, dream-thought, and containing capacity for further epistemological exploration and transformation of the unbearable traumatic unknown (TK, mode 2), the depths of the unknown and unknowable emotional reality of mental catastrophe (Bion, 1970) and of the unthinkable, unexperienced early breakdown (Winnicott, 1986[1963], 1983[1965]), are beyond the limits of the level of representations and analytic thinking (Vermote, 2011). The "dark night of/to the soul" (words Bion borrowed from St John of the Cross) is a "'dark night' to K" (Bion, 1965, p.159), and, thus, can be reached only when the analyst allows himself/herself to experience the "dark night of the soul": "let the dark come upon you . . . with a movement of darkness on darkness" (Eliot, 1974a, p. 200). The unthinkable cannot be thought, but only relived and gone through with the analyst. Real psychic transformation happens in mode 3 at the level of the radical ontological experience of patient and analyst's being-at-one. For only the great intensity of be(com)ing at-one-with the patient's unknown and unknowable emotional reality can reach these innermost annihilated–annihilating states, and create a new experience within the depths of core catastrophe, unthinkable breakdown, and madness. Eigen similarly writes, "More is involved than the capacity to know. . . . A capacity as deep or deeper than the sense of catastrophe must be called forth if healing or profound change is to occur" (1993, p. 219). This capacity is also conveyed in T. S. Eliot's beautiful words evoking "a further union, a deeper communion / Through the dark cold and the empty desolation" (Eliot, 1974a, p. 204).

I believe that the analysis which I have described, and especially its most difficult fifth year, illustrates the necessity of going through and beyond epistemological exploration and understanding (mode 2—knowing) to two-in-Oneness in the experiential, undifferentiated mode 3. Only this made it possible to reach the dark depths in which the unthinkable, unexperienced breakdown comes into being. It was my being there, within the grip of the deadly process, and the eventual emergence of my interconnecting presence or "withnessing", becoming at-one with the patient's agony and annihilation, that enabled the transformation O→K within me-and-him.

I would like to conclude by referring to Dante's journey through *Inferno* (the first part of *The Divine Comedy*, 2008). Dante is guided and protected by the Roman poet Virgil in their descent, circle by circle, through the nine circles of hell, which are teeming with wickedness, horrifying tortures, and unending lamentation.

It is a most critical moment of Dante-with-Virgil interconnection, in which Dante, "more afraid of death than ever", and Virgil had to be lowered by the giant Antaeus into the last, bottom circle of hell, "the lowest point of all evil". Virgil, already in the grasp of the giant's hand, called out to a horrified Dante "'come close, so I can take you'; Then made one bundle of himself and me [Dante]" (canto XXX: 134–135, p. 181), and the giant thus placed them in the bottom pit. Similarly, I would suggest that the analyst and the patient *become one bundle* in order to go through the "collapse into being with the deepest states" (Eigen, 2006, p. 38) of the patient's emotional reality, mostly unknown, unthinkable and unexperienced; a terror too terrifying to be experienced alone.

## *Notes*

1. Tustin and her followers (Spensley, 1995) stress that Tustin's patient John, the little autistic boy, introduced this term some years before physicist John Wheeler introduced it in 1968.
2. In T. S. Eliot's words, it is "Never and always": "Here, the intersection of the timeless moment . . . Never and always" (1974b, p. 215).
3. Israeli astronaut, killed when the space shuttle Columbia was destroyed upon re-entering the earth's atmosphere in 2003.
4. I would like to add an intense description by Eigen (2010) of annihilation, which is closely related to the agonizing experience expressed here:

> Annihilation is not a static state. It goes on and on and on. It's electrifying. I don't have the words for it. It's like being in an electric chair with the current continuously on, or being suffocated but

> you never die. You keep getting more and more suffocated . . . I felt that this is partly what babies must feel, in their own way . . . Screaming and screaming and then the scream fades away. (pp. 26–27)

5. In Ogden's recent words on Winnicott's "Fear of breakdown": "The patient is not alone when he is with an analyst who is able to bear the patient's and his own experiences of breakdown and primitive agony" (Ogden, 2014).
6. It is interesting to note that this kind of undifferentiated "becoming" may be seen in the Biblical description of God's relating to the crying out of the children of Israel from their slavery in Egypt:

> and the children of Israel sighed from the labor, and they cried out, and their cry ascended to God from the labor. And God heard their cry, and God remembered His covenant with Abraham, with Isaac, and with Jacob. And God saw the children of Israel, and God knew. (Exodus 2: 23–25)

These verses contain a sequence of verbs, moving from "God *heard* their cry", "God *remembered* His covenant", "God *saw* the children of Israel", to the last one, "God *knew*" "**וידע אלהים**", which, unlike the other verbs, has no object following it (my italics). I understand this to mean that when a deep knowing of a devastating state is reached, there is no longer a differentiation or divisibility between subject (God) and object (the children of Israel).

## References

Akhtar, S. (2009). Black hole. In: *Contemporary Dictionary of Psychoanalysis* (pp. 38–39). London: Karnac.

Ansky, S. (2002). *The Dybbuk, or Between Two Worlds: A Dramatic Legend in Four Acts*. In: D. G. Roskies (Ed.), *The Dybbuk and Other Writings*, G. Werman (Trans.) (pp. 1–50). New Haven, CT: Yale University Press.

Bibring, E. (1953). The mechanism of depression. In: P. Greenacre (Ed.), *Affective Disorders* (pp. 13–48). New York: International Universities Press.

Bion, W. R. (1965). *Transformations*. London: Maresfield Library/Karnac.

Bion, W. R. (1970). *Attention and Interpretation*. London: Tavistock.

Bion, W. R. (1992). *Cogitations*. London: Karnac.

Bollas, C. (1995). *Cracking Up: The Work of Unconscious Experience*. London: Routledge.

Dante Alighieri (2008). *The Divine Comedy: Inferno*, C. H. Sisson (Trans.). Oxford: Oxford University Press/Oxford World's Classics.

Eigen, M. (1993). *The Electrified Tightrope*, A. Phillips (Ed.). Northvale, NJ: Jason Aronson.

Eigen, M. (1999). *Toxic Nourishment*. London: Karnac.

Eigen, M. (2001). *Damaged Bonds*. London: Karnac.

Eigen, M. (2004). *The Sensitive Self*. Middletown, CT: Wesleyan University Press.

Eigen, M. (2006). The annihilated self. *Psychoanalytic Review, 93*: 25–38.

Eigen, M. (2010). *Eigen in Seoul: Volume 1, Madness and Murder*. London: Karnac.

Eigen, M. (2014). *Faith*. London: Karnac.

Eliot, T. S. (1974a). *Four Quartets*: East Coker. In: *Collected Poems: 1909–1962* (pp. 196–204). London: Faber and Faber.

Eliot, T. S. (1974b). *Four Quartets*: Little Gidding. In: *Collected Poems: 1909–1962* (pp. 214–222). London: Faber and Faber.

Eshel, O. (1998a). 'Black holes', deadness and existing analytically. *International Journal of Psychoanalysis, 79*: 1115–1130.

Eshel, O. (1998b). Meeting acting out, acting in and enactment in psychoanalytic treatment, or: Going into the eye of the storm. *Sihot—Dialogue, Israel Journal of Psychotherapy, 13*: 4–16.

Eshel, O. (2001). Whose sleep is it, anyway? Or 'night moves'. *International Journal of Psychoanalysis, 82*: 545–562.

Eshel, O. (2004a). Let it be and become me: notes on containing, identification, and the possibility of being. *Contemporary Psychoanalysis, 40*: 323–351.

Eshel, O. (2004b). From the 'Green Woman' to 'Scheherazade': the becoming of a fundamentally new experience in psychoanalytic treatment. *Contemporary Psychoanalysis, 40*: 527–556.

Eshel, O. (2005). Pentheus rather than Oedipus: on perversion, survival and analytic 'presencing'. *International Journal of Psychoanalysis, 86*: 1071–1097.

Eshel, O. (2006). Where are you, my beloved? On absence, loss, and the enigma of telepathic dreams. *International Journal of Psychoanalysis, 87*: 1603–1627.

Eshel, O. (2009). To be 'included' in the silence: on the silent patient and the analyst's 'presencing'. *Sihot—Dialogue. Israel Journal of Psychotherapy, 23*: 221–235.

Eshel, O. (2010). Patient–analyst interconnectedness: personal notes on close encounters of a new dimension. *Psychoanalytic Inquiry, 30*: 146–154.

Eshel, O. (2012). A beam of "chimeric" darkness: presence, interconnectedness and transformation in the psychoanalytic treatment of a patient convicted of sex offences. *Psychoanalytic Review, 99*: 149–178.

Eshel, O. (2013a). Tustin's "diabolon" and "metabolon" revisited: further clinical explorations. The Frances Tustin Memorial Prize, the 18th Annual Frances Tustin Memorial Lectureship in Los Angeles, California.

Eshel, O. (2013b). Patient–analyst "withness": on analytic "presencing", passion, and compassion in states of breakdown, despair, and deadness. *Psychoanalytic Quarterly, 82*: 925–963.

Freud, S. (1937d). Constructions in analysis. *S. E., 23*: 257–269. London: Hogarth.

Green, A. (1986). The dead mother. In: *On Private Madness* (pp. 142–173). London: Hogarth Press.

Gribbin, J. (1992). *In Search of the Edge of Time: Black Holes, White Holes, Wormholes*. London: Penguin Books.

Grotstein, J. S. (1986). The psychology of powerlessness: disorders of self-regulation as a newer paradigm for psychopathology. *Psychoanalytic Inquiry, 6*: 93–118.

Grotstein, J. S. (1989). A revised psychoanalytic conception of schizophrenia: an interdisciplinary update. *Psychoanalytic Psychology, 6*: 253–275.

Grotstein, J. S. (1990a). 'Black hole' as the basic psychotic experience: some newer psychoanalytic and neuroscience perspectives on psychosis. *Journal of the American Academy of Psychoanalysis, 18*: 29–46.

Grotstein, J. S. (1990b). Nothingness, meaninglessness, chaos and 'black hole'. I: The importance of nothingness, meaninglessness, and chaos in psychoanalysis. *Contemporary Psychoanalysis, 26*: 257–291.

Grotstein, J. S. (1990c). Nothingness, meaninglessness, chaos and 'black hole'. II: The black hole. *Contemporary Psychoanalysis, 26*: 377–407.

Grotstein, J. S. (1993). Boundary difficulties in borderline patients. In: L. B. Boyer & P. L. Giovacchini (Eds.), *Master Clinicians on Treating the Regressed Patient, Vol. II* (pp. 107–142). Northvale, NJ: Jason Aronson.

Grotstein, J. S. (2007). *A Beam of Intense Darkness: Wilfred Bion's Legacy to Psychoanalysis*. London: Karnac.

Grotstein, J. S. (2009). Dreaming as a "curtain of illusion": revisiting the "Royal Road" with Bion as our guide. *International Journal of Psychoanalysis, 90*: 733–752.

Grotstein, J. S. (2010). "Orphans of O": the negative therapeutic reaction and the longing for the childhood that never was. In: J. V. Buren & S. Alhanati (Eds.), *Primitive Mental States* (pp. 8–30). London: Routledge.

Hawking, S. (1988). *A Brief History of Time: From the Big Bank to Black Holes*. London: Bantam Books.

Hawking, S. (1993). *Black Holes and Baby Universes, and Other Essays*. London: Bantam Books.

Hernandez, M. (1998). Winnicott's "Fear of breakdown": on and beyond trauma. *Diacritics, 28*: 134–143.

Ogden, T. H. (2004). This art of psychoanalysis: dreaming undreamt dreams and interrupted cries. *International Journal of Psychoanalysis, 85*: 857–877.

Ogden, T. H. (2014). Fear of breakdown and the unlived life. *International Journal of Psychoanalysis, 95*: 205–223.

Spensley, S. (1995). *Frances Tustin*. London: Routledge.

Tustin F. (1972). *Autism and Childhood Psychosis*. London: Hogarth Press.

Tustin F. (1986). *Autistic Barriers in Neurotic Patients*. London: Tavistock.

Tustin, F. (1990). *The Protective Shell in Children and Adults*. London: Karnac.

Tustin, F. (1992). *Autistic States in Children* (revised edn). London: Routledge.

Vermote, R. (2011). On the value of "late Bion" to analytic theory and practice. *International Journal of Psychoanalysis, 92*: 1089–1092.

Vermote, R. (2013). The undifferentiated zone of psychic functioning: an integrative approach and clinical implications. Presentation to the European Psychoanalytical Federation (EPF) Conference, Basel, March 24. Also: Vermote, R. (2013). The undifferentiated zone of psychic functioning. European Psychoanalytical Federation. *Psychoanalysis in Europe Bulletin, 67*: 16–27.

Weininger, O. (1903). *Sex and Character*. Bloomington, IN: Indiana University Press, 2005.

Winnicott, C. (1974). Editorial note. Fear of breakdown, D. W. Winnicott. *International Review of Psychoanalysis, 1*: 103.

Winnicott, C. (1980). Fear of breakdown: a clinical example. *International Journal of Psychoanalysis*, 61: 351–357.

Winnicott, D. W. (1979). The mentally ill in your caseload. In: *The Maturational Processes and the Facilitating Environment* (pp. 217–229). London: Hogarth Press.

Winnicott, D. W. (1986)[1963]. Fear of breakdown. In: G. Kohon (Ed.), *The British School of Psychoanalysis. The Independent Tradition* (pp. 173–182). London: Free Association Books. Also in: C. Winnicott, R. Shepherd, & M. Davis (Eds.), *Psycho-analytic Explorations* (pp. 87–95). Cambridge, MA: Harvard, 1989.

Winnicott, D. W. (1988). *Human Nature*. London: Free Association.

Winnicott, D. W. (1989) [1964]. The importance of the setting in meeting regression in psychoanalysis. In: C. Winnicott, R. Shepherd, & M. Davis (Eds.), *Psycho-analytic Explorations* (pp. 96–102). Cambridge, MA: Harvard University Press.

Winnicott, D. W. (1989)[1965]. The psychology of madness: a contribution from psychoanalysis. In: C. Winnicott, R. Shepherd, & M. Davis (Eds.), *Psycho-analytic Explorations* (pp. 119–129). Cambridge, MA: Harvard University Press.

Winnicott, D. W. (1992)[1954]. Metapsychological and clinical aspects of regression within the psycho-analytical set-up. In: *Through Paediatrics to Psycho-Analysis* (pp. 278–294). London: Karnac.

CHAPTER FOUR

# Autistic states in patients with a narcissistic structure

*Anna Oliva De Cesarei*

In her book, *Autistic Barriers in Neurotic Patients*, Tustin (1986, p. 13), referring to "the encapsulated, well nigh impenetrable, autistic part of the personality of neurotic patients" described by Klein (1980, p. 395), notes that "some readers may have difficulties in accepting the thesis that neurotic patients can have autistic impediments" for different reasons. In this chapter, building upon Tustin's observations about two adolescent girls with anorexia nervosa and Ariadne (p. 270), who, as an infant, "had had an overly caring mother who had been grief-stricken as the result of the death of an earlier boy child" and upon my own experience with a small group of patients, I draw attention to the many autistic characteristics that may be found in certain patients with a narcissistic character structure.

These patients had in common an implacable autarchic proclamation, "I don't need anything and anybody", and were trapped in a frozen or "stony" identity (e.g., like a block of marble), in a hard metal shell, or "some kind of cement injection, an inorganic, lifeless, grey substance that takes the colour away from things although it ensures constancy". It was as if they wanted to be perfect and spotless (as any imperfection or "stain" was felt as a flaw in their sense of omnipotence), but, as we shall see, their bodies intervened to signal an excess tension, something distressingly alive, that had shifted to the soma. They immediately conveyed to me a condition of radical hopelessness and a robot-like image that implied the presence of significant areas of unrepresented functioning. In each of them, however, a somatic symptom (e.g., migraine with aura along with olfactory and visual phenomena, stenocardiac crises with angina, fainting fits . . .) had unexpectedly opened a gap in this rigidly structured, seamless system and often became the "motivation" for their asking for an analytic treatment.

As background, these patients each had in common the traumatic experience of a fractured mother–child unity in the very first months of life, a sudden and premature appearance and experience of the "not-me", which, for various reasons, left them precociously alone to deal with traumatic doses of intolerable anxiety. They become aware of this traumatic element only gradually during analysis, whereas, as observer, I often sensed this serious "original" damage from our very first encounters, as a feeling of non-life, or de-animation that I perceived in the stiffness of their bodies, their motionless posture, their blank dull gaze . . .

Gradually, their life stories would reveal events such as a serious maternal depression, an early separation, or emotional disinvestment in the mother–child bond due to a new, unexpected pregnancy or other life events. There was no father to support the mother–child pair in this difficulty, either because the father was physically or emotionally absent, or because he himself was in serious difficulty. These patients survived narcissistic catastrophe by means of a cognitive–emotional dissociation accompanied by hypertrophy and a precocious development of intellectual processes that enabled them to rise to elevated intellectual and cultural levels, and often to hold prestigious professional positions. The formation of an autistic shell protected them from everything that threatened to overturn the system.

In an earlier paper (Oliva De Cesarei, 2005), I described a "narcissism–autism bipolarity", marked by precocious ego development and bi-dimensional identifications, where sensory archaic memories (Bick, 1968; Mitrani, 1998) are deposited, immobile and totalizing, in the formal aspects of character and earlier good emotional experiences leave only a weak trace, that might occasionally be merely glimpsed. In this constellation, we see a dissociated, undifferentiated, autistically encapsulated structure overlaid by a more "normal" looking pseudo-neurotic layer of functioning. If the analyst sees only the "evolved" superficial aspects as being "healthy"—since they allow for good adaptive functioning—without taking the underlying dissociations into account, she could support a pseudo-growth, instead of working in the direction of a progressive transformation of the entire personality. Such a failure would also run the risk of countertransferential collusion with, and repetition of, the actions of the parents, who could not recognize or take care of their young child's worry, anxiety, and deep disturbance.

### *The first years of analysis*

Initial clinical work with these patients reveals the breaks, lacerations, and holes in the psychic background, when the protective maternal screen fails in its function of containing and, thereby, modulating the infant's experience, when the "sensation-object" (Tustin, 1981) imposes levels of separateness that are intolerable for the infant and beyond its capacity to bear. In early trauma, a destructuring situation can result, which has been called "fears of the unthinkable" (Bion, 1962), "primitive agonies" (Winnicott, 1974), and "anxiety at losing the self" (Gaddini, 1969). This anxiety is of an invasive type and, since maternal receptivity is defective or lacking, the object cannot be enlisted to help to shape these primitive fears and agonies into an anxiety signal. What remains is only the endless threat of repetition of a traumatic anxiety state. The faults in the original protective environment, at the boundary between the somatic and the psychic, prevent the possibility of initiating symbolization processes. There is not any "inside" where the event can leave its imprint. Consequently, we do not have any traumatic memory or fantasy about traumas that can be identified, any hidden or underlying formation in which we might encounter and discover the connections between memory, affects, and representation.

Being faced with patients with severe damage to the possibility of representation is a challenge for psychoanalysis and to our criteria for analyzability. With these patients, our function as commentators on an internal world with conflicting but defined characters and roles is ineffective and limited. The fracture of the possibility of representation reflects the presence of a primal repression: a blackout, a gash in the backdrop, a "hole in the paper" instead of "traces in the notebook", missing pages or an eradication of memories. There is no organized screen for a specific trauma. Therefore, the foundations upon which to dream or the screen on which to establish and project a psychic scene are missing. If repair is to be effected, it must come via the development of these capacities by way of the intersubjective workings of the analytic relationship.

In the treatment, this closed system produces immobilization, stiffness, frozenness, or a sense that the patient is petrified. These states reflect the patients' attempts to "contain" the threat of a devastating hemorrhage, within a system that threatens to repeat its traumatic collapse all the time. In the face of this threat, a rigid and immovable "shield" must constantly be maintained as a protection against irreparable breakdown.

A first, long phase in these analyses is characterized by a total incorporation of the analyst into an undifferentiated, indistinct situation, in which analyst and patient are felt to be at one in belonging to an "Olympus" of superior persons: in the stratosphere, ethereal, spiritual, "a mental thing". The sphere and the egg, as images of a totally protected situation, recur to indicate an uncontaminated place, endowed with an original purity (i.e., not "contaminated" by the irruption of the not-me). Within the analysis, these patients repeat their customary mode of self-protection, using knowledge as *opera omnia,* as an encyclopedia, according to individual preferences, to communicate to us the products and constructions of educated, esthetically sophisticated minds. They use their intellect as a domain in which they find a sense of absoluteness and certainty, a place without time that guarantees stability and cohesion of the self, as well as a means for mentally seducing the analyst to join them at this protective level and disregard the chaos and terror that it is intended to shield.

Alongside these aspects, the patient reactivates, in a clinging and totalizing way (and often to the extent of creating a setback in the analytic function, as a possibility of maintaining an asymmetrical level) the other part of the pathological "solution" that they brought to the early trauma, which is inherent in the hard, metallic, repelling aspects of their armor. For a long time, this could impose on the analytic relationship the form of the inadequate, depressed, glacial, or scornful mother with whom the patient has become one. The danger arises that, for both analyst and patient, each might be perceived to be, or to become, the archaic icy or dead maternal object/self.

In lifeless, mental fusion with the analyst and in assimilating the analyst into the autistic shell, gripping him tightly in an inanimate, robot-like, mechanical relationship, these patients look for a perfect union, a circular time (though in a container that is solid and compact in its irremovability, in which we often feel physically and mentally restrained), through an on–off mechanism regarding absence and every interruption, through a break in thought so that breaches cannot be introduced into the system.

In the analytic setting, Freud created for neurotic patients a physical and analytic environment with coordinates that ensure the respect for the para-excitatory system (lights, noises, constancy, etc.), a protected space that corresponds to an intrapsychic space that facilitates good dreaming. For these patients, however, the setting is a reification of the traumatic experience and the autistic shell needed to protect oneself against it (e.g., the couch is an "iron crib" or "a couch with a corpse"). Faced with such patients and such situations, how can we look for a berth on the rocky isle or a footing on the slippery glacier? How can we construct the experience of a space as a condition for continuity and safety (like the earth under our feet and the air that we breathe) and help provide a prelude to an internal space that allows the hope for new possibilities to grow?

The construction of an internal space might begin with an experience with the analyst who enables the patient to pass through the analyst himself, who must allow him or her self to be colonized and infected by an imposing symmetrical relationship between the patient who "makes a wall" in presenting himself as the impenetrable parent and the bewilderment, the feeling of hopelessness, the frequent difficulty in thinking experienced by the analyst. At risk in this movement is the danger of immobilizing the analytic process itself.

In the analyst's reverie, it is important for the analyst to observe the fetish-mind of the patient fractured by affectivity, the sensory impressions, and the auto-sensual forms, but to keep these observations to himself and, when the time is right, to communicate to the patient the embryos of illusion that the patient has managed to maintain alive—rhythmic sensations in his rocking, traces of experiences of an indistinct background that has been lacerated by the irruption of the not-me. In this way, the analyst acts as an amplifier, within herself, of the weak signs of life that the patient has maintained. She is a "lucky archeologist" (Pontalis, 1981) if she manages to gain access to, and enter into, this biological bedrock.

The analyst must dwell "in" the situation that the patient imposes and, at the same time, maintain or recover a free terrain when it is lost in the storms of the relationship, cultivate a transitional area, offer a source of emotional resources to be introduced into the setting. Furthermore, she must receive and restrain what is estranged, alien, totally other than the self (in the sense that otherness is connected with what cannot be represented) for the patient. To give it back too early would indicate a problem of incontinence on the part of the analyst, provoked by a difficulty in living "the effects", the annihilating pain, the sense of death in feeling expelled. Thus, we must experience and provide the profound need of a vital breath investment in a "first person" for a very long time, without inducing a rupture or rejection that could provoke the interruption of the analysis.

Even as we concentrate on guaranteeing the protection and homeostasis necessary to the patient, we must also create possible openings on the horizon. It is important to allow nascent idealization to develop freely, as many authors point out (for example, Kohut, 1971; Winnicott, 1958, 1971), to take therapeutic advantage of the potentially positive function of illusion, to actively take part with annotations and expanding meaning, for example, by paying attention to the alternating traces of adhesive fusion and fracture in the patient's relationship with the partner, to let the patient feel how we understand that, for him, not needing anyone is the only way to maintain a sense of unity and cohesion, to respect slow times, and to create the foundations and the ground for a possible "experiencing for the first time" of the trauma.

For the analyst, there is the need of a *pictorial* use of words, to draw a background or form lively images, so that the analyst's words are not drawn into the identical impossibility of using language, as the patient does, as "dead letters". In this way, the analyst's words can function in ways that are similar to Winnicott's line drawings in his "squiggle game". At this stage, there is no room for interpretation, there being no place for "the other". To offer interpretations prematurely might result in denial or, even worse, might be incorporated by the patient as another intellectualized hypothesis or story that goes adhesively along with the countless possibilities already available to him. In these severe pathologies where the compulsion to repeat imposes automatic repetitions, we can see various degrees of mentalization and different scenarios in which the complex mechanism of *Nachtraglichkeit* cannot be readily engaged.

As we are dealing with "sensory memories" and rigid automatisms, it is necessary to form a first time prior to the trauma, to build an area "uncorrupted" by the invasion of the trauma, re-finding and drawing together once more the threads of the primal illusion, re-establishing fundamental trust in a passivity connected to trusting expectations and in the experience of a para-excitatory dimension capable of transforming an automatic anxiety into an anxiety signal. I would like to emphasize the importance for these patients of the restoration of a situation of harmonious merging containment with the analyst/object, a nature environment, "a humus", a biological ground that reopens and strengthens a profound trust in a "promised land"; a nature represented by harmonious images with lively, fertile, and luminous colors, in order to restore the sense of going-on-being and rebuild a skin that can function as a container of an internal space.

This reconstruction of the background of sensory and affective memories, of a pattern that acts as a screen on which everything that was previously expelled can be deposited, is the prerequisite for coming out, in *après-coup*, from the grip of pathological identifications, and for introducing a transformative temporality. In order to accomplish this, a painstaking underground work is needed: an imperceptible flowing of vital elements that gradually constitute a fabric weave that fills in the gaps and allows the patient to breathe in a new atmosphere and to open up his channels of reception in external relationships, via some kind of "imitation" of a new relational quality experienced with the analyst.

This phase, often shown by more relaxed posture or facial expression and a more lively gaze, is described as breaking loose from the totalizing armor or from the plaster cast that entirely envelops the body. What was once a bottomless pit, a black hole starts to become defined: a hard core with edges. It obtains a form and is located inside the body. At this point the anxiety of fragmentation and annihilation (falling and fainting, dissolving, being pulverized . . .) no longer appears as a one-way path. This development can be considered a sign that the experience of being held by the analyst is working and can open up new perspectives.

Now, I shall examine carefully a delicate phase of the analysis: despite a work of several years in preparing the most appropriate terrain for trust in opening a breach in the "autistic core", the transition often has the nature of a sudden fracture that repeats the old irruption of the not-me, with specific characteristics in relation to the individual personal stories. It is a critical point, because the "hard core" is a stronghold of omnipotence felt as a protection against breakdown, but it can bring about a turning point if strong sensations and passions can be tolerated and held by a present and affectively alive and engaged psychoanalyst. Having assumed via the transference the role of the traumatizing object, it is the analyst's task to tolerate and graduate the weight of anxiety that the patient can bear, to carry out a function of para-excitation, and to be a new object who opens up the possibility of a different story. The transition to the not-me has the characteristics of a sudden fracture that repeats the old break-in of the not-Self, which can entail hopelessness imbued with icy death (Alba), repeated threats of interrupting the analytic treatment (Sara), or it can engender a two-phase analysis, as in the case of Iacopo.

## *Alba*

Alba is forty years old and asked for analysis for blinding migraines that drove her berserk and which would only pass if she isolated herself in the dark, devoid of contacts and in a sleep oblivion that completely cut her off from everything, interrupting all current life events. The headaches totally disrupted her customary altruistic and hyper-willing lifestyle and disrupted the image of herself as a person who, thanks to her lucid rationality, managed "to do everything", both at home and at work.

The dramatic event in her early history occurred when she was just forty-five days old: she "lost" her mother, who was engulfed by pain following the death—in tragic circumstances—of her firstborn child, a son twelve years of age. A few days later, Alba's father left for work and was absent for two years.

Alba's long and complex analytic story (at a rhythm of three sessions a week) encouraged her, after six years, to break loose, in relationships, from automatic roles imposed by the trauma, and to pass from a totalizing two-dimensional armoring to the development of a hard internal core. Alba leaves me with the feeling that one could move indefinitely around this nucleus, with the fantasy of a never-ending analysis. On the other hand, every now and then she urges me to do something strong in order to "break this shell", give her "a shock that would provoke a brusque re-awakening", "a sharp turn that would permit a sudden swerve".

"Shake, break, smash into pieces . . ." are words also used to describe her pounding migraines (the body thus bears witness to the violence of the impact with the other) and refer back to the early laceration, when the maternal adhesive protective shell was unexpectedly broken and the premature irruption of a third, an unrecognizable mother, obliged Alba to have recourse to a shell carapace (Tustin, 1986). The hypertrophic and unpierceable wall of the hard core serves to seal areas of fragmentation, unthinkable aspects not held by the eye-window of the mother, a void of representation. For this nucleus, Alba tells me, "I am not able to grasp the possibility here of being recovered and rebuilt; I don't think I have an internal structure that is emotionally able to grasp this opportunity." The analyst's words come up against a gap that cannot be filled, a representational void that refers back to a lack of the experience of feeling her vital states held, the feeling of existing before everything else. Alba reacted to the lack of her mother's eye with a similar denial, in her turn, becoming "a face without windows".

In one session, Alba, seeing that I was wearing a thick jumper, asked if I was cold, and then spoke to me about rationalism, philosophy, and the poems of someone she knew, and whom she congratulated for their synthesis of form and content. One poem was entitled "Schizophrenia" and the other "Asocial". As she spoke to me of a wall that needed to be broken down, because it prevented her from bearing her desperation, I felt a violent blow in the stomach that prostrated me and made me feel as cold as ice At first I was afraid I would faint, then I fantasized about going home to prepare something hot, and immediately felt worried at leaving Alba alone . . . In the end I curled up in my armchair, slowly got myself warmer and gradually regained a normal temperature. With this blow in the stomach, I resonated with the brusque and traumatic irruption of the otherness in Alba's story, and with the unexpectedness and violence of the setback she suffered.

In my turn, I felt threatened in my psyche–soma unity, confronted with an area of fainting that the body "takes upon itself" to signal. I was the one unexpectedly hit, in a helpless situation.

I tell Alba that she is afraid she will find a mother in me who speaks out of cold reason, and yet she hopes that I can feel this icy death that is in her, that I can tolerate it and can warm up such strong sensations, to be able to differentiate myself from a mother who "fails" in front of the desperation of her baby, dumping her and fleeing, and to hold open the possibility of recomposing a bridge between the sky-nest and the earth-fall.

Alba replies, "But if you feel this, I can no longer believe in a magic solution that cancels my story, that erases the mark . . . if you feel my iciness, my despair, I place something important in you and consequently it isn't true that I don't need anyone . . . perhaps I can't bear to make you suffer for me; I did make my mother suffer and then she left; if you are empathetic with me I will make you feel feelings that are too strong and primitive, I am afraid of upsetting you with my madness, I would see you annoyed, overworked—you would feel "these patients are real bloodsuckers".

But what is this iciness in the body? Starting with the concept of "breakdown" introduced by Winnicott (1974) to describe the state of an unthinkable thing that belies the defensive organism, it is vital to let the patient "live" the experiences depleted of representation in the session and to recover the naked affect connected with the traumatic experience. In the specific case, the unthinkable has to do with psychic death, as a violent and unexpected irruption of a loss of energy. There is no more current (according to an on–off functioning). We have arrived at the need for reproducing the violent, unexpected impact, having the characteristics of an outburst, of the trauma as a hinge for freeing creativity from its confusion with destructiveness, and the analyst suffers the effects on her own person.

In trying to explain the violence of some countertransferential moments, I agree with Steiner (quoted by Rosenfeld, 1987, p. 157) when he describes in the infant uncontrollable processes of absorption of the mother's psychic processes that are remarkably similar to osmosis. Alvarez (1992) quotes Bateson when she speaks of mood-signs as being "thought to be like sexual odours—automatic, involuntary, but outwardly perceptible events which are part of the physiological process which we have called a mood" (p. 58).

### *Sara*

Sara was an unwanted baby and she experienced the early abandonment to a nanny from the age of three months to three years. At that point, her mother came back into her life, but was unable to feel her needs and left Sara to herself and to learn the art of getting by. Her father was a loving man, but had difficulty in filtering his own passions. These elements characterize the history of Sara, a young woman deeply involved in her professional and philosophical interests, accustomed to putting mental images between herself and the world that have always allowed her to tell many stories with a variety of outcomes. For Sara, the word was used as total knowledge, taking phrases from books "pasted like pieces of identity".

A nightmare from the early stages of her analysis—"the image of a warrior, face immobile, like a wax mask, lifeless, just through the mouth mice enter and exit, giving the impression of being even bigger, the mice are the only living thing"—is emblematic of a penis fecal word, with destructive aspects, erected as a means of survival against an atrophic contact, without life. She will tell me, later, of "a tone of voice compressed by a straitjacket". Thus, she described and became an object impenetrable as crystal, ungraspable. This was the image of herself reflecting that of her mother, who seemed caught up in her own world, but cold and inaccessible to Sara: "it was like clinging to walls of ice". Sara, in turn, feels herself a surface, a vertical wall, on which whatever has to do with feeling slides away.

Sara feels I am transparent for her for a long time. She cannot materialize me, just sees me in a superficial two dimensions (like a painting), without depth like a sculpture. For a long time, she tries to seduce and wrap herself around me, using images of beauty and narcissistic perfection from the psychoanalytic church, a sacred but cold atmosphere, made up of mental images that give her the sensation of existing and that I perceive as being drawn into a necrophilic labyrinth of ideas and mental theories.

After more than four years of analysis, the blinding light of the city of mirrors, the sensation of running through many scenes but not conceiving any cure for herself, bring some vital germ of illusion, the hope of living the analysis as an "incubator". The opening of the autistic core happens in an acute way. Sara has just started living in a "state of grace" during the session. She dreams I am pregnant with a little girl, the fruit of her parents' desire. At the same time, an inconsolable desperation emerges, especially during absences, accompanied by a furious anger because she cannot stand "being a wreck".

She arrives late to one session, tells me she is determined to stop coming. I have got it all wrong since she had been perfectly all right before. She had been perfect and now she feels depleted. She will turn to an expert (whose ideas are known to Sara and used as a stick fetish in an adhesive–imitative way) and, she adds, it is pointless for me to try to stop her, because I will never succeed in having her soul or standing her violence. I am absolutely stunned by the way she speaks to me, so that I hardly follow the meaning of her words, feeling a blind rage. I feel carried away by a sudden fury, annihilated in my existence.

In response, I re-create within me a place for reflection to restore something that will at least filter the violence of my emotions, and, in a firm tone of voice, I say, "I think that something fundamental is happening between us, we shall both stop here and try to understand your peremptory assertions of today."

Sara leaves calmly. Once the working day is over, Sara comes back to my mind and I am still restless, upset, dissatisfied, a state of mind that finds relief only when I realize that she has enacted her old abandonment, having formed an omnipotent pair that knows everything, that sees everything clearly. She has made me feel what it is like to be driven out without having any clues for understanding what is happening. With this thought in mind, I have gained from my response, not wholly consciously, a basic foundation, a deep confidence that we two could now be together in a new possibility.

A strong interpretation could set forth a premature integration of the dissociation, counting on libidinal parts that have not yet been fully established, but are still embryonic fragments that have been gathered in, rescued, and reinforced in order to constitute a storyline, a foundation, a base. It is not by chance that we often hear our patients' perplexity at the possibility of "filling the voids of a previous non-life".

The analyst, searched as a source of well-being, breaks the "inanimate" mirroring relationship and presents a not-me, before which Sara, for now, can only show the old fracture, the need to smash everything, a rage that is blind in as much as it is scattered and undirected. There is an evacuation of the fear of death, of self-annihilation, which I feel for myself, while she looks for life elsewhere, in a mental process, a father-phallus of which she knows the ideology. She entrusts the analyst with the possibility of interrupting the automatism of repetition, by helping her build the confidence required to renounce the old way of fracturing her global experience.

Faced with the threat of her precipitously leaving, I used the word "interruption" as the possibility to build a transformative bridge between the old and the new. Sara tries to flee from/toward the analyst as the agent of a mind–soul integration, and yet the watershed of the interruption is the hope of new possibilities. Episodes of such fury have occurred earlier during the regression Sara underwent during her analysis, especially when she felt defenseless and the analyst became the reified image of the traumatic not-me. I have considered this blind anger as the final scream, a form of life if compared to the anxiety of disappearing, dissolving, not existing; a way of Sara's crying out "I exist" through her scream.

Experience has taught me to remain vigilant for whatever might have made the patient feel injured, in such a way as to make her so angry and destructive. If their defenses give way, these patients are overwhelmed with panic and hopelessness. Anger seems to be their only way of feeling alive and they are remarkably incapable of focusing on what it is that makes them feel uncomfortable. The rapid time needed for an acute rationalization gives way to an amorphous and totally inert part and it is exclusively our task, at certain moments, to meet and accept this hopelessness and help regulate their tension.

Forever split into two areas, an internal one of primordial material, an agitated part, and an external armor, "a marionette dressed as a king", two separate channels that are absolute and uncontaminated, the prospect of bringing together reason and the emotions is seen as contaminating the purity of each of them. The analyst is considered as the boatman that joins the two banks, "on one side, hell and, on the other, the light, the two banks being oval, two parts of a sphere", to guide the transition from a penetrative word, invested with magical–omnipotent power, to listening to the language of the body, which is much more blurred, at times indecipherable. This is a fundamental stage, marking the possibility of entrusting something that has long been kept protected, enabled by the possibility of finally starting to live passivity as something freed from an identification with a directionless state that is chaotic and agitated, or with a state of inanition and death (states of mind that, previously, she had just thought of as having to "vomit" out, otherwise she would explode).

Joining the two banks provokes an enormous anguish that Sara fears will suffocate her: "I thought you would take me by the hand from this no-man's land, lift me up from this dangerous place and take me away." If I am not there, if she is more anxious, if the frustration increases, she feels desperate, without anything to hold on to and she starts to claim once more that she is doing everything alone. She tells me that if the re-composition is made up of such flaws, she refuses to carry on, and identifies herself with a vertical self-wall that lets everything slip away, an identical Self to that of her mother, who had let her fall headlong.

Sara has learned to identify this automatism "within me, there is a vertical destructive part, like a laser, I freeze everything, as if this part had a life of its own. I can't control it. It is like saying 'you try now' and I go from an absolute calm to a blind rage . . . All I can do is vomit, to prevent myself exploding."

I now report one of my own dreams from that period: Sara leaves the session in a hurry (as she does when she is upset and releases her anxiety by fleeing into her mind and/or by becoming hyperactive), while I am hanging on a vertical wall, a hard rubber surface that is smooth and black, where, in order to make headway, I must make holes that break the rubber wall, dig out a handhold to grasp and then, with great effort, make other holes in order to climb up. All the time I am worried about holding on tight to avoid falling. While I am making all this effort, I notice that Sara is near me, calm, safely supported on a platform, and I think that the analyst is me.

It is clear the difficulty I am having in making progress on this firmly repelling identification, that makes everything slip away, the difficulty in creating some foothold in order to proceed, and the need to remind myself to keep my thinking faculty alive in the face of such strong emotions. The more I take upon myself Sara's catastrophic anxiety about falling and I create for her a safe base where she can stand, the more it is possible to enter and break this identification with a mother that rejects the requests of the little girl and lets her slip away "like a wall of ice". Counting on the libidinal possibilities that have now been achieved and reinforced in our relationship, I dig into the wall as Sara had done in vain with her mother, to transform her, to humanize a cold and ungraspable "wall", in a battle that is lost from the start since it comes up against the refusal of them both.

The image in the dream recalls the siege of a fortress. Perching on a rock can be a defense, but also a need . . . I have the impression that only by offering an alternative experiencing model to that of the refusing object, taking it upon myself and giving sense to Sara's anxiety, until she is able to hold on to it instead of just running away from it, that trust can be created to give her a support to stand on, to build a connective tissue over the laceration.

This new experience of feeling her anxiety, sensations, and feelings about no longer falling into the void, but being preserved and kept, brings her a sense of well-being and calmness. It re-awakens her emotional capacity, an activity that previously was concentrated in her intellect, but which can now be lodged in the emotional dimension. Repetition becomes a way of learning and opening up different qualitative possibilities: "It's good to feel that you are doing things for me," Sara says.

Apart from the threat of interrupting the analysis, a further two years of analysis were necessary to create an internal space suitable for accommodating the "two banks". For a long time, actions and body language "troubled the waters" and conveyed significant communication. At the end of this period, Sara told me, "You have held and rescued me, and now I want to thank you for having been there when I didn't want to see you. About all my attempts to get away, now there is a horizon, the sky and the land, no longer abysses, as if the earth had closed over . . . having overcome the black holes, there is no longer a sense of irrevocability, just a feeling that this wound could open again, even though it seems to me that I can see the bottom and take stock of it all. Today I feel a sense of belonging that I didn't have before."

## *Iacopo*

At the beginning of his analysis, Iacopo talks about himself as "a corpse lying on the anatomic table, an object of scrutiny by an organic analyst–doctor who studies the different evidences under the microscope." Detached, impassive, imperturbable, the analyst is seen by the patient as being identical to himself, lacking all differentiation in terms of feeling (ataraxia of feelings).

I have wondered at length about this deadly start of Iacopo's analysis, a "dead", stiff body forced to gesture, a tightened threat, a blank, sometimes very sad gaze, and a lively, bright mind that is rigorously shattered by the affects that are experienced as truly alien in the situation. In my countertransference, I find a feeling of non-existence alternating with a sensation of being cornered, smashed against a wall, leveled out. If I consider my own transference to this new relationship, the image of a stiff and cold object to look at (as Winnicott said, rather than to look into) feels impending. As I fantasize about these aspects within myself, the representation of a relationship with a withdrawn mother who gives cold and mechanical care and does not allow her child to touch her is dominating. The child looks for life and connection, but experiences a crashing relationship of aggression and intrusion.

After four years of analytic work the patient has a dream:

> I was coming back home and found my wife lying in bed. She had been released from a plaster cast covering her from the neck to the feet. On her skin there were inscriptions written by her friends that I could not read. By my side X (one of his co-workers) stood and I did not want him to read the inscriptions.
>
> *Iacopo*: The plaster simulacrum is a form of autism, a windowless monad where the invader silences and mortifies all feelings . . . Other times, there are openings, as if some exchange is possible, when I feel your attentive, balanced gaze looking at me as a person. Last night I spoke with a friend and was able to help her express her sorrow.
>
> *Analyst*: You felt you could do with your friend what we are doing here. The wife is a bodily and affective Self that we release from the plaster cast here on the couch. On the skin there are relational traces that have been and are still there. You feel embarrassed when you experience the relationship, because of the shame of showing yourself too naked, and an even stronger presence of an invader mistreating your feelings, dominates. It is not easy to shift to the indecipherable writings, since you are so used to referring to your mind as a certainty.

I find the image of the plaster simulacrum very expressive to convey how his totalizing armor is hiding all the traces of contact that Iacopo has experienced, in his life history, with his meaningful nanny. These traces, although shapeless, indecipherable, and unrecognizable, are a necessary graft for the analytic relationship. Now they appear as experienced inscriptions on an ego that is coming back to life.

In the dream, the plaster armor seems to be easily removed, whereas his relational experience of the humiliation of the narcissistic foundations of the Self has left a bleak, devastated, hopeless world. The "friendly" inscriptions are too few with respect to the huge actualization of the depressed object (at Iacopo's birth) who wanted a genius son and mistreated his feelings.

Often, Iacopo talks about his need to have an extended session, lasting half a day, to strengthen something that he can take away, otherwise everything disappears, as the tearing is too wide. At the limit, the faint appearance of his wish to "let the desert blossom", to enliven blank pages in his life history, is smashed by a metal-walled Self, adhesively identified with a harsh, cold mother absorbed in her depression. And yet, in his life there is a progressive softening of his relationships with himself, his children, his partner, with whom he lives an exclusive "greenhouse love" fully protected against all kind of upheaval.

Almost seven years into his analysis, he asks me to plan termination, as he feels "purified by a truth based on firm certainties". "You succeded in enabling me to reconstruct myself from within. I didn't open up or trust you, but I let you carry out an endoscopy. On the other hand, I myself don't want to see some of my aspects that I don't accept, although we have built many bridges." His decision to terminate appears after a long stalemate, "stumbling block on which no light could be shed", bleak areas lacking all vital breath connected with maternal depression.

The core issue of this premature termination seems to be his anxiety about the breakdown of his identity based on his self-image "sitting on a pinnacle" that might entail an unbearable psychic breakdown (his brother had a breakdown a few months earlier). We have put his omnipotence back into perspective, but a "smaller tower is still standing". The analyst has to carry the burden of a vertical fall and the failure of not being able to help him open up fully and revive him (just like Iacopo, who had not been able to revive his mother and bring her back to life). In a dream, the analyst–trainer with a paraglider crashes and dies as Iacopo flies with a glider and is totally detached from what is happening.

To act on a transition, a gap between the past and the present, by terminating analysis prematurely, means to repeat the original fall in the reverse role. It is a way to cut out a symmetrical transference: the analyst carries the burden of being left "half way through", with the affects and drives that he has to bear.

Around one year later, Iacopo returns: "I am back to light the flame, but don't push too much, as the ataraxia is ready and I am ready to extinguish the flame. You'll need to be very patient." This second time, we shift from the cortex to the paleoencephalon and the "second brain" (one billion neurons in the intestines), from the sea of ice to the underlying magma, trying to give shape to its primordial matter. As Winnicott (1974) says, only the actualization in the transference can access the primitive shapelessness. "The only way to 'remember' in this case is for the patient to experience this past thing for the first time in the present, that is to say, in the transference" (p. 105). A dream that Iacopo has three years after resuming his analysis makes it explicit how, in this second analysis, the perceptions and signals—which used to be "missing" because of a state of deafness and blindness—can, in fact, develop in the presence of the other.

Here is a dream:

> A crazy young woman kidnapped my daughter in an institution for mental disorders. I go around in the city and look for any trace of the child because she did a poo, cleaned herself, and left the paper on the ground. Like a detective, it occurs to me that she has been kidnapped once already, and we feared that the woman would kill the child. I had said, "If she kills her, we'll make another child", but my wife was shocked (upon the first abduction). Now I am terrified for that child in the hands of a crazy woman.
>
> *Iacopo*: I am the girl, strangled by my crazy part (my brain detached from the rest). By the way, I thought of calling a psychologist.

Now, events and memory traces may be experienced (*Nachtraglichkeit*) and Iacopo wants to defend and protect his recovered Self. From a frozen and blocked time, we have shifted into a transformative time.

## *Final considerations*

When the patient is able to show the analyst an opening to the hard core, it means that the patient does not consider the hard core as the only hinge of his identity. The explosion and overflowing of the psychological and physiological tension that Tustin (1986) mentions invades the analytic relationship.

In making a breach in the hard core, the old tearing of a precocious appearance of the not-Self opens again. It is the fracture of the symmetrical relationship that initiates the transition to the not-Self, a process which has been prepared by a previous work of reconstruction of a trustful background through the establishment of an internal space built on the founding experience of feeling that one's once abandoned needs and destructuring anxieties have been met. We can see an acute form of transition to the not-me for Alba and Sara, and a slower one with some chronic aspects, I would say, for Iacopo, where the analyst experiences an action of strain and running out of resources that leads her to feel drained, worn out, fatigued to the point that she is ready to surrender. (That is, the analyst experiences the transition that had led the patient to a definitive withdrawal.)

At the end of the first analysis, Iacopo said, "I feel that you want to help me get in touch with my hard core, but I can't." This area of "events that have already happened, but have not yet been experienced" (Winnicott, 1974, p. 104) is the area of the unrepressed unconscious, where memories are said to be implicit memories. This archaic communication (like communication from unconscious to unconscious, fusion-like states, osmosis, telepathic phenomena, etc.) appears suddenly within the analyst's psyche and has an effect on her mental or somatic functioning. The analyst takes in the lava and tries to give a filtered light back to the patient.

It would be omnipotent to think of getting to the "translation" of whatever has to do with the non-verbal and pre-verbal. Many aspects can be held over, others will be developed by the patient, so long as the analysis sets off a change in the experience towards the basic needs of being and the world of affects. As Tustin (1986) describes, "In the interactive coexistence of Phase 2 in which healing becomes possible, there is dawning awareness of 'me' and 'not-me', but the 'not-me' can sometimes be so unbearable that it is 'blacked out'" (p. 304).

When Alba starts to mention termination, she tells me, in the Monday session, three dreams where the element three appears. She had "three dreams on three successive nights". I focus on the first dream, which is specifically about the topics I have tackled in her session (the two other dreams talk about situations where chaos and confusion are finding some organization through the recovery and the re-investment in vital aspects, opening the possibility to control the abuse and the interference of an identification with the dead mother better).

In the dream, she says,

> I had a fourth child. He was afflicted with Down's syndrome, a baby in swaddling clothes lying in bed. The doctor shows it to me. He has three hands, one is ordinary but the left arm has two hands. His face is terrifying, yellowish, with a dead mask and a hole in the left temple. They are feeding him, he is spilling the milk, he has slimy tears and I feel disgusted. I think, "Better that he spills the food, so that he'll die sooner." I am crying and the doctor tries to comfort me. My husband arrives. As he looks at the baby, some cleaning tissue falls in the hole and he takes it out.

We can understand this dream as the representation of an early break-in of the third as not-Self (three hands) that cannot be metabolized (the hole, the deformity). It is a sudden, vehement, sinister (not only because it affects the left side),[1] upsetting hole that cannot be mentalized at that time, like the mask of psychic death. We cannot speak of an ego that masters the event, but, rather, a state of transition between being a mother who cries about her hopelessness and wants to throw herself as a child out of a window and someone who now has a doctor by her side who comforts and supports her and allows for new potential developments, such as the possibility of introjecting the relationship with a caring parent who is close, involved, comforting the wounded patient and helping to deal with annihilation anxiety. The doctor has contributed to the formation (in the very sense of giving form) of what was stuck in the immobility of the autistic core, helping to put the old event in the temporality of representation. It is a psychic work that enables the patient to overcome the "quick fix" as a one-way path and opens new possibilities for the future. It attests to the psychic work that we have woven together to integrate the infantile dissociated areas within a temporality that gives meaning and depth to her life history.

The malformed child, a dream construction of the traumatic event, not only points to the need to give better form and thinkability to the events connected with the introduction of the third in the ensuing analytic work, but also reflects the breakdown of an image that is so difficult to accept for these patients. They shift from a perfect, absolute, omnipotent sense of Self, to a hole in their Self-image, a stain, "like being damaged forever", something that cannot be erased, the sign of an event that can be dealt with through renewed strengths but that the omnipotent narcissism would just want to deny. I think that the malformed child means that, whatever effort we make, there are insurmountable limits to the representation of these psychic areas.

> Ultimately, it is beyond the power of mind to study itself, or to express non-verbal mental experiences in words . . . But we are driven to go on trying, even though we know that the only certain knowledge is that we can never know "ultimate reality". We have to accept being surrounded by mystery. (Tustin 1986, p. 168)

## Note

1. In Italian, the word for left is *sinistre,* hence the pun: *sinistre*/sinister.

## References

Alvarez, A. (1992). *Live Company: Psychoanalytic Psychotherapy with Autistic, Borderline, Deprived and Abused Children*. London: Routledge.

Bick, E. (1968). The experience of the skin in early object relations. *International Journal of Psychoanalysis, 49*: 484–486.

Bion, W. R. (1962). *Learning from Experience*. London: Heinemann.

Gaddini, E. (1969). On imitation. *International Journal of Psychoanalysis, 50*: 475–484.

Klein, S. (1980). Autistic phenomena in neurotic patients. *International Journal of Psychoanalysis, 61*: 395–402.

Kohut, H. (1971). *The Analysis of the Self*. New York: International Universities Press.

Mitrani, J. (1998). Never before and never again. The compulsion to repeat, the fear of breakdown and the defensive organization. *International Journal of Psychoanalysis, 79*: 301–316.

Oliva De Cesarei, A. (2005). Early trauma and narcissism–autism bipolarity. *International Journal of Psychoanalysis,* 86: 657–675.

Pontalis, J.-B. (1981). *Frontiers in Psychoanalysis: Between the Dream and Psychic Pain,* C. Cullen & P. Cullen (Trans.). New York: International Universities Press.

Rosenfeld, H. A. (1987). *Impasse and Interpretation: Therapeutic and Anti-therapeutic Factors in the Psychoanalytic Treatment of Psychotic, Borderline and Neurotic Patients*. London: Routledge.

Tustin, F. (1981). *Autistic States in Children*. London: Routledge & Kegan Paul.

Tustin, F. (1986). *Autistic Barriers in Neurotic Patients*. London: Karnac.
Winnicott, D. W. (1958). *Through Paediatrics to Psycho-analysis: Collected Papers*. London: Tavistock.
Winnicott, D. W. (1971). Mirror-role of mother and family in child development. In: *Playing and Reality* (pp. 111–118). London: Tavistock.
Winnicott, D. W. (1974). Fear of breakdown. *International Review of Psycho-Analysis, 1*: 103–107.

CHAPTER FIVE

# Sensual experience, defensive second skin, and the eclipse of the body: some thoughts on Tustin and Ferrari

*Riccardo Lombardi*

Tustin underscored the fact that children with psychogenic autism have no sense of self-identity, and she favored a working through based on their need for primary self-definition. For her, the absence of a working through of an early developmental phase in which identity is built up leads to the construction of an autistic shell that makes it possible to circumvent this dark zone of failed early development. Tustin later extended her discoveries to adult patients with autistic characteristics who feel unreal and perceive life as a sort of dream. This is not, of course, a creative dream, but, instead, the condition Bion indicated in which one is neither awake nor asleep.

Tustin sensed how central recognition of the body is to helping these patients define an identity of their own. An interest in the importance of the body in primitive development is a point of contact between Tustin's perspective of infantile autism and my own clinical research, conducted primarily on adolescent and adult patients with serious forms of psychosis containing very often clear autistic components. In fact, in my writing, I have tried in various ways to show how "the perception of the body is the decisive element of differentiation and a first principle of reality which can stimulate awareness of the body-self and of the other" (Lombardi, 2005). Following Ferrari's (2004) hypothesis of the eclipse of the body, I consider two parallel relationships within the analytic relationship: the "horizontal" analysand–analyst relationship and the "vertical" body–mind relationship. In primitive mental states, I attribute a central role to the working through of the "vertical" body–mind relationship: my approach involves deliberately not giving priority to the aspect of transference interpretation, while bearing in mind that the most urgent clinical need is to establish a "transference to the patient's body", together with the rudiments of a functioning mental metabolism and of representation and consciousness of self in the patient.

Experiences focused on the body are a challenge for the analyst to describe and convey, because of the difficulty both of having access to them in the context of analysis and also the absence of words available to the analyst to adequately describe and convey somatic experience that might be sensorially based, vaguely sensed, and relatively ineffable. That is, words seem hardly up to the task of describing this primitive hodgepodge of non-verbal experiences, so that we often find ourselves in a quandary when we set out to verbalize this mysterious dimension. Bion maintained that one of the biggest problems related to the transference was its being "ineffable", that is, practically untranslatable for those extraneous to the experience shared by the analysand and the analyst. When we write or speak about the psychoanalysis of so-called primitive mental states, we seek, with great difficulty, to violate the ineffability of these levels of experience, counting on the experiential complementarity of our listeners.

Tustin has described the primitive anxieties connected with the first bodily experiences, such as falling, spilling, and dissolving. Some patients prefer to seek death—and only in some cases succeed in surviving dramatic suicide attempts—just to avoid unthinkable sensations of this kind. In the course of my clinical experience, I have observed many violent paranoid conditions in which the analysand, when emerging from an autistic state, persistently attacks the analyst for years, with screams, insults, and various forms of emotional violence. Such attacks might be linked to an attempt to contain the impact of unthinkable sensations by calling upon the analyst for concrete participation in this untranslatable condition of sensory suffering. To the extent that the analyst is able to bear a sensory bombardment comparable to the liquid lava issuing from a volcano in eruption, and frequently associated with feeling belittled, useless, and contemptible, the analysand can develop trust in the possibility of bearing the impact of his own undifferentiated sensory world with its attendant anxieties. Matte Blanco (1988) spoke of situations in which "the wrath of hell seems to fall on the psychoanalyst for years and years" (p. 163), a statement that leads us to wonder to what extent his clinical experience with undifferentiated primitive mental states contributed to his theory of a mental world dominated by the disintegrating action of the principle of symmetry and also by the complementary asymmetric orientation of consciousness.

Confrontation with the ascendancy of undifferentiated sensory phenomena, together with the emotional violence associated with it, led me to reconsider, in a less absolutist way, Bion's idea of an alpha function capable of processing proto-emotions. In fact, if taken literally, the idea of an alpha function is in danger of seeming unrealistic when faced with the almost unrestrainable hurricane that the analyst encounters in the course of certain analyses, not least of which occurs during the run-up to the experience of separation and the end of the analysis (Rhode, 2012). Indeed, especially in the most difficult cases, the working through of the end of the analysis seems to start at the beginning of the analysis: a way of distributing the catastrophic change associated with the discovery of limits and separation over a period of years, facilitating a working through of what would otherwise seem un-work-through-able. In various cases I treated, the course of the analysis was accompanied for years by proposals and threats of interruption, which served to transmit an oppressive feeling of insecurity and instability. This panicky sense of insecurity and threat of loss the analyst experiences goes well beyond any possible rational explanation, both because the analysand, in fact, continues to appear despite his threats, and because these are analysands whose interruption would, alas!, result in a great sense of relief for the analyst. Out of this incandescent and undifferentiated jumble, a first image of the patient's body and a first real identity are constructed, so that the angel who was flying over the city—as a patient of mine once put it—is suddenly falling under the bridges.

When I followed some seminars Frances Tustin gave in Rome in the early 1980s, I was struck by her distinction between a sense of the body and an image of the body. According to Tustin, the child's body is associated by the child with a gaseous state and "the early flux of uncoordinated sensations" (1986, p. 226) and is experienced like fluid lava. Tustin wrote that "unrelieved panic and terror were experienced as being turgid with fluids which overflowed in an uncontrollable, water, waterfall-like fashion" (1986, p. 220). In my experience, certain patients come close to representing in dreams these primitive anxieties through the onrush of enormous avalanches or gigantic waves (see Niemi & Lombardi, 2008).

Only later, when the primordial image of the body begins to emerge from the baby's undifferentiated cosmos, can it be associated with a liquid flowing within confines, like water in a system of pipes (Rosenfeld, quoted in Tustin, 1986), a yet more rudimentary image than that which Esther Bick described in relation to the containment function of the skin. The latter was taken up thereafter by Anzieu (1985) as *moi-peau* (i.e., skin ego).

"The 'system of pipes' body image implies awareness of 'insides' and also awareness of outside situations and identification with them", Tustin points out: "It is a movement away from undifferentiated autism to a transitional awareness of 'me' and 'not me'" (Tustin, 1986, p. 216). Tustin underlines beautifully the revolutionary step of differentiating "inside" and "outside". From my orientation, I read this revolutionary step as the patient's emergence from a condition of symmetry establishing a first mental act of differentiation between the wide class of inside and outside (Matte Blanco, 1988), a step that should not be confused with the recognition of otherness: that is a more complex realization that needs, in my view, more time and working through to be realized.

So, Tustin has shown us that primordial sensory states are of central importance in the development of a body image and a sense of self. When the primitive body image more closely resembles the actual body, as happens, for example when a baby recognizes himself in the mirror or in a photograph, he is moving towards a significant consolidation of his own identity.

## *The body–mind conflict in Sergio and Antonio*

I now present for discussion some aspects of the case of Sergio, a hyperactive three-year-old who was unable to speak or play, and was in the professional care of Dr Claudio Paluzzi. For a long time, the patient's inability to establish a connection made it impossible to use language as a form of communication. At the start the only "word" spoken by Sergio was "A-qu" (a tentative utterance of the Italian word for water, *acqua*), with the second part of the word pronounced with the lips pursed and while exhaling through the mouth, giving the impression that he was in danger of dissolving into thin air like the word he was pronouncing. If we hypothesize, in the wake of Tustin, that Sergio's first self-experience was water, then his attempt to give symbolic substance to his sensations by naming water was associated with his anxiety about dissolving. Presumably the word, on these levels, is still too fraught with concreteness, so that *saying* water became indistinguishable from *becoming* water to the point of actually dissolving. Where these primitive terrors held sway, any attempt to evolve towards symbolic usage was apparently not an option. We can now have a look at a moment from this analysis in which Sergio began to play with his own body, wrapping himself up in the rug on the floor. He repeated this activity for many months, wrapping himself in the rug and then unwrapping himself or walking across it.

In one session, Sergio rolled up the rug around himself, with just his head and shoulders sticking out, and walked about the room on all fours. The analyst commented that he seemed like a snail that goes around carrying his house with him. At this point, Sergio stuck his head in as well, his whole body shaking. But when he tried to get out he could not, and so he moved, with violent spasms, towards the analyst, whom he asked for help in pulling himself out of the anxiety of being left trapped inside.

We may hypothesize that the rug served Sergio as a frame, which might refer to the first perception of a boundary of his body. It is interesting to note his desire to withdraw his head as well within the covering or body, like a snail withdrawing into its shell. This would seem to show his anxiety at differentiating his head or mind, which could make him aware of the actual location of his body. What he is setting up, in other words, is a tendency towards body–mind dissociation, by means of making his perceptual epicentre—his head—disappear at the very moment when his body appears as something observable.

The presence of his body seems associated with a great claustrophobic anxiety, to which he reacted by eliminating awareness of his own confines and transforming his body into a sort of trap from which he would then need to escape. His asking the analyst to free him from his entrapment seems a positive sign of acceptance of the real limits of an external relationship that he can call upon.

In the course of Sergio's subsequent development, there appeared in his drawings a little lake, surrounded by two mountains, with a little fish in the middle. Sergio seemed thereby to be indicating his acquisition of bodily boundaries that allowed him to define a liquid area in which a little fish was living. Experiencing water was no longer a boundless flooding for him, but, instead, now had its own definition and containment thanks to his acquiring bodily limits.

Tustin tells us about the case of Antonio, treated by Dr Susanna Maiello, which seems in certain ways complementary to Sergio's. Antonio, after a phase in which he would climb up and down quite fearlessly, began to be frightened by birds in flight. He told his analyst that he would like her to put them in a cage, because he was afraid that they would fly ever higher, until they disappeared. Maiello underlined the importance of "staying down here" and in the office in which the analyst was also present.

Antonio seemed to focus on an "up there", which distanced him from the "down here" of his body. His request that the birds be put in a cage might refer to his intuition of the need for a body/cage which could receive him and protect him from the danger of flying away and dissolving into thin air. Sergio, on the other hand, found a covering/body in which to wrap himself up, but it tended to turn into a "total body": a refuge that, in the end, made him its prisoner.

I am inclined to see the respective positions of Antonio and Sergio as opposite poles of a conflict that pits high against low, up against down, the push towards an attempt at abstraction against the pull of bodily concreteness. Obviously, at the most primitive levels, if the patient fails to find "the down here" of his body first, he also cannot develop a realistic capacity for abstraction that could lead him towards the "up there" of his mind.

My clinical work in exploring some peculiarities of the body–mind conflict and relationship could be summarized as the need to find some harmonious balance between the connection with the confinement imposed by the body and the upward thrust connected to the openness of the mind. This conflict seems of increasing importance, to the point that ever more analysands use it as an area of working through (Lombardi, 2015). And it seems to me that, apart from its relevance to autistic problems, this conflict could reveal a great existential value in terms of being *per se*.

The artist Paul Klee once wrote,

> The contrast between man's ideological capacity to move at random through material and metaphysical spaces and his physical limitations is the origin of all human tragedy. It is this contrast between power and prostration that implies the duality of human existence. Half winged, half imprisoned, this is man! (Klee, 1953, p. 54)

Half winged, half imprisoned: if the relationship with one's body is a requisite of mental development, at the same time that relationship must not remain trapped in a blind, auto-sensual dimension, which would be in danger—like Sergio with his head withdrawn and trapped inside the rolled-up rug—of paralyzing the evolution from the bodily level to the mental one.

When auto-sensual elements are used by difficult patients to promote non-differentiation between the self and the other, in order to mitigate annihilation anxiety due to separateness, I would propose not highlighting the movements connected to the transference in one's comments to the patient, so as, instead, to yield center stage to the passage from auto-sensuality to a discriminative use of sensoriality: this orientation can foster a growth of the mental apparatus which could later create the necessary condition for the recognition of otherness. In fact, focusing on the mental recognition of otherness and taking from the other runs the risk of introducing a kind of working through that is too complex for the resources of a patient who is dominated by primitive anxieties and mechanisms.

So, I shall now proceed to reconsider briefly some clinical cases described by Tustin and other contemporary authors: I hope to show how introducing a focus on the vertical body–mind relationship can facilitate the understanding of some complex clinical developments in autistic children and difficult to reach patients.

## *David and Tessa: defensive second skin or eclipse of the body?*

In the third and fourth chapters of *Autism and Childhood Psychosis* (1972), Tustin describes the cases of David and Tessa as examples of the phenomenon Bick (1968) depicted as a "second skin": the phenomenon of the "muscular type of self-containment" that is meant to take the place of one's actual containing skin. This defensive phenomenon could be linked to what Winnicott (1958) describes as a "false self", and Deutsch (1942) as an "'as if' personality". In all these concepts, the emphasis is on their defensive aspect.

My idea is that the hypothesis of the defensive nature of the second skin that Tustin supported is not consistent with what emerges from most of her clinical descriptions, or indeed with her instinctive manner of reacting to a clinical situation. In other words, I believe that Tustin was making use of Bick's hypothesis because it was the one that, at the time, most closely resembled what she was encountering in her clinical work; however, some fifty years further on, that hypothesis no longer seems appropriate to the available clinical evidence, and, most particularly, fails to tally with the distinctly evolutive impact of the working through involving the body in which these child patients are involved. In fact, if we were to make a more consistent attempt to comprehend the evolutive character of Tustin's clinical descriptions in the light of more recent hypotheses, we would find before us not a defensive phenomenon, such as a "second skin", but, rather, an impelling form of the mind's first recognition of the body, that is, a first emancipation from a body–mind dissociation (Lombardi, 2003) and a first eclipse of the body and the sensory levels in the subject's perceptual orientation (Ferrari, 2004).

How can we explain this apparent erraticism in Tustin? Personally, I feel that it might just come down to the spirit of the time and the unconditional monopoly that traditional theories of object relations exercised during the 1960s and 1970s, and, consequently, we should not be astonished that a person of Tustin's caliber was unable to free herself conceptually from the influence of a mainstream notion. The same object-relational conditioning led Tustin to emphasize the importance of bodily separation for the autistic child, using a mode of thinking that presupposes an ability to recognize relational otherness even in a clinical context such as autism, in which the first problem would not seem to be separation so much as the subject's incapacity to recognize his being located within his own body.

Moreover, Tustin's faithful reference to object relations theory here is in distinct contrast with the growing emphasis, introduced by her, on the primary sensory integrations—hard–soft, light–dark, hot–cold, rough–smooth—in view of the establishment of a self sensation. It is worth noting, for example, how Tustin (1981, Chapter 12) recalls a passage from the therapy of John, in which she interprets his placing his colored pencils so as to form a cross, which he calls "breast", as an expression of the child's desire to construct a breast for himself made out of his own body (!!). The reference to his own body here takes the place of the maternal breast as an external object waiting to be internalized. Passages of this kind show us a Tustin who is willing to go beyond the Kleinian concept in order to emphasize the relationship with the body—or what we would now call the vertical body–mind relationship (Ferrari) or transference on to the body (Lombardi)—since she was consistently more attracted by the organizing potential of clinical references to the sensory self than by emphasizing the "not-me" external world and the external object/mother/breast.

In this context we can now consider some details from the material about David and Tessa that Tustin has provided.

Close to the Christmas break, David asked Tustin for a large cardboard box so he could make a body and dive into it. David's explicit reference to the body and to entering into it revealed an openness towards a level of working through that manifestly involved the body and the body–mind relationship. He was able to make a hand and a head of armor out of the cardboard he was given. He "took" his father's hair, ear, and nose for the head. Tustin sees his reference to his father as the defensive appropriation of a person with muscles, whose "muscular" characteristics he has snatched away so as to be able to construct a defensive second skin for himself which would be muscular in nature. I find that I am not really convinced by Tustin's defensive and muscular interpretation of the father/body. Looking at it in terms of the vertical relationship, I would instead tend to stress both the body representation suggested by the figure of the father and also the child's creative effort in attempting to construct a realistic corporeal reference (with hair, ear, nose, etc.) so as to approach a first conscious perception of the existence of his own body, within whose limits he might be able to recognize himself.

At David's request, Tustin let him have her chair. Although this is what she chose to do in the actual session, Tustin is critical *a posteriori* of this choice, which she regards as a mistake. I, however, cannot see Tustin's action as clinically mistaken, because her choice provides the patient with *de facto* permission to proceed with his working through, while also involving the analyst in his laborious attempt to place himself within his own bodily confines. Further along in her book, Tustin herself explicitly recognizes the developmental value of the child's perception of his body, even if this takes place through the mediation of the projection of his own body on to someone else's. So I would emphasize the use that David made of his "horizontal" relationship with Tustin as a springboard and mediation for drawing nearer to the problematic area of his own "vertical" body–mind relationship.

Drawing nearer to his body seems desired by David because of its being a warm nest, but, at the same time it is hated, because he associates his body with feces and with his anxiety about other people possibly leaving bits of feces on their chairs. Hence, placing himself in Tustin's chair seems desirable as the means of being situated in a reassuring nest, which opens the way to placement within his own body, as well as being a first sign of his ability to tolerate an imaginary contact with bodily matter such as feces, which is also part of this kind of working through of body–mind integration. However, leaving the metaphor aside, we see that David gives signs of managing to tolerate his hatred and disdain for his own body, to the point of seeing it as a nest in which to place himself. That such a working through should take place on the eve of an analytic break for vacation seems consistent with the fact that the imminent separation spurs him towards a realistic recognition of the confines of his own actual body in contrast to the undifferentiated level on which he experiences his relationship with Tustin.

It should be noted that although Tustin feels the conceptual appeal of stressing the defensive component of the armor David has constructed, she is simultaneously aware that that armor represents a step forward. Her positive evaluation is paradoxically overshadowed by her emphasis on the defensive aspects, so that David is seen as constructing a defensive second skin for himself. As far as I can understand the defensive mechanisms in the David material, they seem secondary compared to the greater consistency that shines through when I read the material from the viewpoint of his recognition of his own actual body. The reference to other people's bodies (his father's and Tustin's), would seem to be the expression of the activated processes of symmetrization (Matte Blanco, 1988)—fairly common at these levels of functioning—according to which other people's bodies are, at the deepest levels, indistinguishable from one's own. Hence, the most powerful aspect of the material appears to me to be the dawning of David's awareness of the existence of his own physicality.

In the next chapter, Tustin presents the case of Tessa, a ten-year-old girl observed by her teacher, Margaret Sampson. Tessa had presented almost monosyllabic speech with disconnected verbal references to her belly or her veins, when, for the first time, she expressed a desire to make a doll she could get into. Tessa was then helped by Sampson to make a cardboard dress that could cover her completely, but, after a short while, Tessa rejected it, murmuring the word "material". Once she had been given some material, Tessa set about sewing a dress that pleased her much more than the cardboard one. After she had created the cloth dress, Tessa began to use a first person singular pronoun and to look at herself in the mirror, even reaching the point of recognizing the color of her own eyes and hair. Finally, she alluded to her growth, by measuring her hand against her teacher's, showing some sort of perception of the effect of the passage of time on the dimensions of her body. Tustin, even while underscoring the encouraging steps forward that this psychotic child had made, offers the case as an example of the construction of a second skin.

On the whole, in the cases of David and Tessa, Tustin presents a collection of elements from which one can deduce how important recognizing the body is for the development of children on the autistic spectrum. At the same time, we should note that the role of the body remains, for her, below the threshold of theoretical recognition, since she underlines the defensive role of the second skin and overlooks the real importance of the body–mind relationship, despite the fact that her material definitely focuses on a working through of the presence of the body and its actual confines. The connotation of defensive second skin seems even more paradoxical if we consider the fact that these children had shown no signs of integration on the body–mind axis before these developments.

## *The underrated and under-theorized emergence of the patient's body in analysis*

An increasing amount of clinical evidence has become available about the propulsive role played by the integration of the body in so-called difficult patients, but one often encounters a large gap between practice and theory, and, in fact, its theoretical formulation is really rather fragmentary in contrast to the specificity of the clinical data.

In "Finding a center of gravity via proximity with the analyst" Eekhoff (Chapter One, this volume), for example, describes the case of Kay, a patient who wanted to be analyzed "because she said something was missing in her" and, after a period of compliance with the analyst's expectations, started to show that "none of her thoughts seemed to begin inside of her". This phase was followed by a serious physical deterioration, including the collapse of a lung, which required two operations, and threatening dermatological conditions: the situation was so grave as to suggest that her life was in danger. After these episodes, Kay began to give signs of her physical presence at her sessions, and to give up lying like a dead body on the couch, demonstrating instead an ability to move her hands quite expressively. During this phase, her analyst was disconcerted to note that "it seemed there was room in the session for only one of us at a time". At a certain point, Kay developed the delusional conviction that her analyst wanted to kill her. This period was replaced by one in which she could see, right there in the analytic office, her own double, who was threatening her. Eekhoff interprets this development in relation to the appearance of anger and disappointment in the transference, with the result that she felt inadequate as an analyst and discouraged about psychoanalysis in general. After this unstable and dramatic phase, the patient was able to develop like "a real woman" and to achieve a perception of the analyst as separate from her.

Eekhoff, although she recognizes that "these patients demonstrate little awareness of being in their bodies", conceptualizes the importance of proximity to the analyst in these developments, to the point where "the analyst becomes the center of gravity for the patient, enabling a floor for experience to develop". In the wake of Ferenczi, Klein, Bion, Meltzer, and Mitrani, Eekhoff asserts that "introjective identification is the vehicle for becoming a center of gravity".

Considering Eekhoff's case from a perspective that focuses psychoanalytic attention on the body would have the advantage of helping to orientate the analyst dealing with the mysterious evolution that takes place in analyses such as this. The patient passes, in fact, from an initial absence of any bodily referent and the related impossibility of situating her thoughts within her subjectivity, to the entrance of the body into the analytic evolution by means of explosive physical phenomena that could even put her life at risk. Tustin had noted the value of autistic children's somatic illnesses, which are capable, in analysis, of evolving towards less impenetrable forms of defenses exposing the children to a physical permeability to infections. From my point of view, this bespeaks not only a reduction of autistic defenses, but also an actual ontological emergence of the body, which is crucial to the patient's identity and thinking. It is as if the body, during these phases of somatic illness, were to assume a primitive hatred towards itself from a period in which the patient did not yet have the tools for representing herself and her conflicts. This could be an example of the possible creative interaction between the two subsystems, body and mind, which we witness in analysis: the one (the body) can come to the assistance of the other (the mind) when the latter's resources are still insufficient or in the process of being formed. This is very different from a "psychosomatic" interpretation, according to which the mind unloads on to the body the proto-emotions/beta elements, which it wishes not to have anything to do with (Meltzer, 1982).

In the light of this perspective, I think we should bear in mind that the center of gravity, which is being constructed with such dramatic difficulty, is *inside* the patient, so it ought to be no surprise that "there was room in the session for only one of us at a time". In these phases, the urgency of building a vertical body–mind relationship implies the necessity of putting off until later the working through of the "two" in the horizontal analysand–analyst relationship. The ensuing discovery of the body also leads to the discovery of one's bodily weight and of gravity (and not in the metaphorical sense!) as acquired rights of membership in nature and the physical world. This discovery of the weight and gravity inherent in the body is very movingly condensed in the final moments of the film *Gravity* (Cuarón, 2013), in which Dr Ryan Stone (Sandra Bullock), just back from her space odyssey—which is both particular and personal, and general and human, as Kubrick described in his films, starting with *2001: A Space Odyssey* (cf. Lombardi, 2004)—feels the almost unendurable weight of her own body stretched out on the water's edge, as the expression of her discovering that she inhabits a heavy and earthbound body.

Eekhoff's presentation is only one example of the problem that I generally find in contemporary psychoanalytic literature, which lacks a conceptualization of the body with its own specific metapsychological state, an error which Ferrari's hypothesis (2004) of the "concrete original object" would seem to put right (cf. Lombardi, 2002). Just by attributing a central role to the analysand's body, one becomes able to conceptualize the appearance of somatic phenomena in analysis as the expression both of a first perceptual act of approaching an actual body and of an eclipse of the body which can create a center of gravity within the person which is otherwise absent in this kind of analysand. This conceptualization throws light on a very primitive level, of which Freud (1914c) was already aware, as we can see from his emphasis on the importance of a new psychical action for bringing about the transformation of autoeroticism into narcissism: a very problematic passage which has been obscured by object relations theories focused on the introjection of the mother's breast as the organizing nucleus of the ego.

Kay's delusion, described by Eekhoff, that she was about to be killed by her analyst offers an interesting chance to explore the radicality of the body–mind conflict that emerges at primitive levels and, thus, makes the construction of a passageway to narcissism that Freud describes problematic. Kay's delusions provide a projective representative form for her homicidal hatred towards her own body, and also for a first drawing near to the death anxiety (although with paranoid features) consequent upon her discovery of having a body of her own.

In the light of the interest and abundance of this kind of clinical phenomenon, distinguishing between the vertical body–mind axis and the horizontal analyst–analysand axis becomes crucial for positioning the facilitating role of the analytic relationship without obscuring the importance of phenomena belonging to the body–mind relationship and their primacy in the organization of a personality whose roots lie in the body of the analysand.

In a style of theoretical exposition not very different from Eekhoff's, Eshel (Chapter Three, this volume) describes the case of P, a patient with severe fetishistic–masochistic perversion, who, during his analysis, develops a sense of non-existence, an obsessive belief that he is dead, and a feeling of the "emptying out of the brain", together with panic at being in a world "that has no center". The situation was able to evolve positively, with a release from fetishism and the activation of an inner sense of existence, after the analysand could work through in analysis the terrifyingly powerful emotion he had felt during physical contact with a prostitute. His next experience of physical (but not sexual) contact with two women reinforced his perception of his own existence, beginning with the perception of his own body, which concretely revealed his entry into being.

The center-less world and the obsession with being dead experienced by Eshel's patient refer, as I see it, to the absence of one's own bodily center and to the consequent sense of death. In such a context, fetishism, rather than a perversion, seems like an emergency contrivance that protects the patient from a sense of total annihilation. And, in fact, he leaves fetishism behind when he succeeds in entering into contact with his bodily dimension, even managing to bear the terror evoked by the ineffable world of his own sensations: the two women could evoke at a concrete level the experience of a dawning primitive duality preceding the differentiation between body and mind. Following the activation of sensory perception, there can gradually take place within him an evolution of his body, affects, and thoughts (Lombardi, 2009), so that he feels that he is alive and that his brain is no longer emptied of all contents.

## *Conclusion*

To sum up, I have attempted to explore some connections between Tustin's contributions (1972, 1981) on the role of sensations and the self-sensation and Ferrari's hypothesis (2004) about the eclipse of the body, as I have personally interpreted it in my clinical writings. Tustin, even though she focuses her research on the sensory levels, nonetheless remains in part concerned about the role of separateness and the external object, together with the defensive function of a second skin. In a more radical way, Ferrari underscores the strategic value for clinical development of using the vertical relationship and the propulsive role of the eclipse of the body that takes place through the interaction between containment and cooling down brought about by sensory perception and the overwhelming and explosive sensoriality, which is ethological in nature.

Maiello (2015) has recently considered the lack of a bodily dimension in autism and recalled that Tustin—in describing the absence of any experience *of* the body and *in* the body in the autistic state—used the term No-body.

I personally find the "no-body" metaphor confusing, given that an autistic child nonetheless has a real body of his own: the no-body metaphor, by asserting the absence of the body, would paradoxically tend to confirm precisely the sort of body annihilation anxieties that torment this kind of child. It would seem more accurate to say, instead, that it is not true that there is an "absence of a bodily dimension in autistic states" (Maiello, 2015) and that only the stamp of the mental dimension in correspondence with the bodily dimension is absent.

Speaking of the body as the concrete original object and of the eclipse of that COO, as Ferrari proposes (2004), seems to me to be a useful epistemological tool, as long as a clear distinction is made between the body as ethological object (the COO in a sensory condition that is still too saturated, and alien to any mental coloration), and the activation of an eclipse of the body (or of the COO), in which the setting in motion of sensory perception within the child makes possible the dawning of bodily self-awareness, while also enabling the child to begin to distinguish among sensations.

In conclusion, I feel that the results of a rapprochement of the different perspectives of Tustin and Ferrari could invigorate clinical research on the centrality of the body in primitive mental states: the valorization of the vertical body–mind relationship and of the phenomena connected to the eclipse of the body—as a primary area of working through in difficult patients-could lead to making better use of the revolutionary potential of Tustin's intuitions about the earliest forms of the sensory organization of subjectivity.

## References

Anzieu, D. (1985). *Le moi-peau*. Paris: Dunod.

Bick, E. (1968). The experience of the skin in early object-relations. *International Journal of Psychoanalysis, 49*: 484–486.

Cuarón, A. (Dir.) (2013). *Gravity*. Film. Warner Bros. Pictures.

Deutsch, H. (1942). Some forms of emotional disturbance and their relationship to schizophrenia. *Psychoanalytic Quarterly, 11*: 301–321

Ferrari, A. B. (2004). *From the Eclipse of the Body to the Dawn of Thought*. London: Free Association Books.

Freud, S. (1914c). On narcissism: an introduction. *S. E., 14*: 73–102. London: Hogarth.

Klee, P. (1953) *Pedagogical Sketchbook*, S. Moholy-Nagy, (trans.). London: Faber & Faber.

Lombardi, R. (2002). Primitive mental states and the body. *International Journal of Psychoanalysis, 83*: 353–381

Lombardi, R. (2003). Catalyzing the dialogue between the body and the mind in a psychotic analysand. *Psychoanalytic Quarterly, 72*: 1017–1041.

Lombardi, R. (2004). Stanley Kubrick's swan song. *International Journal of Psychoanalysis, 85*: 209–218.

Lombardi, R. (2005). On the psychoanalytic treatment of a psychotic breakdown. *Psychoanalytic Quarterly, 74*: 1069–1099

Lombardi, R. (2009). Body, affect, thought: reflections on the work of Matte Blanco and Ferrari. *Psychoanalytic Quarterly, 78*: 123–160.

Lombardi, R. (2015). *Metà prigioniero Metà alato* [Half Winged Half Imprisoned]. Turin: Boringhieri.

Maiello, S. (2015). NO-BODY. Sull'assenza della dimensione corporea negli stati autistici [NO-BODY: On the absence of a bodily dimension in autistic states]. *Richard e Piggle, 22*(4): 347–364.

Matte Blanco, I. (1988). *Thinking, Feeling, and Being*. London: Routledge.

Meltzer, D. (1982). Implicazioni psicosomatiche nel pensiero di Bion [Psychosomatic implications of Bion's thinking]. *Quaderni di Psicoterapia Infantile, 7*: 199–222.

Niemi, T., & Lombardi, R. (2008). Run or die: bi-logical phenomena at the body-mind border. *Scandinavian Psychoanalytic Review, 31*: 95–104.

Rhode, M. (2012). Whose memories are they and where do they go? Problems surrounding internalization in children on the autistic spectrum. *International Journal of Psychoanalysis, 93*: 355–376.

Tustin, F. (1972). *Autism and Childhood Psychosis*. London: The Hogath Press.

Tustin, F. (1981). *Autistic States in Children*. London: Routledge.

Tustin, F. (1986). *Autistic Barriers in Neurotic Patients*. London: Karnac.

Winnicott, D. W. (1958). Psychoses and child care. In: *Through Paediatrics to Psycho-Analysis* (pp 219–229). London: The Hogarth Press and the Institute of Psycho-Analysis.

CHAPTER SIX

# "Emotional" storms in autistoid dynamics

*Bernd Nissen*

In autistoid organizations, projective identification fails because the hope of a containing object has been given up. But what happens if the self has abandoned hope of a containing object and no longer has the possibility of an explosive ejection? What happens if pre-psychic, not thinkable, unqualified, and unconceptualized parts remain in the self, but cannot be digested or transformed, made useful? How can a person find a way to deal with such elements, which might also potentially dissolve more mature connections?

Tustin (1972, 1981, 1986, 1990) investigated these dynamics and arrived at her important results, which today belong to the canon of analytic thought. Thus, if the most primitive of mechanisms, excretion and incorporation/digestion, are no longer possible, only encapsulation remains—quite similar to physical encapsulations—but never providing real security (see also S. Klein, 1980). The earlier encapsulations are formed, the more precarious the inner emotional situation and further development become. A self that has not yet developed is then lastingly weakened and highly vulnerable. Tustin, and, before her, Winnicott (1971), clearly realized this. The "breast", which, in my interpretation, is conceptualized as a mother–child encounter, becomes the central point of autistic and autistoid events. If the child experiences sustained disruptions in this relationship, words will hardly be able to capture the experience: going-on-being is jeopardized, the emergence of black holes, feeling torn off, falling, dissolving, falling to pieces, are only attempts at getting around these states. Such experiencing persists in pure presence and finds no connection in the psychic system. Similarities with traumatic events are evident, yet there is one difference: traumatic crises are also experiences in pure presence (see Baranger et al., 1988), and a receiving object can no longer be thought at this moment, so that the ego is confronted with total helplessness. Yet, the primal phantasy, or the conception of the breast, need not be basically damaged, as is the case with autistic and autistoid encapsulations. Put simply, every autistoid encapsulation is traumatic, but not every traumatic encapsulation is autistoid. Therefore, traumatic experiences can also be communicated by projective identification.

Normally a preconception (Freud's primal phantasy) encounters its realization, that is, a "presence moment", in which something is there in order to become. The presence is transferred into the presentational (presentational symbolism, Langer, 1942), finally becoming representation (cf. Levine's reflections, 2013). The pre-conception of the breast finds its realization. Mother and child are then there in order to become. A conception arises and, at the same time, prepsychic elements (beta-elements) are qualified, becoming potentially combinable in the conception (alpha-elements).

Let us paraphrase the world of the baby: it expects the breast, that is, a relationship in which it feels unconditionally accepted. From this presence moment (Bion's O), mother and baby then become. At the same time, states of agitation of the physical (with Freud, source of the instinct; Bion's elements) are qualified, such as excretion, hunger, and finding pleasure in being breastfed. The formation of the conception, together with the qualification, is a creative act on the part of the pair. In the conception, the elements come together, are related to each other, and, joined in this way, safeguard the conception. Here, mental nuclei (conceptions) are formed, which, in the presence of the object, can remain and exist. It is very important that at the moment of presence, that which should become confronts the mother–child pair as something created by the pair, yet still remaining an independent third.[1] The dyadic and triadic dimensions are inherent in the moment of the being one. The mother, with her developed psychic apparatus, is able to name this third. From this figure, benign dependence emerges, since the third, the fatherly, exists.[2] Dependence is benign because the third works like a catalyst and allows autonomy and separateness to appear. This complex emotional experience forms a memory trace, which is not yet available to thinking. For this, the thought must outlast the absence of the object, meaning it must develop an apparatus for thinking thoughts.[3]

We now have to investigate exactly what disruptions mean in these events (assuming, for the sake of simplicity, a failing object, aware that disruptions are mostly multi-layered). Let us imagine someone dying of thirst in the desert who, in a hallucination, mistakes a *fata morgana* and sees a water hole before him, rushes to it and stuffs a handful of sand into his mouth. With his emotional equipment, he will, despite his desperation and anguish, at least recognize the reality. Yet, what is the situation of a baby who has a pre-conceptional expectation of the breast which, as Freud (1900a, 1915e) and Bion (1970) taught, resembles hallucination? It now encounters a bottle suspended in a wire frame, not a loving mother. His psychic apparatus is not yet developed. He would think the sand was milk, something dead for the living relationship he yearns for. He would believe he was with an understanding mother, whereas there is not only nothing to understand but no self and no object, no beginning and no end.

It is important to understand these dynamics precisely: for the one dying of thirst, on the emotional reference level the expectation of water is the expectation of the breast. But he has a conception of the breast that enables him to think. The expectation of the breast/of the water becomes a preconception that encompasses both the fulfilment and the absence. The sand in his mouth represents a presence moment in which there is a reality (no water, no breast) that he can recognize. The pre-conception[4] of the baby requires, existentially, a positive realization, that is, an accepting, loving object. In my view, it was for this reason that Freud attributed his primal phantasies to self-healing powers. He defined primal phantasies as ". . . phylogenetically inherited schemata, which, like the categories of philosophy, are concerned with the business of 'placing' the impressions derived from actual experience . . ." He continued, "Wherever experiences fail to fit in with the hereditary schema, they become remodelled in the imagination . . . We are often able to see the schema triumphing over the experience of the individual . . ." (Freud, 1918b, p. 119). But this self-healing has its limits.

Let us try to speculate what might be the situation of the child whose mother, for example, is severely depressive, in whom emotion and vitality have died away. She will endeavour, aware of her condition, to carry out feeding and remove the excretions (excrement, urine, saliva, wind, and air from the stomach) hygienically and carefully, but she is not able to take in and take away emotional distress and to give love. The baby fails in its attempts to make the object emotionally alive, just as his strengthened projective identifications do not find any resonance. The realization that he existentially expects remains absent. Experienced reality cannot be adapted to match the schema. This means two things: neither a conception nor $\alpha$-elements can emerge. The security of an understanding mother–child relationship does not arise, only a nameless deformation; elements stay on a $\beta$ or bizarre level. I suspect a disruptive tension arises together with devastating confusion, and there is a danger of dissolution and annihilation. The rudimentary self must hang on to that which is there, as the longed-for relationship/breast/milk, even if it is not there but is something dead, or sand. Otherwise the going-on-being is jeopardised. At the same time it is felt that the pre-conception does not become the conception. There is something present there, but no presence emerges. The pre-conception cannot evolve to join with a realization and become a conception. The situation roughly corresponds to one in which the person dying of thirst clings to the belief that the sand is water. The consequences are devastating: with the absence of a sufficiently good realization, neither a conception nor emotional elements emerge. A secure self-object differentiation in the presence of a third object (interpsychic dimension) cannot unfold and a differentiated internal order cannot arise (intrapsychic dimension). A thought, not only a nucleus of the emerging self, but the basic element of any emotional differentiation, does not emerge, in fact, it must not emerge, for otherwise reality would be recognizable and it would mean annihilation. If no thought exists, no apparatus for thinking thoughts can develop, no secure self and no idea of a containing object and an object relationship; the important function of the third object is missing. Ultimately, both the traumatic inner world and reality and any form of separation are feared. The traumatic states are encapsulated, reality is abandoned. The objectal remnants that exist even in the most severe autistic formations have retreated to a corner of the psyche (Freud, 1940a [1938]). Autistoid mechanisms begin to form that are very similar to autistic ones: second skin formations, including addictive and perverse excitations, autistic objects and shapes, psychosomatic capsules, etc.

Yet, what is the situation of the autistoid inner world when a person has abandoned hope of a containing object, but, in fact, needs it, both to digest unbearable inner states and to obtain emotional nourishment? From my work with patients who have formed severe autistoid organizations, I know that they suffered as children from states akin to nightmares and psychoses, for which the objectal orientation was missing. They report catatonic dormant states, panic fears, animals devouring their insides, blood erupting from the walls, physically disruptive tensions, and fear of their bodies disintegrating into small pieces. Such states, which are frequently dramatically shown in the post-autistoid psychotic phases (Meltzer) during the treatment, are, in my view, subsequent formations with which the mute but threateningly perceptible presence of the death instinct finds its expression.

It is evident that what we have defined here in terms of basic research is, in reality, a great deal more complicated. Children have astounding resilience (as Mächtlinger (2012) demonstrated in her brilliant paper about the Bulldogs Bank children, who survived the Theresienstadt concentration camp) and can make use of the little that is there for emotional survival and for development. In my view, there have to be very unfavourable constitutional and/or objectal conditions to induce the formation of severe autistic and autistoid states. For autism in early childhood, I suspect constitutional damage to the pre-conception "breast". The primal fantasy of an understanding mother–child encounter is so severely damaged that an adequate conceptional change cannot occur—with all the outlined consequences for emotional thinking and being-in-the-world. In the autistoid, in which the pre-conception breast exists, we must assume severe object relationship disturbances, which are frequently reciprocal: a lack of primary motherliness in all its forms (premature separations from the primary objects, depressions, abuse, addiction, etc.) on the one hand, constitutional weaknesses in the child (such as frustration intolerance, envy, deficient utilization of what is emotionally available) on the other hand. Striking, in this group of patients, is that the fathers are often absent (divorce, work, addiction) and the mothers were prone to boundary violations and, not infrequently, to sexual border transgressions.

If autistoid features gain psychodynamic and structural dominance, we speak of autistoid disorder. If they control the personality for a long time, a pathological organization emerges. This is clearly distinguished from the narcissistic organizations which at first Freud and Abraham, later Meltzer, and particularly Rosenfeld and Britton, describe; they are also distinguished from the emotional retreats which Steiner conceptualized as remaining between the depressive and paranoid–schizoid position, secured by romantic, narcissistic, or sexual perversions. The most important feature of autistoid organizations is the absence of projective identification because the hope of a containing object has been abandoned. I see projective identification as an interpenetrative process between subject and object that reciprocally provides complexity for developing structures (see Luhmann, 1987) in which a third is created.

I shall now illustrate some of these aspects using a case example from an initial interview.

## *Clinical example*[5]

A patient books by telephone in the normal way. She appears as a young woman dressed in student style. She makes hardly any contact, seems uncertain, tries to hide behind a friendliness that is almost embarrassing. She looks disoriented, but instantly takes over the entire waiting room. I straightaway find myself in a raging chaos: her paraphernalia is everywhere: hat, scarf, gloves, jacket, bag, a packet of cigarettes and coins falling out, coffee mug, etc. are scattered throughout the room. She seems to stay put nowhere, she talks incessantly, without my being able to hear her words. My breathing is constricted, I almost come out with nonsense such as "It really is pretty cold out there," though I cannot remember which season it is and if it really is cold. Suddenly, the patient steps in front of the mirror (that hangs in the waiting room) and it is quiet, as in the eye of the hurricane. When she steps back from the mirror, I almost bundle her into the treatment room and shut the door hastily, as if trying to banish the raging chaos. "Inside", it remains calm on the surface. Her eyes flit over my face. Then she spreads out her fragmented mental world: she still bears the name of her father, whom she does not know. He had cheated on her mother during pregnancy, after which the mother left and took back her maiden name. My patient did not enjoy her studies, but she completed them. She is a hypochondriac, afraid of having breast cancer. She examines her breasts for hours, visits several doctors a day, the fear remains. I start again to perceive, to grasp what is fragmented, to intuit her threatened self, feel that she has no place in a relationship. After her birth, she had gone to her grandparents for several months; her mother had "joined the hippies". "Commune, free love, always other men, I was often there—sorry, I forgot my tissues out there!" She jumps up; struck by fear, I want to call, "But you do not need . . . I have . . ." She is already in the waiting room. It remains calm, quiet, a moment too long. I know that she is looking at herself in the mirror. She comes back and I ask very directly, "Have you been looking at yourself in the mirror again?" For a split second she looks at me. She admits it. I say, "You are afraid of drowning in all this chaos, of dissolving into the fear. In the mirror, you make sure of yourself." She nods, looking briefly at me. She breathes heavily and falls silent. I take her into treatment.

I understand the whole situation, from the moment of arrival to the final interpretation, as one scene that is divided into several sections: first the raging chaos as a re-enactment of the abusive primal scene experience in objectal abandonment, in which I take on the role of the suffering child threatened with dissolving disintegration, then the self-focused reassurance of the self in the first self-mirroring, and, afterwards, the communications in the treatment room about her fragmentation, parallel to my rediscovering of analytical thinking and concurrent intuitive participation, then her associative approach to the traumatic primal scenes, that makes us both afraid, followed by the silence and my comprehension of the scene, and, finally, the first "naming".

Let us look in detail at the dynamic under the working hypothesis of the autistoid. In the first sequence, there is chaos raging in the waiting room, into which I am literally dragged. Many months later, when she, for the first time, began to grasp the sexual border violations emotionally, I learned in the treatment that she felt that the way to the practice, a densely planted, winding garden path, was like an intimate, seductive intensification, which put her into a state of great tension. This stress weakened her self and opened up the way to the traumatic primal scene experiences. The intimate–sexual, abusive experiences with the mother did not constitute enigmas for the patient as defined by Laplanche (2003, p. 83), but blocked the psychic processing, not only of these experiences but the processing of the requirements which the primal fantasies represent for every child. For the conceptualization of these primal fantasies, the child needs deeply unconscious loving, containing objects, precisely those that were not sufficiently available to the patient: let us recall the early separation traumatization. In the analysis, we reconstructed that, in the first three years of her life, she lived for more than one and a half years with other people, going soon after her birth not only to the grandparents, but to people who were complete strangers to her. We can assume, therefore, that the pre-conceptions of the breast in the patient, of the primal scene and of the oedipal, are likely to have encountered pathogenic misrealizations. The formation of these conceptions is then barely satisfactory. Interdependently, the elements included in these spheres and developmental stages have also not been sufficiently qualified. It can, therefore, be assumed that encapsulations have been formed in which these elements have been accommodated.

To the weakening of her self and the exposed priming of encapsulated abusive elements, the patient reacts by switching over to an automated mode: she talks incessantly, amiably, but almost causing embarrassment, with which the weakening of the self is accelerated. I suspect that it is during this phase that the contents of the capsules are released. The patient no longer manages the favored shift into the hypochondriac organ. Hallucinatory residues of the primal scene experiences gush tangibly into the waiting room.

The traumatic impressions of the primal scene, having emerged at times she can remember, are sensually present in fragments, are draped in this form. Since the primal phantasy "breast" is deeply deformed, objectal hopes have been lost and communication from unconscious to unconscious is no longer available. This is why I would not conceptualize this scene as projective identification, but as an inductive process of becoming involved. In the relinquishment of the fragments, I become the child who, dissociatively pushed to the edge of loss of the self, experiences the traumatic–abusive primal scenes de-personally, de-really, spinning, confused, somatically constrained.

Bion wrote that there are people who "feel the pain but will not suffer it and cannot be said to discover it" (Bion, 1970, p. 9). Would I have been able to discover this impending dissolving disintegration?

Let us do a thought experiment: suppose the patient had gathered up her belongings before the first mirror scene and fled the practice. Would this scene have ever attained emotional significance for me? I do not think so. With the knowledge gained from experience, I would have hypothetically filed it among my empirical knowledge, banished it with a few words, such as "The waiting room scene", but emotionally it would not have become significant. It would have remained mysterious and strange in my psyche. However, neither would I have been able to forget it. The patient staged precisely this emotional state: traumatic–abusive impressions that cumulatively threatened her self. They were never symbolized, not even presentationally (Langer, 1942). They remained excluded from projective identification because they had found no container into which they could have been projected. What appears almost like the film scene of sexual passion—things scattered around the room, cigarettes, mug—is, in fact, an expression of an autistoid thought disorder in which the patient has access to $\beta$ elements and bizarre objects, but no emotional elements. She is unable to process these impressions either consciously or unconsciously. Neither can they be dreamily intuited by the object, because they have dropped out of unconscious communication and can only be in some way experienced, to return to Bion.

Let us examine the second sub-scene: the patient looks at herself in the mirror. I absolutely do not know at this moment what is happening, only feeling that I have escaped the storm for a moment. I have to save myself, to get by. Here, I come physiologically close to the patient (e.g., my constricted breathing). I am far away from a dreamy intuition, and, thus, from ideas of what the mirror could represent mentally. It was only after months in analysis that I knew that "looking in the mirror" had two functions for the patient: first, to stop everything, to see that she is physically still there, is not deformed. She watched the primal scenes, in which she was to some extent involved, in anxious, masturbatory arousal. As a result, she experienced her body as quite literally deformed, bent, distorted, torn. On the other hand, mirroring functions as a second skin (Bick, 1968). When she was not sliding into anxious arousal at the sexual activities of the mother, she fixated herself in a floor-length mirror that stood next to her mattress. A trance-like fixation is set against the risks of the dissolution of traumatic involvement. This second skin formation centers the sensations and is experienced, at least for a few moments, "as if . . . [it]

were holding the parts of the personality together" (Bick, 1968, pp. 484–486).

After my intuitive skill has been restored in the third sub-scene, I notice that the patient presents her ideas as she had draped her clothes around the waiting room. When she mentions her hypochondria, the mosaic pieces begin to fall into place in me and I sense a possible diagnosis. Based on my clinical experience and theoretical considerations, severe hypochondria is an autistoid pathological organization (see Nissen, 2000, 2003, 2007, 2008, 2010).

A brief digression, with some general comments.

We had presumed that autistoid components were not digestible and dropped out of the hope of objectal understanding. They are encapsulated, yet such encapsulations are never lastingly safe. If such encapsulations are opened, the self is threatened with dissolution and has to take action. The hypochondriac organ in the framework of such a dynamic can function as a substitute capsule for the volatile capsule contents. In displacement, the hypochondriac organ becomes a collection container for the elements that destroy connections. The organ then, having become malicious, must be examined again and again, located at the same time in the tactile or examinable sphere. Yet, despite and because of the means of control, the fear of annihilation remains persecutory. In clinical reality, it is, unfortunately, not so easy: Rosenfeld observed, in his clinical brilliance, that patients initially do indeed try to cast off these fragments projectively (see Rosenfeld, 1958, 1964). I have observed that maternal objects or substitute objects (mostly in the imagination) are chosen. This means there are in some hypochondriac dynamics projective rudiments, which then disintegrate in the subsequent regression. For these objects are experienced by the patients in such a way that they take possession of what is projected and distil out of it the dimensions that bring about meaning and relationships. The remnants, which have lost their last psychic significance, are forced back into the patients. This is experienced as concretistic reintrojection (it is important to recall Fenichel's [1982] astute observation that in hypochondria introjection is very close to the body, oral, anal, occurring by inhalation or through the skin). Induced *inter alia* by the plundering of the emotional and the concretistic–physical introjection of the remnants, a renewed projection fails (M. Klein, 1932) referred to this failure). All that remains is final displacement into the organ.

Back to the example: when the patient reports on the severity of her hypochondria, my conceptual knowledge preconsciously unites with the experienced scenes. In this way, I obtain a view of the patient. It remains unclear whether the patient notices my regained emotional composure. This aspect is important because, in the next sequence, the patient comes closer to the traumatic abuse (hippies, free love). Is this small movement due only to the association, or is there a minimal shared agreement between analyst and patient? Does the patient dare to take this associative approach because she hopes the object that she has glimpsed is potentially a container? Her hasty departure into the waiting room is certainly an attack on the emerging connection and on my reviving ability to think, which, in the first moment, promptly collapses again. But if her flight is integrated in a previous objectal movement, it should be evaluated diagnostically and indicatively quite differently.

The silence in the waiting room now becomes the key scene in the interview. In my view, it is a presence event, a moment of O being, in which the K dimensions are absent. The silence was a moment of standing firm in which the patient's forlornness and fear of dissolution existed without being named or knowingly grasped. My knowledge that she is watching herself in the mirror is already a transformation towards K. Presence (O) precedes evidence/the presentational (K) (see Nissen, 2009, 2012, 2013). In the presence of the silence and of the mirroring lies the analytical third, which can be grasped and given a name by the analyst, which then appears in the presentational interpretation: the mirror, the reflection in the mirror. (Incidentally, the term "mirror" became a key technical term in the treatment.) This presentational interpretation then introduces a presence event—the moment in which the patient looks at me. As I have said, I know at this moment only about the physiological silence of the mirroring but virtually nothing of the functions that mirroring has in the emotional life of the patient. Nevertheless, the patient feels recognized and recognizes the analyst, whom she looks at and sees. In this looking and seeing, we can sense something of the third, how the patient experiences it emotionally: there is something clear, sober (Rhode's vertical), a reality there.

It is important that pre-conceptional and elementary dimensions exist in these presence events, which encounter the analytical pair as the third. In mirroring, the patient's worlds are revealed and, with the presentational interpretation, this third is created so that this revelation occurs in the relationship. With this objectal bridge, the preconception "breast", as we have defined it, is realized. A receiving and containing object is there and with it the relationship, the patient as the subject and a name created out of the scene. This object has qualified some basal elements, which are fear of dissolution and forlornness. The words chosen in the subsequent interpretation circle this qualification with concepts such as chaos, drowning, fear, dissolving, mirroring, and self-reassurance. With this, the delicate seed of a thought is sown which I intuitively offered to the patient. With this intuition, the other misrealizations, such as the primal scene, can also more easily be identified. A thought is there which can become the nucleus for the relationship and for emotional understanding.

I feel, however, that the patient was hardly listening to my words. She seems rather to have been contacting her last remaining hope that there is an object that is trying to understand her. I experience this as an indicative change of direction: if the hope of a containing object has not been completely destroyed, if the patient in the first session of an interview is in a position to feel the hope, a holding and containing object relationship can almost certainly be established in treatment.

The connection of these intrapsychic objectal hopes with a present object occurs in the analytical process over many months in holding (see Nissen, 2013). Analysand and analyst adjust to each other, a complementary, bipersonal alignment process in which an analytical field emerges and the autistoid contents will—one hopes—be shown. With this patient this was achieved, even though the treatment was to take many years.

## *Notes*

1. Here, there are areas that overlap with Ogden. He sees becoming in the light of Hegel's dialectic (1994, pp. 98–101): since both the projecting one and the recipient are partially and temporarily negated in their subjectivity, are, therefore, ego and not-ego, they create in this way a new subject:

> . . . projective identification can be understood only in terms of a mutually creating, negating, and preserving dialectic of subjects,

> each of whom allows himself to be "subjugated" by the other, that is, negated in such a way as to become, through the other, a third subject (the subject of projective identification). (1994, pp. 100–101)

This intersubjective third subject then opens up new moments of understanding. In a subsequent publication (2001), Ogden expands this version and postulates

> that the dreams and reveries being generated by analyst and patient at the frontier of dreaming draw not only on the unconscious experience of analyst and analysand as individuals, but involve a set of unconscious experiences jointly, but asymmetrically, constructed by the analytic pair. (p. 11; see also Ogden, 2004)

Contrary to Ogden, I do not conceive this process dialectically and think the dynamic is about O, which I set as the origin. See also Levine's discussion of Ogden's approach. According to Levine, Ogden describes processes ". . . in which representations have already been formed and linked to chains of meaning" (2013, p. 59).

2. It is reasonable to assume that this third, which can be grasped and named by the mother, is felt very concretely in the child, for example, "what is hard" in the " 'nipple–tongue' combination" in which Tustin detects the "disciplining fatherly authority" (1986, pp. 286–287) (see also Rhode's reflections on the autistic level of the Oedipus complex: for example, 2004).
3. Bion (1963) distinguishes between "failures in the development of thoughts themselves" and "failures in the development of an apparatus for dealing with thoughts" (p. 30). With this, two "thought concepts" become necessary: he distinguishes "a primitive 'thinking', which is active in the development of thought, from the thinking required to use thoughts. The thinking used in the development of thoughts differs from the thinking required to use the thoughts when developed" (p. 35).
4. Here I follow Grotstein (2007, e.g., p. 63 or p. 87), who points out that Bion distinguishes between pre-conception (with a hyphen) and preconception. The pre-conceptions are *a priori*, not thinkable cores of the unconscious, which make themselves felt in the emotional as an expectation, while the *posteriori* preconception had already encountered realization.
5. The clinical material first appeared in 2014 in the *Jahrbuch der Psychoanalyse, 68*. My thanks to the publisher, Frommann-Holzboog, for kindly permitting the copyright release.

## *References*

Baranger, M., Baranger, W., & Mom, J. M. (1988). The infantile psychic trauma from us to Freud: pure trauma, retroactivity and reconstruction. *International Journal of Psychoanalysis, 69*: 113–128.

Bick, E. (1968). The experience of the skin in early object relations. *International Journal of Psychoanalysis, 49*: 484–486.

Bion, W. R. (1962). *Learning from Experience*. London: William Heinemann [reprinted in *Seven Servants*, London: Karnac, 1977].

Bion, W. R. (1963). *Elements of Psychoanalysis*. London: William Heinemann [reprinted in *Seven Servants*, London: Karnac, 1977].

Bion, W. R. (1965). *Transformations*. London: William Heinemann [reprinted in *Seven Servants*, London: Karnac, 1977].

Bion, W. R. (1970). *Attention and Interpretation*. London: Tavistock [reprinted in *Seven Servants*, London: Karnac, 1977].

Fenichel, O. (1982). *Psychoanalytische Neurosenlehre* (The Psychoanalytic Theory of Neurosis, London 1946) Bd. 2, Olten: Walter Verlag

Freud, S. (1900a). *The Interpretation of Dreams. S. E., 4–5*. London: Hogarth.

Freud, S. (1915e). The unconscious. *S. E., 14*: 161–215. London: Hogarth.

Freud, S. (1918b). *From the History of an Infantile Neurosis. S. E., 17*: 7–121. London: Hogarth.

Freud, S. (1940a[1938]). An outline of psycho-analysis. *S. E., 23*: 139–208. London: Hogarth.

Grotstein, J. S. (2007). *A Beam of Intense Darkness. Wilfred Bion's Legacy to Psychoanalysis*. London: Karnac.

Klein, M. (1932). *The Psychoanalysis of Children*. London: Hogarth.

Klein, S. (1980). Autistic phenomena in neurotic patients. *International Journal of Psychoanalysis, 61*: 395–402.

Langer, S. K. (1942). *Philosophy in a New Key*. Cambridge, MA: Harvard University Press.

Laplanche, J. (2003). *Die unvollendete Kopernikanische Revolution in der Psychoanalyse*. Gießen: Psycho-Sozial.

Levine, H. B. (2013). The colourless canvas: representation, therapeutic action, and the creation of mind. In: H. B. Levine, G. S. Reed, & D. Scarfone (Eds.), *Unrepresented States and the Construction of Meaning. Clinical and Theoretical Contributions* pp. 42–71). London: Karnac.

Luhmann, N. (1987). *Social Systems*. Stanford, CA: Stanford University Press.

Mächtlinger, V. (2012). Resilience: Psychoanalytische Überlegungen zur späteren Entwicklung der sechs Kinder, die als Kleinkinder Theresienstadt überlebt haben. (Die 'Kinder von Bulldogs Bank'). In: B. Nissen (Ed.), *Wendepunkte. Zur Theorie und Klinik psychoanalytischer Veränderungsprozesse* (pp. 25–51). Gießen: Psychosozial.

Nissen, B. (2000). Hypochondria. A tentative approach. *International Journal of Psychoanalysis, 81*: 651–666.

Nissen, B. (2003). Zur Behandelbarkeit der monosymptomatischen Hypochondrie. In: B. Nissen (Ed.), *Hypochondrie—eine psychoanalytische Bestandsaufnahme* (pp. 333–385). Gießen: Psychosozial Verlag.

Nissen, B. (2007). Autistoide Rückzugsdynamik bei schwerer Hypochondrie. *Psyche, 61*: 1–21.

Nissen, B. (2008). On the determination of autistoid organizations in non-autistic adults. *International Journal of Psychoanalysis, 89*: 261–277.

Nissen, B. (2009). Die Geburt des Seelischen. In: *Die Entstehung des Seelischen. Psychoanalytische Perspektiven* (pp. 213–235). Gießen: Psychosozial.

Nissen, B. (2010). Hypochondrie—Versuch einer konzeptionellen Zusammenfassung; Forum Psychoanalyse.

Nissen, B. (2012). Diesseits der Deutung—Zur paradoxalen Figur der Präsenz in psychoanalytischen Prozessen. In: T. Storck (Ed.), *Zur Negation der psychoanalytischen Hermeneutik* (pp. 197–213). Gießen: Psychosozial.

Nissen, B. (2013). On mental elements. Based on the example of an autistoid perversion. *International Journal of Psychoanalysis, 94*: 239–256.

Ogden, T. H. (1994). *Subjects of Analysis*. London: Karnac.

Ogden, T. H. (2001). *Conversations at the Frontier of Dreaming*. Northvale, NJ: Jason Aronson.

Ogden, T. H. (2004). The analytic third: implications for psychoanalytic theory and technique. *Psychoanalytic Quarterly, 73*: 167–195.

Rhode, M. (2004). Different responses to trauma in two children with autistic spectrum disorder: the mouth as crossroads for the sense of self. *Journal of Child Psychotherapy, 30*: 3–20.

Rosenfeld, H. (1958). Some observations on the psychopathology of hypochondriacal states. *International Journal of Psychoanalysis, 39*: 121–124.

Rosenfeld, H. (1964). Die Psychopathologie der Hypochondrie. In: *Zur Psychoanalyse psychotischer Zustände* (pp. 209–233). Frankfurt: Suhrkamp.

Tustin, F. (1972). *Autism and Childhood Psychosis*. London: Hogarth.

Tustin, F. (1981). *Autistic States in Children*. London: Routledge.

Tustin, F. (1986). *Autistic Barriers in Neurotic Patients*. London: Karnac.

Tustin, F. (1990). *The Protective Shell in Children and Adults*. London: Karnac.

Winnicott, D. W. (1971). *Playing and Reality*. London: Tavistock.

CHAPTER SEVEN

# "The very same is lost": in pursuit of mental coverage when emerging from autistic states

*Joshua Durban*

The pursuit of a safe bodily–mental container, alongside the development of a defining psychic membrane, is a life-long, arduous task for the ASD child and fraught with danger. The more the child approaches the possibility of change in the analysis when he begins to emerge from the soothing, addictive sameness of his autistic organization, the more he is faced with the horrors of reality and with the threat of losing shape and protection. His "hyper-vulnerability" as Tustin (1981) put it, is fully exposed. What we encounter then is an oscillation between a fear of disintegration and a fear of integration. The child then tries to ward off nameless dread and more advanced death anxieties by establishing various substitute formations through the use of the analyst. I shall describe one such mode of mental coverage, which I call "mantling", in detail. It is created by ASD children in the process of emerging from their autistic states. These formations can calcify and seriously hamper further development, bringing the analysis to an impasse or to what might be described as an autistic negative therapeutic reaction. However, if met by an appropriate understanding and interpretation, this inevitable mantling could become a transitional phase on the child's journey from his psychic retreat toward seeing and being seen (Steiner, 2011).

Rachel, a young woman who has been in analysis with me since she was three years old, has recently moved into a special home for ASD adults. After her first week there, she arrived at her session looking distraught and typed the following sentence on her iPad: "The very same is lost. Now my self my self!" In her silent, almost poetic way, Rachel was able, like many other ASD patients in analysis, to convey with an almost uncanny precision her experience of painfully emerging from the safety of her encapsulation while losing the comfort of her autistic objects and sensation shapes. She began to have a sense of reality and with it the anxieties and frustrations of dependence, transience, separateness and psychic responsibility. Rachel feared disintegration. She went through a one-year period of violent psychosis from which she finally emerged. Now she typed 'my" and "self" separately twice, as if trying to regain through instant doubling the "very same" she had lost. She expressed her confusion and her attempts at adhesive identification by typing in quick, unpunctuated succession "my self my self", as if no differentiation were possible. She was able to feel, if only briefly, a budding depressive vulnerability, with moments of grief and mourning for her lost autistic objects. The emergence of "[her] self" immediately evoked the terror of separation and the pains of reality, which she previously covered by rage and violence. Earlier that week, her carers at the home where she was living told me that she stood by the fence, observing youngsters laughing and playing on their way to Scouts. She pointed at them and started crying bitterly. One of the carers said that it was clear to all of them the Rachel was mourning her condition, being damaged and excluded. She was experiencing the pain and shame involved in seeing and being seen. Rachel showed me what she had typed and her accusing stare made it perfectly clear that she held me and the analysis responsible for this difficult state of affairs. I was reminded of Bion (2005) saying, "It took me a very long time to realize that the actual experience of being psychoanalysed was a traumatic one and it takes a long while before one recovers from it". In fact, the process of acquiring an analyst-based coverage can prove to be quite traumatic for both child and analyst.

For the ASD child, emerging into the world of human relationships is a terrifying experience at worst, an uncanny one at best. The realities of separateness, dependence, mental boundaries, transience, and triangulation often shock the child back into the familiar, "very same", retreat of the autistic encapsulation. Furthermore, the process of change itself, which requires a capacity to tolerate shapelessness and uncertainty, might prove to be just too much for the child. Winnicott (1965) described the process of individuation in the healthy-enough child thus:

> I suggest that this I AM moment is a raw moment; the new individual feels infinitely exposed. Only if someone has her arms round the infant at this time can the I AM moment be endured, or rather, perhaps, risked. (p. 148)

It is often the analysis and the analyst that need to provide these arms around the patient.

These processes involve constant oscillations between despair and hope within the analyst, not only with regard to the possibility of development of the individual patient, but within the analyst's belief in the efficacy of psychoanalysis as a therapeutic tool. Furthermore, as we are working in primitive, newly explored recesses of the non-evolving mind, we are often confronted by the need to come up with inventive new modes of reaching the child (Alvarez, 2012).[1] These sometimes evoke anxiety in the analyst, as he or she might feel that they are not "analytic" enough or that their technique is only "an introduction to analysis" and not the "real thing".

As I have tried to demonstrate in a previous paper on despair and hope (Durban, 2014), these are present throughout the analysis of the ASD child and are best detected with the aid of the analyst's countertransference and what I call "total bodily presence". Their manifestations vary from the most concrete, bodily, and hallucinatory to the more discernible projection–introjection-based ones. In its most chaotic phase, one can describe an analysis in which a "leaking" child is met by an "absorbing–gathering" analyst, or what Houzel described in his important paper as "transference onto the container", utilizing its capacity for integration (2004). Later on, the analyst might gradually be able to work through the "analysis of infantile transference" and, perhaps, even work through "the transference neurosis", however unstable (Houzel, 2004).

The movement, in the analyst, between states of despair and hope often reflects a similar one in the child. Despair is mainly triggered by both severe states of dismantling in the child as well as by the shift during analysis from dismantling to mantling. However, the very existence of a movement signifies the child's "autistic hope" of finding a container and, as a consequence, arouses hope in the analyst.

## *Some dangers on the way to I AM-ness*

There are three main defensive pathological organizations that are frequently encountered in the process of emerging from autistic states while seeking substitute mental coverage. All of them might impede further development in the analysis and, in their extreme forms, become the equivalent of an autistic negative therapeutic reaction. The first is the creation of what I call "mantling", or an autistic "false self". The child seeks bodily and mental protection by annexing (Rhode, 2012), in unconscious phantasy, the carer's "external" layers: his mental and bodily traits. The child imitates them while ceasing to develop internally, thus keeping a withdrawn, autistic core intact. Although there are encouraging signs of the capacity for imitation, this is not yet internalization or true identification. It is the nature and function of this mantling process that is the main topic of my chapter and I shall return to it.

The second danger is of developing a full-blown psychosis as a means of organizing the new, overwhelming experiences with the help of newly acquired massive splitting, projective identification, and obsessive manic mechanisms, all of them unavailable to the pre-analysed child. This is often accompanied first by violence and, later, by a phantasized retreat into a bodily "claustrum" or orifice (Meltzer, 1992), usually the anus, oral cavity, or the urinary tract. This bodily retreat soon becomes persecutory. Thus, for example, following the marked development of her communication, her relatedness, and her internal phantasy life, Rachel became terrorized by her teeth and her dentist, whom she equated with me and with her mother. She tried to pull out her teeth, attacked mine, and soon it became clear that she retreated into her mouth where she felt herself to be her tongue trying to hide there. Rachel would roll back her tongue and gag whenever she saw her teeth, or anyone else's. This eventually subsided and she went back to seeking other, more benign, forms of coverage. Another form of psychosis, although more organized, is the obsessive preoccupation with making impossible reparation described recently by Weinberg (2016), such as trying to go back in time, sticking fallen leaves back to the tree, and trying to fix totally damaged objects while denying the damage.

The third danger is that of collapsing into a confusional, schizophrenia-like "twilight zone", as described by Tustin (1981), where not even psychosis is possible. Tustin used to say that hallucinations in the child were a sign that communication was beginning, though her initial reaction was to be alarmed (Rhode, 2013). There was a good reason for her alarm. While mantling and psychosis can both turn out to be transitional phases and lead to further emerging and development, this confusional state is often tragically permanent. For the ASD child, transformation is equated with destruction, since it necessitates an inevitable measure of formlessness, unpredictability, and helplessness (Ogden, 1988). Development is not possible, neither is containing nor reverie, without this capacity for formlessness. This poses a real threat, as it evokes the initial trauma of an early disruption of being and is equated with death (Durban, 2012). Since there is still an absence of stabile, containing good internal objects and there is an intense hostility towards the existence of a separate object whose live-presence might support the process of change (Alvarez, 1992), the child experiences a catastrophic threat. Change for the autistic child is perceived as a primary dread of losing form, distorted as it might be, and remaining formless with no new form in sight. While the former use of autistic objects and shapes creates a self-generated, "organized" chaos[2] which is somewhat controllable, alive, and, thus, made tolerable, change is experienced by the autistic child as a catastrophe which is unpredictable, uncontrollable, and, therefore, totally annihilating. Finding a shelter, or regressing to the use of the former autistic shapes and objects is no longer possible because of the dawning perception of separateness and otherness already achieved in analysis and the budding internalizations and identifications that come with it. Furthermore, there is a breakdown of, or an active, "attack on splitting" because of the inevitable harsh realities of separateness that the mechanism of splitting entails. The child is faced with intolerable anxieties and tries to defend himself with the use of a shattered, disorganized "armor" of previous, now inefficient, autistic defenses. The confusional child is, thus, stuck in a state of agitated emptiness, severs all previous contacts or modes of communication, and is terminally unreachable. Tustin (1981) provided us with a detailed catalogue of the confusional state's characteristics: an inextricable confusion between "self" and not-"self" where fragments of the self are felt to be dispersed and scattered: uncoordinated bodily movements, the child looks clumsy, muddled, and confused, softness and flaccidity of muscle tone, shifts between responsive eye contact and a bleary, unfocused stare, alternations between bodily rigidity and melting, a tendency towards respiratory, circulatory, metabolic, and digestive difficulties or physical illnesses, hyperactivity mixed with limpness, preservation of sameness, hallucinations, an autistic "armor" lacking homogeneous quality, chaos, pseudo-speech and play.

Haag (1993) supplies us with further insight into these conditions. She writes,

> In my experience, those encapsulated autistic children who emerge from their armor seem to do so in rather long transitory stages and following one of two principle tracks . . . either into post-autistic obsessionality or into a more boisterous manner, so called psychotic or schizophrenic, and in any case of hyper-penetrating symbiosis, which is quite destructive. (pp. 70–71)

She tries to differentiate between the schizophrenogenic elements characterized by an explosion into minute splitting and those elements derivative of manic–depressive problems, characterized by non-explosive projective identification which uses the different bodily compartments for the purpose of re-penetration and sexualized co-excitation.

As the analysis progresses there are often oscillations between mantling and psychosis—much in the same manner that there is an oscillation between the paranoid–schizoid and the depressive positions in the course of normal development.

## *Mantling*[3]

I shall focus on the clinical phenomenon of mantling. Meltzer and colleagues (1975) described "dismantling" as a slow, *passive* crumbling of the psyche's connective tissues, which are the affective, sensory, and perceptual links within the mind and with the object, which makes phantasy, imagination, and triangulation virtually impossible. Mantling, by contrast, is the advanced *active creation* of bodily and mental coverage. It appears in the analyses of ASD children and adolescents when they approach the possibility of change, which for them is often catastrophic. The analysis might seem to be progressing quite well at this point: the child slowly emerging out of his autistic encapsulation, exhibiting more relatedness, communicating, and sometimes even beginning to play and to respond to interpretations. The parents report good progress at home and at school. However, all progress is then suddenly brought to a halt, followed by a collapse, a regression to severe, earlier autistic states or to psychosis. In a way, what is being witnessed by the analyst now is both a repetition and an enactment of the initial autistic catastrophic breakdown witnessed by the parents in early infancy. At first, the infant seems to be developing quite normally. Suddenly, around 6–18 months, there is a collapse into speechlessness, non-communication, and a disappearance into an impenetrable array of self-generated stimuli. It is as if the infant survived initially by taking on an external functioning membrane, an autistic "second skin" (Bick, 1968), but did not really develop internally. In the analytic mantling process, the child, feeling pressed for communication and relatedness, and beginning to desire it himself, is faced with intolerable anxieties. He then retreats, while "covering" himself and hiding under a special kind of autistic membrane. This type of coverage, more advanced than his initial use of autistic objects and sensation shapes, is a combination of the external "normal" traits of the analyst and some of the carer's characteristics. These are combined with a finer version of his original autistic objects and sensation shapes and with projections of an internal autistic, bizarre primary object. It is at this juncture that the analyst might realize that most of the progress has been organized superficially around such defensive "false forms", based on adhesion, annexation, and mimicry and accompanied by contempt and fear. In this sense, mantling resembles an autistic precursor of a manic defense.

The analyst might have felt hopeful and as if significant work was being done before gradually becoming aware that, in the meantime, the child has secretly withdrawn, attempting, often unsuccessfully, to keep his autistic core intact. The child's secret secondary withdrawal, which is sometimes accompanied by what appears to be a kind of perverse, sadistic pleasure, is similar to what Joseph has described as the patient who is difficult to reach (1989a) and as an addiction to near death (1989b).

It is as if the child has "unwillingly" changed in analysis and is now seeking a way back into the "safety" of complete autism. This, naturally, gives rise to feelings of despair, meaninglessness, and futility in the analyst. Bion (2013) described the misappropriation of the analysis by the patient as a "bogus cure":

> The bogus cure in a sense is so effective that it gets in the way of getting to the real trouble. And it is so ineffective that it makes it impossible to live like that. I would think that you would almost certainly have essentially a great deal of despair and depression, that the situation is really hopeless. (p. 122)

The process of mantling involving "false forms",[4] often serves as a primitive, defensive, autistic pathological organization or psychic retreat (Steiner, 1993) against the inevitable, unpredictable, and uncontrollable temporary formlessness which is a crucial pre-condition for transformation. As such, mantling easily turns into an autistic negative therapeutic reaction against catastrophic change and nameless dread. However, mantling might also be a hopeful sign—a primitive personal creation of the child's. It is an initial recognition of a self and an object, an amalgam of a withdrawn self and other, which creates temporary form and coverage.

Thus, if detected on time and interpreted, the process of mantling can also become a necessary transitional organization leading to further growth and change, to the development of more authentic forms, and to the crucial acquisition of containing mental coverage originating from introjections of, and identifications with, a rudimentary good analytic object.

## *Mantling as primitive psychic retreats*

By suggesting the concept of mantling, I wish to expand Steiner's ideas regarding the creation of the pathological organization as a psychic retreat and apply them to the autistic spectrum. It is surprising that this link has not been made before, although many authors have described the various forms of autistic anxieties and defenses and their manifestations in protective bodily–mental forms.

Autism, being a well-defined defensive pathological organization of a damaged organism constantly on the verge of breakdown, is first constructed as a concrete physio–mental retreat. It defends the child against anxieties of being, that is, those involving the child's earliest experiences of existing as a cohesive, bounded, and continuous entity within a safe constitution. In ASD children, constitution itself becomes a persecutory presence. Due to a complex interplay of deficits, traumas, developmental vicious circles, and the ensuing failures in establishing splitting, differentiation, separateness, object-relations, and identifications, the child cannot inhabit his body–mind safely. This non-integrated, persecutory body is equated with the mother's and, in turn, with any other human presence. Since the body is our primary coverage, our relationship with it forms the prototype for any consecutive experience of a safe, protective organization.

The pathological organization described by Steiner (1993, 2011) as a rigid, nearly impenetrable narcissistic set of defenses, serves as a double protection from persecutory paranoid–schizoid anxieties regarding the object as well as from the inevitable anxieties and psychic pain involved in the depressive recognition of reality and loss. In other words, the acceptance of reality entails the suffering of dependence upon the object, neediness, separateness, transience, loss, and the oedipal situation. The pathological organization offers a seductive, anxiety-nullifying retreat. However, it soon turns into a tyrannical bunker cum prison in the service of destructive narcissism. It amounts to an attack on all the tender, needy, helpless, and feeling parts of the self and to a massive denial of the realities inherent in relatedness and links. Steiner shows how the pathological organization as a psychic retreat is linked to a wide variety of pathologies: borderline, perverse, obsessive, and depressive. He sees it as an outcome of internal and external traumas, of a primary failure in establishing normal splitting or its collapse into a confusional state. The psychic retreat is simultaneously a defense, an unconscious phantasy, and a psychic structure. Without proper analysis, it might consolidate and stop the necessary movement between the paranoid–schizoid and the depressive positions (PS-D).

The autistic psychic retreat, however, is non-symbolic, very concrete and observable, due to the disturbance in symbol formation and the regression to symbolic equation (Segal, 1957). It is experienced through what I call "mantling", as a defense against "dismantling" (Meltzer, 1992, 1994). Mantling protects the child from the dread of falling into bits, dissolving, losing shape, freezing, burning, suffocating, falling, losing his membrane, the sense of cohesiveness and of orientation. The child then concretely covers himself with autistic objects and sensation shapes and, thus, avoids relationship, communication, and an unbearable reality. The autistic psychic retreat has two phases: it appears initially as autistic encapsulation and then as more developed mantling when the child, snail-like, begins to emerge from his primary encapsulation only to retreat again back into his shelter.

The autistic pathological organization thus brings to a halt not only the movement between paranoid and depressive anxieties (PS–D), but mainly between anxieties of being and paranoid anxieties (B–PS).

In the course of the psychoanalyses of ASD children, it is important to try to distinguish between the different forms of autistic psychic retreats and interpret accordingly. While the primary autistic retreat of encapsulation is concrete, using autistic objects and sensation shapes and characterized by a massive confusion between self and object as a defense against separateness from the object and its proper internalization, the secondary psychic retreat of mantling manifests the beginning of object perception and relatedness. Primary encapsulation protects the child from nameless dread and catastrophic annihilation following a lack of sufficient sense of "the body as a safe mother". Secondary mantling protects against catastrophic change and psychic pain in a dawning reality of dependence, transience, and otherness. The primary encapsulated retreat wards off anxieties of being and paralyzes the movement towards paranoid anxieties. The retreat of mantling prevents the movements towards depressive anxieties and mourning.

## *Mantling in unconscious phantasy*

Unconscious phantasies of seeking coverage exist throughout life in many different forms: covering-up with the womb, the breast, the skin, different parts of the body (soft and hard), and by the other's mind and understanding.

Mantling begins with an active forceful annexation (Rhode, 2012) in unconscious phantasy of the analyst's outer physical and mental layers. This echoes the infant's initial tendency to first detect contours of stimuli and relate to them. It is involuntarily accompanied by severe anxieties about a bizarre, mutilated, and dangerous retaliating object that the child tries to expel through motor and perceptual evacuations and acting-out. The quality and content of the unconscious phantasy of mantling brings to mind that of envy. The violent, anxiety-laden appropriation of the object's properties and assets, alongside the accompanying simultaneous fears of retaliation and annihilation, are all characteristic of envy. Both envy and mantling are born out of the realization of separateness and the existential dangers it entails. Both are aimed at the obliteration of that realization and at eradicating self–object boundaries. However, while envy is directed primarily towards the object's goodness, creativity, and abundance, mantling aims at the appropriation of form—of a cover taken forcefully from the object. In this sense, mantling might be an autistic precursor of later ordinary developmental envy.

When psychic development occurs in analysis, the phantasized coverage might gradually change from appropriated persecutory forms to more authentic and benign ones. This change is characterized by to-and-fro movements in the analyst between despair and hope (Durban, 2014).

The gradual recognition of the other is first experienced by the analyst as mimicry, or as an adhesion to the analyst's surfaces. For the child, the gradual recognition of the other provokes unconscious phantasies of a forceful annexation leading to "combining" of elements. Later on, through incorporation and concrete introjections of the analyst's properties (Sodre, 2004), it is experienced as a "getting into" and "getting to know". In this sense, for the ASD child, mantling, which relies heavily on the bodily–mental presence of the analyst, might be another crucial developmental step in the long and complex process of assuming a contained physio–mental form.

## *Dana's pursuit of analyst-based coverage*

Dana's analysis[5] began when she was almost three, and a non-verbal ASD child. During the first two and a half years, she was largely impenetrable, immersing herself in constant, obsessive hand-waving, bobbing her head up and down, or turning it around and around. She used to bite and lick herself as well as most of the objects she encountered. She would usually carry around empty boxes that she shook and rattled. At other times, she would push herself against table corners, radiators, and walls. There was almost no eye contact. She was either in a state of self-stimulation with her "organized chaos" of autistic objects and shapes, or limp and completely withdrawn, slowly rubbing saliva and mucus on to her body, on to mine and on to the furniture. What I then noticed was that she never actually put her fingers inside her mouth or her nose but just used and smeared the fluids she appeared to generate almost at will. It seemed as if she either avoided or did not have a sense of "inside" her body, defined by external surfaces and noise. During that initial period, I was aided mainly by my countertransference, which took the form of bizarre, bodily near-hallucinatory sensations and images. I would feel myself melting, losing shape, or becoming numb and paralyzed. On occasion, I felt my tongue sticking to my palate or saw it being torn out of my mouth. I had recurrent images from violent films or would imagine Dana in a faded photograph, smiling and communicating. I fluctuated between therapeutic despair and hope. Much later, I came to understand all of these reactions as echoing Dana's split-off and projected experiences of both her initial violent breakdown and of her autistic hopes for reparation, that is, for becoming whole again through gaining some sort of a rudimentary bodily and mental container (Durban, 2014).

During the third year, much work was done on her terror of separateness, from which she tried to shield herself with non-stop stimulation so as not to lose shape and feel torn into bits. She then became simultaneously obsessed with, and terrified of, holes, gaps, expanses, and the color white.[6] In sessions, while maintaining her preoccupation with water, saliva, mucus, and boxes, although to a lesser degree, she would also cut big gaping holes in the middle of a sheet of paper with a pair of scissors. She would appear to be completely blissful, impenetrable, and non-communicative. She would use the scissors without so much as looking at them or the paper. At times, she would suddenly start screaming with her mouth shut tight and try to stab holes in her skin with the scissors and then look at me in a terrified way, sometimes trying to stab me. I interpreted this behavior to her as an attempt to show me the white, the hole, or the gap in her mouth and in her heart by cutting holes. I said she felt I had torn parts of her mouth and pieces out of her middle and stuck them on to me. She was afraid I would cut some more. She was also terrified that I might try and take these parts with me, so she tried to cut them out of me in order to get them back and get rid of me. On other occasions, I added that these holes, in turn, become angry, dangerous, cutting things that threaten her and try to cut her up, as well as me, so that we become nothing. Dana would then approach me, still avoiding looking at me, but relaxing her mouth and not screaming. I told her that maybe only after having seen me survive could she try to seek me, so that I would help her. After many such interpretations, she calmed down. In later sessions, she would signal towards the scissors and scream in a terrified way. I tried to tell her that the scissors separated things from other things and that this terrified her. She wanted to be one, glued and spread all over and merged with me, like her saliva and mucus, and not cut separate into two. I thought of this as enacting her traumatic separation from the breast, experienced not as a clean tearing apart, but with parts of her left in the breast and parts of the breast in her. I interpreted her mode of defending herself at that time through gluing, spreading, liquefying, and sticking. At the same time, this adhesion to surfaces manifested her deepest anxieties regarding loss of shape, formlessness, and annihilation.

After the emergence of an adhesive identification, Dana began using my bodily presence in a concrete form. She would run towards me and shove her head tightly underneath my jacket. She would then fall to the floor and lie there, frozen. She would do this repeatedly and it took me a long time to understand. Eventually, I told Dana she was trying to get into me, like a Joshua-mommy with an inside, so that she could be my baby and be born from me again. But something did not let her and made her frozen. That something, maybe the white hole, or perhaps the scissors, kept her not moving, not speaking, paralyzed, and she wanted me to do something to it so that she could live. Dana seemed to react to this and the jacket ritual stopped. Soon after, she began putting things into her boxes and taking them out. I felt she was beginning to have some more sense of her internal space after being assured of my presence and mantling herself with my body and its insides. Dana progressed well outside the analysis and became more communicative and alive in it.

We are now in the fourth year. Dana's encapsulation has assumed more advanced mantling forms. She is seven years old and has taken to wearing black shirts, jackets, and baseball caps. She has begun to speak, but in a strange high-pitched voice. She takes great care to say "hello" and "goodbye" in a robot-like voice upon arrival and departure. She has begun to play with two dolls, a mother and a baby. After some time, it became clear, however, that this is not real play. The dolls mainly say hello and goodbye mechanically, sit opposite each other, or open and close doors. Sometimes, the mommy doll pretends to speak (mainly gibberish) while moving all around the doll's house. The baby is thrown on the floor or out of the house. Dana has a new autistic shape: she pulls the corner of her eye to the side, squinting, at the room and at me. When I try to do it, I see the world distorted, alien, and out of focus. She also has a new autistic object: an old watch which she holds tightly in one hand or whose hands she moves back and forth. I understand this as a left-over of her addiction to autistic sensation shapes and objects, as her attempt to maintain a kind of autistic, blurry comfort zone, while she progresses slowly towards contact with the world.

When I meet the parents, I notice that the father is wearing a baseball cap and he points out to me that Dana adores black jackets and shirts: "just like you". The parents are relieved and grateful. Their little girl is speaking now, goes to a special school, and even meets friends in the afternoon.

It is wintertime. Leaving my clinic, I suddenly notice a trail of jelly-like stains on the road leading to its door. When I look closer, I discover a line of crushed slugs that have obviously been destroyed deliberately. The next day I can see Dana coming with her carer and, although she is being warned not to, she looks for slugs and snails and crushes them under foot. She seems thrilled and laughs. When she enters the room, wearing another black jacket and saying, "Hello, how are you", it sounds strange, like a contemptuous, sadistic mimicry of my own welcome. I am able to see now that she has managed to really "get into my jacket", has torn parts off my external surface and speech and, in unconscious phantasy, annexed them to herself, but not in order to change and develop, but, rather, in order to keep something secret, static, out of my reach. Dana opens the dolls' house and starts moving the mother and the baby around aimlessly. This time, the mother is wearing a bizarre head-cover made from cloth with bits of Dana's mucus stuck to it. She attempts to lick my hand and then licks the head cover. This takes some time and I realize that almost half an hour has passed and that we are approaching the end of the session. I say, "You are moving the mommy and baby dolls about so that I will leave you alone. You are giving me the Dana you think I want, dressed up and talking like me. You are wearing Joshua. But in a secret, far place you are keeping the crushed slug which is you, Dana. This is what you don't want to feel like: without a shell, without a form. So, you behave as you think I want you to, but it is all strange, blurred and twisted." Dana carries on moving the mother and the baby dolls, looking vacant. I realize that she is also trying to communicate to me what constitutes a quite accurate impression not only of her internal mother, but of her real mother as well. Her mother is always busy doing things, quite mechanically or manically as a defence against her inner chaos. At the same time, she is often detached, distant, and absorbed in her own world. I am somewhat encouraged by Dana's reality testing. I think that Dana must be doubly frightened: not only of me becoming identified with this mother, but of her becoming like mother and, thus, losing all hope of a safe, responsive container. So I go on, "I've become frightening and strange like the mommy-hat. You feel you have taken all my thoughts, my jacket, my eyes, hand, and voice and now I have become a wounded and dangerous Joshua-mommy full of holes. I cannot cover Dana. You are afraid you will fall out, like the baby. You are afraid I will hurt you."

The next day she arrives with her mother, who looks red-eyed and distraught. The mother tells me Dana has been wild and uncontrollable throughout the day. She refused to participate in the school's activities and became violent towards her teacher and towards her mother. She further reports that, for quite some time now, Dana has been spending a lot of time in the toilet shoving toilet paper into her anus and vagina screaming that they mustn't let Dana fall out. It seems that she is desperately and psychotically seeking, like Rachel and her tongue, some new coverage inside her anal and vaginal claustrum. These new shelters are meant to substitute for the primary damaged container and for the secondary one supplied by me, but it seems they fail. I also note the absence of the father, who exists only as a baseball cap covering her head, and Dana's terror of not finding a container outside of the ruptured Dana–mother dyad. Her move into temporary psychosis does not supply the safe coverage she needs. I feel this is related to my growing awareness of her use of the analysis and me as a "false form" within a wider process of pursuing bodily coverage (through my jacket, her anus, and her vagina) and mental coverage (through the concrete mommy-hat, daddy's baseball-cap, and the annexation of my voice and wishes). I wonder whether Dana feels that I am her only way out of this but fears that I, too, have become a vacant mother or an absent father. Furthermore, there is no possibility of joining these damaged part-objects. I also feel she fears that her using bits of me as cover have left me damaged, mutilated, and, therefore, dangerous.

When Dana enters the room, she is limping strangely. She does not say her usual "hello" and crouches, fetus-like, on the couch, holding on to her watch tightly. When I approach, she hides her head under a blanket and screams with her mouth and eyes shut. I tell Dana, "You need to hide from me. You fear I will rip off your Joshua-cover and crush you like the slug. If I take back my jacket and my speech and see what's going on in Dana's head, she will lose everything—all the blankets, the jackets, the voice, the eyes, the hand, her leg, the saliva, and the mucus. This is the reason you scream and scream with your eyes and mouth shut. You are afraid you're disappearing." Dana opens her eyes and becomes quiet. I wait a few minutes, and when I see she is calmer I go on, "I am the Mommy who doesn't really care, talking gibberish while Dana is thrown out. I am the baby thrown out while Dana is doing things and doesn't care." Dana looks at her watch and then gives it to me. I say, "You'd like me to stop time with your watch so all these things will not happen again. But this is impossible. But now that I know all of this, perhaps you'll let me near you so that I can hear you and you can hear me. We can be together."

It takes many more months to work through all of this. Dana improves: the mantling through false forms has nearly disappeared and she is beginning to develop her own style in clothes, to find her own voice and personality. Dana is also able to seek out her father when he is away and say she misses him "because she needs the hat and daddy underneath". She has invented a new game where daddy, mommy, and she wear each other's hats. She asked her parents for a pet turtle and when she got one she named it Jo.[7]

## *Discussion*

Dana's case is but one of many where I have witnessed this process of mantling taking place when the child begins to emerge from a severely autistic state. It is often accompanied by a temporary relapse into psychotic organizations. In some cases, there is a collapse into an often incurable, confusional state. The analysis of such children might be described as a constant to-and-fro movement, often accompanied by intense feelings of despair and hope in the analyst, between a search for protective covers and attacks on this search. Within these attempts at creating and securing a rudimentary bodily and mental container, the analyst's total body–mind presence and availability become the crucial focal points of the child's primary adhesive and, later, projective identifications.

Tustin (1981, 1990) has taught us that the creation of a protective shell, composed of self-generated, idiosyncratic, autistic sensation objects and autistic sensation shapes, is the preferred initial mode of protection, organization, and self-regulation for the child. It appears upon facing early, unthinkable anxieties about premature traumatic separateness, formlessness, chaos, and annihilation. These objects and shapes provide a semblance of going on being, a reassurance of sorts to the patients that they continue to exist. They provide strength and self-soothing while simultaneously blocking out communication, development, and reality.

The use of mantling, however, can be more advanced, as it often appears when there has already been a degree of progress in the analysis and when there is some communication that reflects a measure of self and object differentiation. The analyzed child becomes capable of splitting. There are even some autistic precursors of envy, manic defenses and attempts at primitive, although delusional, reparation. It is then that the child might develop an external "false form" aimed at keeping the analysis from progressing so that no real change will ensue and, thus, the inevitable anxieties are avoided.

As I see it, the main terrors of the autistic child involve formlessness and loss of shape. These have been described by Klein (1984a), Winnicott (1975), Bick (1968, 1986), and Tustin (1972) and include such experiences as falling forever, losing orientation, liquefying and spilling out, having the skin torn away, burning and freezing, and of falling into bits or losing parts of the body when feeling physically or mentally prematurely separate from the mother. These terrors, quite evident in Dana's early phase in analysis, in turn block out any possibility of transformation and change. This is an understandable outcome of a complicated, multi-factor interaction between inborn deficits in perceptual and sensory–motor self-regulation, alongside hyper-vulnerability and a deficit in drive regulation and deficiencies in modulating anxiety and environmental care. A vicious circle is established between the withdrawn child and the gradually despairing parents.

Psychoanalytic work with autistic children clearly demonstrates that, experience-wise, the child tries to deal with this multi-determined trauma of living in a catastrophic and incomprehensible world by doing his best to maintain some kind of balance, continuity, and form, be it self-generated or taken over from the inanimate and human environment. These attempts, however somatic or concrete they might be, are aided by, and encoded in, unconscious phantasy.

As seen in Dana's case, the process of mantling is mainly somatic, adhesive, and obsessive in nature. The unconscious phantasies accompanying it are of warding off a deadly, mutilated, and bizarre object that has been attacked repeatedly and sadistically by the child in the course of his appropriating its outer layer, and whose aim is to destroy the child by retaliating and robbing him of his autistic organizations, thus propelling him into formlessness. It may also be regarded as a proto paranoid–schizoid fear of integration (Klein, 1984b), masking a deep fear of a second breakdown, this time due to the possibility of change and the inevitable restructuring of internal and external modes of being it would entail.

Dana attempted to create the illusion of change and progress while internally stopping time, blurring and distorting reality-based forms, deadening the objects by robbing the analyst's exterior, and turning him into an empty shell.[8] This also echoed Dana's perception of her primary object as alternatively hollow[9] or obtuse and mainly non-attuned. When this was detected by the analyst, it failed. Dana was then threatened with re-experiencing her initial breakdown and the failure of her primitive reparative attempts. She then resorted to psychosis and to finding cover within her own bodily orifices. Following further working through, mantling evolved into a primitive personal creation, an amalgam of a withdrawn self and other, which created temporary form and coverage. Thus, it might prove to be an important step towards normal incorporation and projective identification.

The appearance of an analyst-based mantling, while threatening to constitute a difficult impasse or a defensive pathological organization, might also pave the way for a better recognition of the psychic, physiological, and behavioral properties of the other and, through him, of the self. Or, as Rachel wrote, "The very same is gone. Now my self my self!"

## *Notes*

1. In a recent paper (2015), I focus on the technical considerations (for some, deviations) regarding interpretations, based on the accumulated innovations arising from analytic work with ASD and psychotic children. I suggest that, within sessions, there is an interplay between: (1) the construction of a bodily container (corporation—inside and outside, spinal and muscular, perceptual and sensual); (2) presenting the analyst as a live companion (personification through enhancement, imitation, emotional echoing); (3) utilizing the linking function (integration between body parts, fragmented part-objects, self and objects and between decomposed unconscious phantasy elements); (4) reclaiming; (5) autistic reparation in action based on pre-symbolic realizations. I further claim that, while working with the ASD multi-determined pathologies, the analyst serves as a developmental reparational object and through him an "object-implant" is achieved into a black hole where "bad-objects" mask a neuro-mental experience of "no object". These kinds of interpretations are needed in order to establish contact with the children, to mobilize their anxieties, and to promote integration and development.
2. It is interesting to note that many children come from quite chaotic homes. Often this chaos is covered up by an appearance of efficiency and false manic organization. A central feature of such chaotic homes is an overdose of constant emotional and sensory stimulation. Since the culture we live in is characterized by this excessive stimulation, I sometimes think that the near-epidemic increase in the appearance of autism is a magnified, tragic reaction to this.
3. I have chosen the term "mantling" because of its immediate implications in everyday language. According to the online "Free Dictionary", mantling means: 1. Covering with, or as if with a mantle, to conceal. 2. To spread or to become extended over a surface. 3. To become covered with a coating as scum or froth on the surface of a liquid. Mantle is the outer covering of a wall; in anatomy it refers to the cerebral cortex; in geology it is the layer of the earth between the crust of the earth and the core.
4. Although the term "false forms" brings to mind Winnicott's description of the False Self defence (1982), the autistic false form is much more primitive and has some characteristics peculiar to autism. As will be seen in Dana's case, it is mainly somatic, adhesive, distorted, and obsessive in nature with the unconscious phantasies of warding off a deadly, mutilated, and bizarre object which has been attacked

repeatedly and sadistically by the child in the course of appropriating its outer layer, and whose aim is to destroy the child by retaliating and robbing him of his autistic organizations and excretion–muscular formations, thus propelling him back into formlessness.

5. The cases presented in this paper are of five sessions per week analyses. The first years of Dana's analysis are described in Durban, 2014.
6. I have elsewhere shown how the white color might sometimes stand for the autistic child's experience of being totally blended or welded with the environment, as well as feeling dominated by death (Durban, 2011, 2012).
7. Besides the obvious reference to my name, perhaps as a first transitional object, the name "Jo" carries an additional meaning. Dana's family is of Argentinean origin and "Yo" in Argentinean Spanish means "I".
8. It might be argued that autistic false forms, acquired or created through the process of adhesive identification and mantling, are an advanced variation of autistic objects and autistic shapes (Tustin, 1981, 1987). However, there are a few important differences: (1) the analyst serves as a central mantling object; (2) there is no complete blocking out of communication; (3) it is not predominantly muscular, excretion-based or self-generated, but, rather, a combination, or an amalgam, of child–analyst characteristics. In fact, it might constitute a budding precursor of the unconscious phantasy of the primal scene (where fluids and surfaces are exchanged or joined together in order to create a new membrane); (4) it is less obsessive and responds well to interpretations; (5) unlike adhesive identification, it entails some experience of a psycho–physical membrane or skin and internal and external space; (6) there are underlying emotions which might be detected.
9. Bronstein (2014) describes the hollow self and the hollow object and its relation to psychosomatic symptoms and the inability to experience psychic pain. The patient encounters profound anxiety as the hated object is also desperately needed for the subject's physical–emotional survival.

## *References*

Alvarez, A. (1992). *Live Company. Psychoanalytic Psychotherapy with Autistic, Borderline, Deprived and Abused Children*. London: Routledge.

Alvarez, A. (2012). *The Thinking Heart*. London: Routledge.

Bick, E. (1968). The experience of skin in early object relations. *International Journal of Psychoanalysis, 49*: 484–486.

Bick, E. (1986). Further considerations on the function of the skin in early object relations. *British Journal of Psychotherapy, 2*: 292–299 [reprinted in: A. Briggs (Ed.), *Surviving Space*. London, Karnac, 2002].

Bion, W. R. (2005). *The Tavistock Seminars*. London: Karnac.

Bion, W. R. (2013). *Wilfred Bion: Los Angeles Seminars and Supervisions*, J. Aguayo & B. D. Malin (Eds.). London: Karnac.

Bronstein, C. (2014). 'I am not crying. I am rubbing my eyes': Annie and the hollow object. *Journal of Child Psychotherapy, 40*(2): 135–149.

Durban, J. (2011). Shadows, ghosts and chimaeras—on some early modes of handling psycho-genetic heritage. *International Journal of Psychoanalysis, 92*(4): 903–924.

Durban, J. (2012). Vergänglichkeit und die inneren Beziehungen zum Todesobject. In: B. Nissen (Ed.), *Wendepunkte: Zur Theorie und Klinik psychoanalytischer Veranderungsprozesse* (pp. 107–135). Geissen: Psychosozial.

Durban, J. (2014). Despair and hope: on some varieties of countertransference and enactment in the psychoanalysis of ASD (autistic spectrum disorder) children. *Journal of Child Psychotherapy, 40*(2): 187–200.

Durban, J. (2015). In the beginning was the Word? The changing shape and use of interpretation in the analyses of ASD and psychotic children. Paper presented to the IPA Congress, Boston.

Haag, G. (1993). Fear of fusion and projective identification in autistic children. *Psychoanalytic Inquiry, 13*: 63–84.

Houzel, D. (2004), The psychoanalysis of infantile autism. *Journal of Child Psychotherapy, 30*: 225–237.

Joseph, B. (1989a). The patient who is difficult to reach. In: M. Feldman & E. Bott Spillius (Eds.), *Psychic Equilibrium and Psychic Change: Selected Papers of Betty Joseph* (pp. 75–88). London: Routledge.

Joseph, B. (1989b). Addiction to near death. In: M. Feldman & E. Bott Spillius (Eds.), *Psychic Equilibrium and Psychic Change: Selected Papers of Betty Joseph* (pp. 127–139). London: Routledge.

Klein, M. (1984a). The importance of symbol-formation in the development of the ego. In: *Love, Guilt and Reparation and Other Works 1921–1945* (pp. 219–233). London: Hogarth Press.

Klein, M. (1984b). Envy and gratitude. In: *Envy and Gratitude and Other Works 1946–1963*. London: Hogarth Press.

Meltzer, D. (1992). *The Claustrum: An Investigation of Claustrophobic Phenomena*. Strathtay, Perthshire: Clunie Press.

Meltzer, D. (1994). Adhesive identification. In: A. Hahn (Ed.), *Sincerity and Other Works: Collected Papers of Donald Meltzer* (pp. 335–350). London: Karnac.

Meltzer, D., Hoxter, S., Brenmer, J., & Weddell, D. (1975). *Explorations in Autism*. Strathtay, Perthshire: Clunie Press.

Ogden, T. H. (1988). Misrecognitions and the fear of not knowing. *Psychoanalytic Quarterly, 57*(4): 643–666.

Rhode, M. (2013). Whose memories are they and where do they go? Problems surrounding internalization in children on the autistic spectrum. *International Journal of Psychoanalysis, 93*: 356–376.

Segal, H. (1957). Notes on symbol formation. *International Journal of Psychoanalysis, 38*: 391–397.

Sodre, I. (2004). Who's who? Notes on pathological identifications. In: E. Hargraves & A. Verchevker (Eds.), *In Pursuit of Psychic Change: The Betty Joseph Workshop* (pp. 53–67). London: New Library of Psychoanalysis.

Steiner, J. (1993). *Psychic Retreats*. Hove: Brunner Routledge.

Steiner, J. (2011). *Seeing and Being Seen*. London: Routledge.

Tustin, F. (1972). *Autism and Childhood Psychosis*. London: Hogarth Press.

Tustin, F. (1981). *Autistic States in Children*. London: Routledge.

Tustin, F. (1987). *Autistic Barriers in Neurotic Patients*. London: Karnac.

Tustin, F. (1990). *The Protective Shell in Children and Adults*. London: Karnac.

Weinberg, R. (2016). The impossible reparation. *Journal of Child Psychotherapy, 42*: 152–162.

Winnicott, D. W. (1965). Group influences and the maladjusted child: the school aspect. In: *The Family and Individual Development* (pp. 146–155). London and New York: Routledge, 1999.

Winnicott, D. W. (1975). Birth memories: birth trauma, and anxiety. In: *Through Paediatrics to Psycho-analysis* (pp. 174–193). London: Hogarth.

Winnicott, D. W. (1982). Ego distortion in terms of true and false self. In: *The Maturational Processes and the Facilitating Environment* (pp. 140–153). London: Hogarth Press.

CHAPTER EIGHT

# Bion and the unintegrated states: falling, dissolving, and spilling

*Celia Fix Korbivcher*

## *Introduction*

In previous publications (Korbivcher, 2005, 2013a,b), I have examined autistic states in neurotic patients in an attempt to introduce a new conceptual category, autistic transformations, into Bion's (1965) theory of transformations. Following a similar line of reasoning, my aim here is to investigate unintegrated phenomena in patients for whom the non-psychotic part of the personality predominates, and differentiate these phenomena from the autistic phenomena that were mentioned in my previous publications. I establish a relationship between such phenomena and Bion's ideas of the primordial mind and describe a further conceptual category, that of unintegrated transformations. To illustrate my proposal, I will present clinical material from three patients whom I believe demonstrate the presence of unintegrated phenomena and discuss the implications and paradoxes that result from my formulation. In so doing, I hope to expand existing psychoanalytic theory so that analysts may better recognize, understand, and address the intense bodily manifestations that have not yet achieved representation in the minds of their patients and that are characteristic of unintegrated states.

## *Unintegrated states*

Winnicott was the first author to emphasize states of unintegration, distinguishing the latter from disintegration and fragmentation. According to Winnicott, disintegration is a defense and can only occur after some degree of integration has already occurred. Unintegration, however, is caused by failure of containment, giving rise to terrifying anxieties.[1]

In 1962, Winnicott stated,

> In the event of a deficiency in good enough mothering the infant is likely to be subjected to sudden or chronic awareness of disconnection, leading to unthinkable anxieties associated with the felt state of unintegration such as the fear of going to pieces, of falling forever, of having no relationship to the body, and having no orientation in space. (p. 12)

According to Bick (1968, 1986), unintegrated states are manifested in all human beings from birth. These states can move toward integration through interaction with an object that fulfills the infant's initial sensorial needs. The latter process provides the foundation for a sense of self. If it does not go well, however, the infant might experience extreme vulnerability and a chaotic state caused by the terror of losing the limits of its own bodily integrity. The latter is reflected and expressed by terrors of falling into a "black hole", dissolving, or spilling away into nothingness.

Through the practice of observing babies, Bick (1968, 1986) developed the idea that infants are not able to bind together their emotional contents because they lack the notion of limits to distinguish bodily substances from mental and internal contents. She proposed the notion of a "psychic skin", which is the projection of, or the mental equivalent to, the bodily skin. Its function is to gather experiences or parts of a rudimentary self in the direction of some integration or cohesion, giving rise to the first fantasies of internal and external space.

The development of the psychic skin depends on the introjection of an external object. From the beginning, this external object interacts continuously with the infant's sensorial needs. Bick suggested that disturbances in the primal psychic skin function, which follow from a failure in the external object's being sufficiently containing and, therefore, "good enough" can lead the infant to develop a "second skin", through which he replaces dependence on the object with a state of pseudo-independence. This is achieved by turning instead to a non-human sensorial object that is used to momentarily hold together parts of his personality. This object can be considered a "second skin", or, in Tustin's terms, an autistic object used in an autistic protective maneuver (Tustin, 1986, 1990, 1992).

Meltzer (1975), referring to unintegration, introduced the notion of the "dismantling of the *self*", in which the individual's attention is suspended, causing the senses to move in the direction of the most attractive sensorial stimuli existent at that moment. In such a state, the mental apparatus passively falls into pieces.

Tustin (1986) sharply described her ideas about unintegration. She stated,

> In psychotherapy, as patients emerge from autism they show very clearly that they are on the brink of "falling" or being "dropped". Breaks of continuity of the physical presence of the analyst, such as weekends and vacations are not experienced by such patients as rejection, as they would be in patients in a neurotic state of response, but as actual physical breaks ... Quite literally and physically they feel they are "let down". The ground seems to have opened beneath their feet, and they feel on the edge of a chasm which opens before them. In these states they talk about such things as bottomless pits, black holes, chasms and precipices. These patients, in their initial experiences, felt that they were falling into a void with nothing to catch them or to break a fall ... For them, the primary wound of the physical separation from the mother ... reappears in the other situations of separation ... (p. 194)

Mitrani (1996) offered an important and detailed study of "unintegration, adhesive identification, and psychic skin", in which she highlighted the contributions of Winnicott, Meltzer, Bick, and Tustin. She noted that while Meltzer and his colleagues understood unintegration as a passive defense against anxiety, according to Winnicott, Bick, and Tustin,

> unintegration may be seen as a normal primary state which is only experienced, felt, and evaded when the needed environment supports, are absent. Here unintegration is conceptualized as a feeling-state

> rather than a pathological development, occurring at the expense of normal mental and emotional growth. (p. 12)

The feeling state that Mitrani refers to is associated with experiences of catastrophic anxieties and annihilation (e.g., the threat of falling forever, spilling, or dissolving). Ultimately, what prevails is the threat of losing the notion of existence itself. According to Tustin (1990), the loss of the latter is likely to be the greatest threat that a human being can experience, and is worse than death itself.

## *Bion and the primordial mind*

In his late works (1976a,b,c, 1977, 1980, 1997), Bion showed a strong interest in the functioning of the embryonic mental states and in the manifestations of primordial phenomena. In 1977, he posed the following questions:

> Is it possible for us, as psycho-analysts, to think that there may still be vestiges in the human being that would suggest a survival in the human mind, analogous to that in the human body, of evidence in the field of optics that once there were optic pits, or in the field of hearing that once there were auditory pits? Is there any part of the human mind which still betrays signs of an "embryological" intuition, either visual or auditory? (p. 44)

According to Bion (1991), the mental equivalents of embryonic remnants of archaic mental states, primitive patterns of behavior, and manifestations can be detected even in the most civilized and cultured individuals. These reflect a state of mind in which ideas or thoughts that had never been conscious and unconscious and whose origins are out of reach could exist. He wrote,

> . . . the nearest I can get to giving it a provisional title, is the *inaccessible state of mind*. . . . Whether it is an awareness of its heartbeat, or an awareness of feelings of terror, of sound, or of sight—the type of sight experienced through pressure in the optical cavities by the changes of pressure in the intra-uterine fluid—everything that can never have been what we call conscious or unconscious . . . (Bion, 1997, p. 50)

In Bion's (1976b) last works, he referred to proto-emotions and proposed the term "sub-thalamic fear". Bion defined this as a type of fear that is not controlled by the mind and, therefore, does not acquire meaning. It refers to bodily manifestations of remnants of prenatal parts involving the adrenal glands and adrenaline secretion, activated at certain moments, leading the individual to unthoughtful fight or flight reactions.

Bion and the other authors that I have mentioned seem to be talking about a similar category of phenomena, that is, unintegrated phenomena, which are the consequences of unintegrated states. I shall now attempt to describe these in relation to Bion's theory of "Transformations".

## *Autistic transformations and unintegrated transformations*

Bion (1962) suggested that the analyst's field of work is "learning from emotional experience" and offered his theory of "Transformations" as an observational theory of mental phenomena that are shared between analyst and patient in this field. By adopting the standpoint of "Transformations" (1965), an analyst can make his observations with the assumption that "the facts to be observed are distorted by the very act of observation" (p. 45), because the tool that he possesses for his work is his own mind, which is susceptible to psychic movements that are equal to those of his clients. Beginning with his contact with these movements, the analyst formulates his version of a particular emotional experience. His participation in the session is pregnant with elements from his own personality and with the baggage he has accumulated through his lifelong experiences. It is influenced by the trained psychoanalytic intuition that he acquired during his own analysis (Korbivcher, 2005, 2013a,b). The analyst's contribution comes about in this field, a field in which the analyst abandons the position of an authority who will give the precise meaning to that current phenomenon. Instead, he offers his own transformation of the emotional experience he is living.

With the concept of O, Bion expanded the analytical field of *knowing* the patient's reality (K) to *being* the reality. He proposed a multidimensional view of the psyche, highlighting different groups of transformations, including rigid motion transformations, projective transformations, transformations in hallucinosis, and transformations in K, –K, and O. This proposal of a multi-dimensional mind offers us a basis for the idea of additional types of transformations, as well. With this in mind, in 2005, I proposed the introduction of autistic transformations. As I conceive them, these develop in an autistic medium, implying the absence of the notion of an object. The relationships between "me" and "not-me" are dominated by "sensation objects" that have no representation in the mind. Some of the invariants in autistic transformations include absence of affective life, emptiness, and auto-sensual activities.

If we adopt the theory of "Transformations" as a reference and agree that it can include additional types of transformations, I propose the possibility of introducing—together with transformations of the neurotic, psychotic, and autistic areas—transformations of an unintegrated area, that is, unintegrated transformations characterized by intense non-mental bodily manifestations. Unintegrated transformations are developed in an unintegrated medium, resulting in the absence of the delimitation of the self and of the notion of a separate object. A state of permanent threat and vulnerability and a state of terror of losing the notion of existence itself are some of the invariants in unintegrated transformations.

It should be emphasized that autistic phenomena evolve from unintegrated phenomena. Thus, they are related but have different characteristics. In unintegrated states, the relationship between "me" and "not-me" is not established by projective identification, as in neurotic and psychotic areas, or by adhesive equation, as in the autistic areas. There is no adhesion or identification with an object, no discrimination of interior or exterior. As a result, the self threatens to "spread" infinitely, causing a permanent threat of falling, spilling, or dissolving. In these circumstances, the individual typically reacts by attempting to create autistic protective maneuvers as a means of obtaining a more cohesive state through his body. In contrast, in autistic states, "sensation objects" ("autistic objects" and "autistic shapes") are used to enforce a kind of unstable patch to form the boundary between me and not-me. These objects are strongly impregnated by sensations and clung to obsessively as a maneuver to avoid the intolerable awareness of corporeal separation from the object. These relations are established by adhesive equation (Tustin, 1990), in which the individual adheres to contiguous surfaces, avoiding any space. The individual, thus, entertains an experience of continuity with the object.

When encountering unintegrated states, analysts do not always easily recognize patients' communications because of their impact on his mind, that is, disturbing the analyst's capacity to think and discriminate. Bion's concern in highlighting different types of transformations was to enable the analyst to identify (in his clinical work) different levels of communication proposed by the patient. The analyst's contact with the emotional experience shared with the patient in the session orientates him to detect the type of transformation that he is facing (Korbivcher, 2005, 2013a,b). Nominating the group of unintegrated transformations provides the expansion of the analyst's observational field to include the unintegrated part of the patient's personality beyond the autistic part. So, the analytical field expands to areas that are not yet integrated, areas in which the notion of a boundary that is capable of holding emotional content together has not been developed.

It is also worth mentioning that unintegrated phenomena, or unintegrated elements, as I propose to name them, have to be distinguished from beta elements. Beta elements belong to the primitive area of the mind, that is, to the proto-mental area, whereas unintegrated elements belong to the primordial area, that is, the embryonic area of the mind. Beta elements are sensorial impressions that were not transformed by the alpha function into psychic elements and, consequently, are not able to be used for thinking. They are undigested elements that should be evacuated to relieve the psychic apparatus from excessive tension. When they cannot be evacuated, they create a beta screen.

As we know, in the area of neurosis, the production of alpha elements allows for the creation of a contact barrier that separates the conscious from the unconscious. In the area of psychosis, the contact barrier that should be there is destroyed, and the beta screen, established by an accumulation of beta elements, is formed instead. In the autistic area, an autistic barrier is constructed that is composed of autistic elements. In the unintegrated realm, on the other hand, we cannot find any type of barrier. There is the absence of a barrier and, thus, a lack of delimitation between interior and exterior space. In this realm, the self spreads without delimitation and the autistic barrier does not form. Relations between me and not-me in the unintegrated area are not established by projective identification, as in the neurosis and psychosis areas, or by adhesive equation, as in the autistic area. Thus, no adhesion or identification with the object is constituted, but there is a state of constant threat of loss of the notion of existing.

As a further hypothesis, I would like to suggest that unintegrated elements arise from tropisms and not from beta elements. The meaning of the word tropism, according to *The Heritage Illustrated Dictionary of the English Language* (2013), is "The turning or bending movement of an organism or a part toward or away from an external stimulus such as light, heat or gravity".

About tropisms, Bion (1992), says,

> Tropisms are the matrix from which all mental life springs. For maturation to be possible they need to be won from the void and communicated. Just as a breast, or its equivalent, is necessary for the infant life to be sustained, so it is necessary a mental counterpart, the primitive breast should exist, for the infant mental life to be sustained. The vehicle of communication—the infant's cry, tactile and visual senses—is engaged in order not only to communicate but also to control the tropism. If all goes well the communication, by projective identification, leads (as Melanie Klein has described) to the deposition in the breast of the tropisms that the infant can neither control, modify, nor develop, but which can be so controlled and developed after they have been modified by the object. If this breaks down, then the vehicle of communication, the contact with reality, the links . . . suffer a significant fate. This applies particularly to the communicating particles that are felt to lie with the enclosed tropisms, rejected by psyche and object alike. . . . The tropism remains enclosed within the vehicle of communication itself, be that sound, sight or touch. (Bion, 1992, p. 47)

Tropisms describe a movement toward an object, which is expected to modify that object into a psychic element. If this object is reached, the resulting psychic primordial element will be an unintegrated element. This element might move toward some integration based on the introjection of an external object. If the latter is introjected, the resulting elements belong to the field of beta elements. However, if the introjection of this object fails, unintegrated elements are converted into autistic elements (Korbivcher, 2013a,b).

Regarding the position of unintegrated phenomena in the Grid (Bion, 1963), I had proposed elsewhere to insert a space directly before

Line A (beta elements) as an area that contains primordial phenomena, tropisms, and autistic elements. This space refers to Line A0. I suggest that unintegrated elements can be placed on this same Line A0. On the vertical axis, these elements are located on the A01 and A06 columns.

## *Clinical material*

Mariela, a young woman in her forties, has been undergoing analysis three times a week. She called me between two sessions to request an extra session on the same day. I was unable to fulfill her request. Therefore, we could not meet until the following day, which was the day of her next regularly scheduled session. In the interim, I became concerned about the reason behind her request and how my refusal might make her feel.

When she arrived on the following day, I noticed that she was very distressed and displayed an expression of terror. She did not lie on the couch that day, which was unusual for her. She was in an uneasy, restless state and had difficulty breathing. She mentioned that she had had an asthmatic episode and that she had been feeling unwell but was now feeling better. She added that she was feeling very nervous and thought that she was taking it out on her children.

As I listened to her, her terrorized condition drew my attention. I thought her state was related to the phone call of the previous day and the fact that I had been unable to see her. When I mentioned this, she promptly answered that it was not a problem at all. I wondered if not lying on the couch that day was a way of avoiding more contact with her pain. I pointed this thought out to her, which allowed us to talk about her suffering and discomfort. She seemed slightly relieved and then lay down on the couch. She lay there for a long time in silence, restless, constantly scratching her nose, fidgeting, and breathing with difficulty. Her discomfort made me feel somewhat uneasy.

After some minutes, immersed in this terrorized atmosphere, she commented,

> "I am looking at this picture [a picture that hangs on the wall in front of the couch] and I see a hole, a black hole that looks like a tunnel. It is very dark! I don't like that! It seems like a free fall, like jumping without

> a parachute. It is a well. It has no wall; it is very dark. The fear becomes stronger, mainly at night."

She added that she felt as if she was falling, rolling down a staircase, without a handrail to hold on to. Her mental state at that moment had changed. She seemed calmer and was breathing better. I suggested to her that through forming and expressing her thoughts about the picture, she was able to translate her vulnerable state of terror and threat into words, and this made her feel somewhat relieved and more comfortable.

Mario is a three-year-old boy; his parents brought him for analysis because he has terror crises. According to his parents, he often seems to be calm. Then, he suddenly starts screaming desperately, as if completely terrorized. He complains of something that bothers him on the palms of his hands, which he says are rough.

During a session in which Mario and I seemed to be very connected, he began to play at the sink with running water, but suddenly started to scream desperately. I felt impacted by his state and unable to contain him. I took him to the waiting room where his mother was. It occurred to me that something might have hurt him somewhere on his body. He continued to scream relentlessly. The mother also became frightened due to his state. We checked to see if there was something wrong with his body, but nothing showed up.

I slowly recovered my ability to think and realized that when we were playing, some water ran down his arm and into his sleeve. I conjectured that there might be an association between his terror and that occurrence. I told him that he looked very scared and that something had happened between us but that we did not know exactly what it was. After a while, I mentioned that perhaps the water running down his arm made him feel as if his whole body would run away with the water. We continued talking, and Mario slowly calmed down and stopped crying, recovering a more integrated state that allowed him to return to the room and resume playing.

Vera is a successful young woman who occupies a position of great responsibility in her job. She is very attractive and careful with her appearance. She has received analysis for four years, attending sessions three times a week. As she arrived to a session, I noticed that she seemed to be content and smiling. I attributed her cheerfulness to her meeting with me.

She lay down and stated (in a concerned tone) that she was not well and that she was worried that she might have a problem. She stated, "I am afraid I am undergoing a regression. I think there is something wrong with me." She mentioned that she had been having nightmares and that she had dreamt of her work several times, which was unusual. She stated she had always slept very well and, therefore, did not know why she was having such restless sleep.

I became somewhat surprised by the discrepancy between her seeming contentment and her narrative. I pointed this out to her and added that she seemed to be glad and relieved to be there with me.

She stated that, on her way to the session, she realized she wavered between two states. On the one hand, she was very happy because her aunt had been awarded an important prize and, on the other hand, she was enraged by her work situation and, thus, could not stop thinking about it.

I informed her that coming to the session, talking to me about her concerns, and having me listen to her are very basic needs. This information seemed to help her.

She agreed and added, "This place seems to be my balance. Only here do I manage to achieve a balance of all this."

At that moment, while she spoke, she turned her back to me and faced the wall, as she often does. She curled up and, in making herself comfortable on the couch, she lay face down, facing the wall. I noticed that her physical movements reflected the mental state of someone who seeks comfort through her body. I told her that when she arrived that day she seemed restless, showing contradictory experiences, but that she found a much more comfortable state, leaving everything that upset her outside.

She stated,

> "That's the problem! This is the only place I experience this. I come here and I hold myself firmly to this couch . . . I feel I lack very basic things in my life . . ."

She then mentioned, in a calmer tone,

> "I looked at the wall and thought: 'Oh, my wall!' You know, I always look at the little dots on the wall and think that if I could, I would rip out the wall and take it with me, but I know I can't do that."

The way that she held herself to the couch drew my attention. She seemed to be stuck to it. Her involvement was intense and she surrendered entirely to the situation. It struck me that she might have been afraid, helpless, and needing to hold me, similar to how she held herself to the couch. I mentioned this idea to her, and she replied, "I wonder why this is so important to me!"

After a while, she became slightly emotional and said,

> "The problem is that when I leave here, I immediately find myself out there, and this is horrible!! I open that door and fall right outside. It is as if I were falling into a huge pit. After that, I spend a long time inside my car, shivering with cold, before I am able to calm down and drive away."

Again, her position on the couch drew my attention. She lay face down, facing the wall, with her feet up and her very high-heeled shoes dangling. She seemed to be completely relaxed and surrendered to the situation. The extremely high heels stood out in the primitive atmosphere that the situation evoked. At that moment, I reminded of her several trips abroad on business and the stories that she had told me about very important decisions that she had to make.

I mentioned that she seemed to be perplexed about finding herself in two such different states. On the one hand, she experienced a state of terror upon seeing herself as a separate person, such as when the sessions end and she feels the threat of "falling into a pit, remaining shivering with cold inside the car before leaving". On the other hand, she must attend to the demands of the world, feeling a state of being overwhelmed. I added that these experiences potentially made her feel, as she stated, afraid of undergoing a regression The session ended, and she stood up slowly and shakily as if she was going to lose her balance and fall. Then, she left the room.

## *Comments*

On arriving for her session, Mariela was greatly disturbed and apparently terrified and threatened. Predominantly corporal symptoms appeared. She mentioned an asthma crisis and added, "I am very nervous and take it out on my children." I suggested to her that this state of distress was possibly connected to her asking to have an extra session the previous day and then not having being seen. In Mariela's mind, however, this experience did not have emotional meaning. My hypothesis was that the asthma crisis and the resulting difficulty in breathing were bodily manifestations that reflected experiences that did not yet reach a level of psychic representation. I suggest that the somatic manifestations produced a certain organization and took the place of feelings of vulnerability, helplessness, and imminent annihilation. The somatic manifestations could be considered transformations of unintegrated states.

Mariela lay on the couch and continued to show great physical discomfort. The presence and emotional availability of the analyst allowed her to use the picture on the wall in front of her to name the experience that she was living; a state of threat of falling in an endless space. As she said, "It is as if I rolled down a staircase without a banister to hold on to." From the experience of feeling contained by the analyst, Mariela acquired a more cohesive state and could translate her experience of vulnerability, falling into a black hole, and dropping into words. Here, the patient´s transformations were unintegrated transformations →K.

Mario was very involved with the analyst and in a state of continuity with her. Suddenly, however, something unexpected happened that escaped his control; water ran down his arm inside the sleeve of his shirt. At that moment, the adhesive use of the analyst was broken and triggered a more catastrophic set of feelings. Because his mind could not contain the feelings that were triggered, Mario experienced intense feelings of terror. I hypothesize that the sensation of the water running down his arm made him feel threatened with losing the limits of his own body and dissolving or spilling and, thus, losing parts of his own self. His terror of the unintegrated state triggered a chaotic state in the room, momentarily causing the analyst to lose her capacity to think. Such reactions occur by a kind of affect contagion and should not be confused with projective identification phenomena.

Mario did not present the notion of a separate object into which he could project his undesirable contents. Rather, he manifested an unintegrated experience in which there was no container or psychic skin to hold together his inner contents. Facing such manifestations, the analyst became anxious and vulnerable. I believe that these states were provoked because of the patient's primordial experience of a lack of self-delimitation, that is, a lack of delimitation between interior and exterior, which triggered an experience of dissolving or spilling.

If the analyst is able to contain such an experience, the patient can move to a more integrated state in which he is able to name what he is living. In Mario's case, the patient's transformations were transformations from K → unintegration. This situation can be observed when the analyst recovered her thinking capacity and interpreted that perhaps that water running down his arm . . . felt as if his whole body would run away with the water. Suggesting this to Mario calmed him down as he was unable, on his own, to perform the transformation O→K. The change in the state of the analyst's mind was an important pre-condition in this process.

In the case of Vera, although the neurotic part of her personality was prevalent, she showed intense manifestations of autistic and unintegrated states. Initially, the analyst noticed that although Vera stated that she was distressed, she seemed to be glad and relieved to be in the session. The analyst stated this, and Vera replied, "It's only here that I can live like this. That's the problem!" At that moment, Vera was physically clinging to the couch and visually to her little dots on the wall. She hung on to the dots in the same way that she clung to the couch. With this maneuver, she maintained an adhesive state of corporeal continuity with the analyst, avoiding the awareness of any separation or space between them, which would cause intense vulnerability and a terrified state. In this case, her protective maneuvers can be considered autistic transformations. Vera then stated that the problem was when she left the session and opened the door. She stated that she felt as if she was falling into a huge pit and that after the session, she spent a long time inside her car, shivering with cold . . . Anticipating the threat of separation from the analyst, Vera translated her terror regarding facing the experience of falling forever into words. We can state that the latter transformations are transformations in K → unintegration.

In the sequence, observing Vera's position on the couch, the analyst indicated the contrast between the adult Vera, with her feet up and her very high-heeled shoes dangling, and the infant Vera, involved in an intense primordial atmosphere, to which she had completely surrendered. This scenario caused the analyst to think that Vera had a premature separation from the object without having fulfilled her initial sensorial needs. Vera had developed a vulnerable structure that is not able to attend to the demands of the world. I hypothesize that Vera had a sense-dominated adhesive relationship with certain physical attributes of the analytic setting; the couch the wall, the dots, and with the analyst as an autistic shape. She established a corporal continuity with the analyst as a means to obtain a more cohesive condition. In these movements, the patient's transformations were autistic transformations. It is interesting to observe that Vera initially complained that she was regressing, demonstrating her perception that she was experiencing primordial states of adhesiveness in her relationship with the analyst and that she perceived that the threat of the loss of these states resulted in a terror of falling into an endless space, of falling into a pit and of the threat of loss of her own existence. These movements indicate unintegrated transformations → K.

## *Discussion*

1. Mariela, Vera, and Mario operated predominantly with their neurotic part of their personalities but also manifested states of unintegration. Mariela and Vera felt the threat of falling into an endless space and were able to use metaphors such as falling into a well or falling into a black hole to talk about their inner experiences. Mario, however, being so young, lacked their capacity to transform these primordial terrors into psychic elements, words, and images, and so manifested a state of terror due the threats of dissolving and spilling.
2. In these patients, we can observe different manifestations of unintegrated states. Some are inaccessible to the patient and analyst (e.g., Mario's episode with the water and Mariela's difficulty breathing), while others the patient—or patient with the help of the analyst—can name through metaphors. I am suggesting that Mario's terror and Mariela's manifestations correspond to Bion's sub-thalamic fear associated with an unintegrated state. After my interpretation allowed Mariela to achieve a calmer state, she was able to name her feelings, referring to a black hole. Mario, after being contained by my interpretation, recovered a more integrated state and was able to continue playing. In her session, Vera dealt with the threat of becoming conscious of her separateness from the analyst by expressing her fears, mentioning the fear of falling into a pit after leaving the session, and stated that

she remains shivering with cold in her car following sessions. Although these states were translated into words, in my opinion, they retained certain characteristics of unintegrated phenomena and can be considered transformations in K → unintegration. I include K (knowledge) here, because it indicates that the patient, despite living an experience of unintegration, is able to communicate that experience.

3. The proposal of unintegrated transformations evokes the following question: can the idea of transformation be applied to the unintegrated area? In other words, to have a transformation, is some integration necessary? As previously stated, unintegrated states are communicated through intense bodily manifestations that express feelings of terror evoked by the threat of losing existence itself. I understand that such experiences, despite not yet being integrated, are transformations of inaccessible states of the mind (Bion, 1997). As Bion claimed, we do not have access to the thing itself, O, but rather to its transformations. As such, I suggest that unintegrated phenomena might also belong to the field of phenomena that are contained in the theory of "Transformations".
4. We can also ask ourselves whether what Bion calls "nameless dread" is equivalent to the states of terror that are present in states of sub-thalamic terror. Bion claimed that when the mother's capacity for reverie fails, the infant reintrojects what it projected and experiences what Bion calls "nameless dread". In addition, the beta screen (i.e., a screen that is situated in an area that corresponds to the psychotic part of the personality) is formed. The unintegrated area is an area that has not yet been integrated and in which the mechanisms of identification, projection, and introjection have not been constituted. The unintegrated area comes prior to the projective identification area. In this area, a "protopsyche" reacts to situations of pressure or discomfort with physical manifestations. Thus, we can ask the following question: how can the analyst reach and speak to the patient´s unintegrated states? Does the notion of reverie apply to these primordial areas of the mind? I raise the hypothesis that the analyst does not dream or daydream about the patient´s manifestations and transform them. Rather, the analyst must gather and join these manifestations together and only then will he be able to dream the contents that have been contained.

5. Finally, it must be emphasized that unintegrated phenomena, which are considered within the vertex of the theory of "Transformations", require a new perspective. These phenomena can be recognized as existing in an infinite domain, in which the analyst's transformations arise in this field as one of many possibilities to be considered in his dealing with the material. The analyst is no longer an outside observer whose function is to attribute meanings; rather, he is actively involved in the analytic situation. Within this approach, unintegrated phenomena are not considered to be isolated. Rather, they are viewed as a link in a chain of successive movements and their consequences, arising from the interaction between the analyst and the patient in the session.

I must state that the ideas that have been developed in this work are intended to continue the investigation of the functioning of the primordial mind, more specifically, the "inaccessible areas of the mind" or unintegrated areas. I am aware, however, that one of the main features of these areas is the difficulty of accessing them and, therefore, the resulting conceptual imprecision to which they are subjected. Despite this difficulty, I am convinced of the importance of daring to enter these areas, as "such manifestations are detected in most civilized and cultured people" (Bion, 1977).

## *Note*

1. Winnicott also used the term unintegration to refer to a normal relaxation state. This state, which occurs only if the infant has introjected a benign internal environment, is not the focus of this chapter.

## *References*

Bick, E. (1968). The experience of the skin in the early object-relations. *International Journal of Psychoanalysis*, *49*: 484–486.

Bick, E. (1986). Further considerations on the function of the skin in early object relations: findings from infant observation integrated into child and adult analysis. *British Journal of Psychotherapy*, *4*: 292–299.

Bion, W. R. (1957). Differentiation of the psychotic and the non-psychotic part of personalities. In: *Second Thoughts* (pp. 43–64). London: Heinemann Medical Books.

Bion, W. R. (1962). *Learning from Experience*. London: Heinemann Medical Books [reprinted London: Karnac, 1984].

Bion, W. R. (1963). *Elements of Psychoanalysis*. London: Heinemann [reprinted London: Karnac, 1984].

Bion, W. R. (1965). *Transformations: Change from Learning to Growth*. London: William Heinemann Medical Books [reprinted London: Karnac, 1984].

Bion, W. R. (1976a). Emotional turbulence. In: *Clinical Seminars and Four Papers* (pp. 223–233). Abingdon: Fleetwood Press.

Bion, W. R. (1976b). Evidence. In: *Clinical Seminars and Four Papers* (pp. 239–246). Abingdon: Fleetwood Press.

Bion, W. R. (1976c). Making the best of a bad job. In: *Clinical Seminars and Four Papers* (pp. 246–257). Abingdon: Fleetwood Press.

Bion, W. R. (1977). *Two Papers: The Grid and Cæsura*. Rio de Janeiro: Imago.

Bion, W. R. (1980). *Bion in New York and São Paulo*. Strathtay, Perthshire: Clunie Press.

Bion, W. R. (1991). *A Memoir of the Future*. London: Karnac.

Bion, W. R. (1992). *Cogitations*. London: Karnac.

Bion, W. R. (1997). *Taming Wild Thoughts*. London: Karnac.

*Heritage Illustrated Dictionary of the English Language, The* (2013). Fifth edn. Boston, MA: Houghton Mifflin Harcourt.

Korbivcher, C. F. (2005). The theory of transformations and autistic states. Autistic transformations: a proposal. *International Journal of Psychoanalysis, 86*: 1595–1610.

Korbivcher, C. F. (2013a). Bion and Tustin. The autistic phenomena. *International Journal of Psychoanalysis, 94*(3): 645–665.

Korbivcher, C. F. (2013b). *Autistic Transformations. Bion's Theory and Autistic Phenomena*. London: Karnac.

Meltzer, D. (1975). Adhesive identification. *Contemporary Psychoanalysis, 11*(3): 289–310.

Mitrani, J. L. (1996). Unintegration, adhesive identification, and psychic skin: variations on some themes by Esther Bick. In: *A Framework for the Imaginary: Clinical Explorations in Primitive States of Being* (pp. 1–26). London: Karnac.

Tustin, F. (1986). *Autistic Barriers in Neurotic Patients*. London: Karnac.

Tustin, F. (1990). *The Protective Shell in Children and Adults*. London: Karnac.
Tustin, F. (1992). *Autistic States in Children* (revised edn). London: Routledge & Kegan Paul.
Winnicott, D. W. (1962). Ego integration in child development. In: *The Maturational Processes and the Facilitating Environment: Studies in the Theory of Emotional Development* (pp. 56–63). London: Hogarth, 1985.

CHAPTER NINE

# Inhibition of curiosity due to concern about the object's response: difficulties in tolerating a "third position" in relation to autism

*David Simpson*

Difficulties with being curious, and showing curiosity, are, in my view, fundamental in those people with autism, or who show autistic states, but are also common in many other people, including those who might seek psychoanalytic treatment.

I am proposing that those with autism, autistic states, and this wider group of people, which includes those with narcissistic and neurotic difficulties, have a common origin to their inhibition of curiosity. This is their fear of engendering an intolerant response from those that are the objects of their curiosity, and that this arose in childhood when they perceive their primary carer, usually their mother, as being unable to bear their curiosity about her, and particularly their curiosity about her feelings and attitudes towards them. Alongside the child's hypersensitivity to his mother's feelings, I think that an important factor behind this is a failure in the mother's capacity to tolerate observation of herself from what Britton (1989) called a third position. Through her being unable to be a witness, this failure of the third position is transmitted to the child, who finds it difficult to be curious. In these people, this scenario has been internalized as a relationship between themselves and their primary internal objects, to be relived in their relationship with significant figures and areas of interest in their later life including, if they become patients, in their transference to their analyst.

These ideas emerged from my work with learning disabled and autistic people where I was struck by how frightened many of these people were to look at and be curious about their parents, perceiving them not only to be unable to bear their curiosity, but fearing that it would expose their parents to painful feelings that they found intolerable. It appeared to me that they often perceived their curiosity as threatening catastrophe. I later noticed a similar pattern in a much wider range of patients, including those of normal intelligence and who do not show an autistic state, hence my belief that this is a more general phenomenon.

My proposal of a common origin to the difficulties in curiosity seen in this wide range of patients is in keeping with my view that these difficulties are a manifestation, and function as part, of the process of psychic retreat that is common to those with autistic states and those without, who would most usually be described as showing narcissistic or neurotic difficulties. I consider the inhibition of curiosity seen in non-autistic individuals to be on a continuum with that seen in autism. This is in keeping with the notion that autistic aspects of personality and autistic mechanisms function as part of, and underpin, other forms of psychopathology (S. Klein, 1980). In my view, autistic defense mechanisms are an important facet in the process of psychic retreat seen across the whole range of human mental functioning and pathology. I suspect they potentially occur in everybody. I distinguish autistic mechanisms from autistic states, which includes the syndrome of autism, where I think these mechanisms operate in more profound ways and with clearly aberrant developmental trajectories.

It follows from this that, in my view, autistic states, like other forms of psychic retreat seen in non-autistic individuals, arise in response to difficulties in object relations. Constitutional vulnerabilities, organic disorders, and emotional problems, including difficulties in parental containment, contribute to this.

Following a Kleinian perspective (Klein, 1975d), I view object relations, including primitive part-object relations and early forms of triangulation and the oedipal situation, as being present from birth. In fact, they predate it, both in terms of fetal experience and their origin, following Bion and Money-Kyrle's idea that these derive from genetically determined inborn preconceptions.

My perspective on the origin of autistic states, which assumes object relations existing from the beginning of life, appears to differ from that taken by Frances Tustin, particularly in her early work. Although she trained in a Kleinian tradition, she originally stressed the importance of a stage of normal primary autism. In this stage, the newborn infant is believed to be in a sensation dominated state, undifferentiated from its mother, with "no experience of the world outside its mother's body and its own" (Tustin, 1981, p. 6). Tustin (1981, pp. 3–12) believed that at this stage the infant was in a hypersensitive state of vulnerability to the impingement of "not self" and that if the illusion of auto-sensual union with the mother was disturbed, for a variety of reasons which could lead to premature awareness of bodily separateness, then pathological autism could result. Although she bases her theory on the stage of primary autism, which is essentially considered to be pre-object relations, even in her early work there are signs of her having a different conception in her statement that

> It is tenable that the primary state of autism not absolute. There are likely to be flickering states of awareness of separateness which, if they are bearable, prepare the child for . . . emotional relationships with people experienced as separate and different from his body. (Tustin, 1981, p. 5)

Towards the end of her life, in her paper "The perpetuation of an error" (Tustin, 2009). She clearly states that the idea that pathological autism involves a regression to a stage of primary autism was a serious mistake. She changes her mind and, no longer holding with the idea of normal primary autism, which lacks scientific credibility, she articulates her view that autistic states arise as a retreat from the problem of relationships to other people. Following Bion's (1977) idea that traumatic patients experience "pain but not suffering", she states that "the pain of trauma leads the autistic child to turn away from people". She suggests that the outcome is a form of early, or primal, depression; a state which she recognizes was similar to that suggested by Winnicott that occurs in infants who are exposed to separation from their mother before they are psychologically equipped for this. This is not far from the notion suggested by Klein's (1975b) early work that autism results from a primary depressive retreat from object relations due to the child's premature exaggerated concern for the effects of his desires, including his hostile wishes, towards his mother. I think Tustin just falls short of a return to her Kleinian roots. I believe the key concept that she does not use is unconscious phantasy, against which I think autistic states are a defense.

Tustin's later views of autism, as a retreat from the problem of relatedness, essentially from object relations, are in keeping with my own and the perspective that I take in understanding the problem of curiosity, in autism and non-autistic individuals, where there has been hypersensitive concern for their mother's feelings and particularly her feelings about them. Essentially, I think that these difficulties emanate from problems that arise in early object relatedness, where the self and object can be separate. To be curious implies this separation.

From a psychoanalytic perspective, Freud (1909d, p. 245), Abraham and Klein described curiosity as a manifestation the epistemophilic instinct, a component of the libido. Abraham (1973) thought that it derived from a transformation of the child's wish to see his parents' bodies (particularly the body of the pregnant mother) and sexual acts. Klein (1975a) developed this idea further and stressed the way that the child's anxieties engendered by his sadistic wishes towards his mother could inhibit curiosity and learning. In "The importance of symbol-formation and development of the ego" (Klein, 1975b,c) she described her work with a young boy with autism, "Dick", to illustrate how intellectual development is inhibited when there is a "premature defense against sadism" following an "exaggerated identification with the object attacked". She introduces the idea that the child's guilt out of concern for his parental objects, which she later called depressive anxiety, is a major factor influencing the direction of his curiosity and cause of his inhibition.

Bion (1962, p. 42) represented the epistemophilic instinct, essentially curiosity, as a link (K) between objects, independent of, but possibly linked to, links in love (L) and hate (H). He introduced the importance of the mother's influence, including her relationship with the father, in the development of the child's capacity for this (Bion, 1962, pp. 36, 90, 1967, p. 114). Following his view, the mother's capacity for containment, to take in and transform the infant's anxiety, is essential for the development of his curiosity and thinking.

Britton (1989), following Klein and Bion's ideas, has suggested an important model, a triangular space which, in normal development, is formed in the infant's mind and which gives a basis for understanding how curiosity and knowledge grow. In Britton's (1998) view, in order for phantasies or ideas to acquire the status of belief and acquire psychic reality, they need to be experienced subjectively and objectively, and this requires the possibility of a third objective position which can allow observation in the mind. This triangular space, which is essentially the internal realization of the primary Oedipal situation potentially present from birth, can provide this. In my view, this development requires the experience of a mother, or primary carer, with this capacity who can relate both subjectively and objectively to her child, which I think requires a mother with the capacity for a separate internal relationship with the father, or paternal figure.

Britton (1998, p. 58) postulates an innate factor in the child which can disrupt this process, which he calls "psychic atopia", which results in an intolerance to psychic differences, an allergy to the products of others' minds. In my view, in psychic atopia, it is particularly the presence of "another in the mind of the other", which represents a link to a father in the mind of mother, which cannot be tolerated. Psychic atopia corresponds closely with Tustin's (1981, p. 6) idea of "hypersensitivity" to "not self", a psychical immunological reaction to otherness seen in autism. Tustin (1981, p. 10) quotes Stein (1967) and Fordham (1976), who have suggested "that pathological autism is akin to the immunological reactions on the part of the body to reject or annihilate alien tissues, it is like an autoimmune reaction to reject or annihilate not self experiences". I think psychic atopia is fundamental to autism being a major force that prevents relatedness.

Psychic atopia is not the prerogative of infants and mothers can also be allergic to their infants. This can be gross (e.g., child abuse) or subtle, when the child displays "otherness" by not conforming to his mother's conception of her ideal child, which can leave a persistent sense of feeling "wrong" (Simpson, 2014). For some mothers, their child's curiosity may be an unwelcome sign of otherness, and the child, perceiving this, may inhibit his exploration of the world.

### *Interaction between the child and the mother in the inhibition of curiosity with particular relevance in autism*

Britton's ideas of triangular space and psychic atopia provide a basis for understanding the inhibition of curiosity in autism, and, more widely, in terms of the interaction between the child and his mother's state of mind, with a complex field of possible factors promoting and inhibiting development. This framework is also helpful in understanding the particular relevance of the child's concern about his mother's response to being observed. The idea that an internal triangular space, with an established third position providing a basis for observation, is essential for the development of curiosity is crucial in this. In my view, these processes, which operate from the beginning of life, are particularly important in infancy in autism, but are also relevant at later stages, particularly where pathological development has already occurred.

From the perspective of the child's contribution, psychic atopia plays an important part in inhibiting curiosity and I think it operates in two ways. The first comes through determining the child's intolerance of otherness and particularly his intolerance of his position in the early oedipal situation as a separate observer of the parental couple, of which the internal triangular space is symbolic. The second comes by interaction with his mother's difficulties through determining the child's hypersensitive concern for her emotional state, which prevents the child taking in, and identifying with, an observing third position

The mother's contribution, in these situations, comes from her difficulties in allowing herself to be observed and known, by herself and her child, due to her difficulties in tolerating objective observation from a third position. This is not only required for self-observation but also to appreciate and bear reality. Parents who cannot bear to know themselves often cannot bear to know their children; the two go hand-in-hand. If parents are unable to be curious about themselves, including bearing to know about their own hostile impulses, it is difficult for them to tolerate curiosity and hostility in their children, with the result that the expression of this will be inhibited.

In some situations, the origin of the problem lies with the mother's intrinsic problem in developing a third position, with a contribution from her psychic atopia, which reflects difficulties in the quality of her relationship with her internal father. In other situations, the dominant factor is the nature of the reality to be faced. This might be too painful and evocative of guilt and shame for the mother to allow herself to be observed, including by herself. In my experience, this is often the case when a child is mentally handicapped. Autism is frequently associated with mental handicap and is itself a form of mental handicap.

Here, powerful defenses are mobilized against the awareness of reality, particularly denial, including denial of the nature and extent of handicap, which is sometimes seen as an advantage (Simpson, 2004). Frequently, a collusive situation between the mother and the child develops where the child inhibits his curiosity, sometimes literally does not look at his mother because he believes the mother cannot bear to know her feelings about the child. As a result, the child cannot be known. The reality exposed by an observing third position is felt, by both parties, to be too painful to bear and this inhibits the development of the third position in the child which inhibits his curiosity and further handicaps intellectual development. The link to the paternal third position in the mother's mind is disabled, which mirrors how, when a child is handicapped, the parent's marriage will often collapse under the weight of guilt and shame, at some level their sexual acts being held responsible. In these situations, the mother's sensitivity to defects in her child interacts with the child's sensitivity to his mother's emotional difficulties in bearing these. When a child is hypersensitive, or even allergic in psychic atopia, this potentiates the problem, which I think is often the case in autism.

I describe two clinical illustrations: an adolescent with severe learning disabilities and autistic features an adult male patient who, although without an autistic state, shows a hypersensitive concern for his object.

## *Sam*[1]

I saw Sam for weekly sessions. He had severe learning disabilities due to a chromosomal abnormality. His appearance was distinctly abnormal and he looked ugly, and this, together with his obsessional, socially aversive behavior and limited repetitive speech, made him stand out as handicapped. He had lived in residential care since he was young.

On first meeting, he presented as a tall young man who surprisingly offered me his hand to shake. This and some other glimpses of meaningful contact were quickly interrupted by his agitated searching around my room and outside. Over time, he became more settled and eager to see me. He concentrated on repetitive play with a set of dolls identified with members of his family. His play, however, did not develop and I was left expectant, finding it often difficult to concentrate. Eventually, I felt that he was doing this to control me and avoid contact by keeping me at a safe distance. He became frightened when I broke through this familiar routine and was more active in my enquiry of him, which could lead to him trying to leave. He appeared frightened of being trapped. I think he found contact unbearable, even when I understood him, and that it was my curiosity about him that frightened him most.

Our gaze avoidance was mutual. He avoided eye contact and I found it difficult to look directly at him. He seemed frightened that I would learn more about him, but was also frightened of revealing his own curiosity about me. In fact, he monitored me closely and was acutely aware of changes.

The following illustrates this.

> Sam was sitting in a full waiting room and greeted me by repeating my name in a high-pitched voice. "Dddd . . . it's Dr. Simpson." Everybody looked at me and I felt uncomfortably exposed. He then looked away. In my room he was withdrawn, playing with the dolls and avoiding eye contact. I said, "I think you are keeping me safe, playing as you always do with the dolls like this, which is safe." He said, "Yes", staring at me for a moment then looking away.
>
> Later, he began fingering the dolls, putting the baby doll underneath his jumper. When I showed interest he looked away. I said, "I think the dolls are safe, much safer than finding out about me." He looked away, and I said, "I think you are interested in being here but are frightened to show it . . . I think you are frightened of really looking at me."
>
> He then seemed calmer, and, while holding a father doll, he smiled briefly and muttered the name of his school, but was not able to look at me directly. I said, "Now you can't look into my eyes for fear of what you might see and you are frightened of what I might say which makes it difficult to speak." He fumbled with the toys for several minutes and then I said, "I think it is very difficult just to be here with me", and he said, "Yeah", looking at me.

Sam considered curiosity, mine and his, to be a dangerous intrusion. He feared that my being curious about him would evoke in me unwanted feelings, including embarrassment, shame, guilt, and even disgust, and he feared that his curiosity in me might result in admonishment for displaying his potential to bring my unwanted feelings, which I suspect he believed would reveal him to be unwanted by me into the open. I think he withdrew following greeting me in response to my embarrassment at being seen collecting him as such an obviously disabled patient. I suspect that this scenario, which led to him protecting me from embarrassment, originated in his relationship with his mother and was being lived out in the maternal transference and my countertransference. Through preoccupation with my state, he sought a safe refuge in a close familiar routine, where curiosity, the corollary of a third position representing father, was felt to be a dangerous attribute needing exclusion.

Despite this, there were surprising moments of enlightenment. Later in this session, we were both surprised when my telephone rang. His safe routine was broken, which allowed me to bring his curiosity about this to his attention. Following my interpreting his fear of losing my attention this led to a freer contact where he showed how he had felt "put out" and sad. Now, I think he was allowing a third paternal position to emerge in the transference. Although a fleeting shift, it was indicative of his growing capacity to use his mind and be curious.

Patients with severe handicaps like Sam are rare in analytic work; however, problems with being curious, and being seen to be curious, are common in analytic patients, who are usually neither learning disabled nor show any clearly identifiable source of trauma in their history. In these cases, the balance of the problem seems to be much more with the mother's intrinsic difficulties in bearing a third observer position, and revealing herself to her child, while the child's difficulties with curiosity and gaze derives, as it does for the handicapped, from his desire to protect his parents from the pain he expects if this emerges.

I believe that Mr A illustrates this.

## *Mr A*

Mr A was a married man who sought analysis because of a chronic sense of dissatisfaction. His mother, a doctor, appears to have been depressed following the birth of his younger brother. She worked long hours, including nights, and their father largely cared for them.

Mr A's mother could not tolerate discomfort and pain, neither physical nor psychological, and he was unable to show her his discomfort from any cause, including his feelings of disappointment and despair when she left him to work at night. Although he sometimes felt like the apple of his mother's eye, she would recoil from his expressions of physical affection, or his curiosity about her. Much went unsaid in his family home. They moved frequently due to his father losing his job, although this was never discussed openly. When older, he learned that she nearly had an affair with a colleague but there were no rows, just an atmosphere of gloomy silence.

Mr A believed his mother could not tolerate his curiosity about her and he avoided showing this. However, he was preoccupied by his mother's state and his curiosity was intense, although inhibited and indirect.

Mr A's childhood relationship with his mother and family was lived out in his analysis with me. The home atmosphere was demonstrated when, following breaks, he would arrive late, with a sense of dread about returning to a bleak, empty house with a cold, unwelcoming analyst. He was often reluctant to speak, wanting to avoid contact or even to flee. At the same time, he was preoccupied with my state, sometimes feeling that I was unwell or self-preoccupied and viewed him as an intruder. He spoke softly, as if not to wake me, which reminded him of keeping quiet when his mother was sleeping following night-work.

The following illustrates this.

> When I collected Mr A in the waiting room, he was just out of my view but looking towards me. He came in, lay on the couch, making little noise, and said that he thought that my house seemed silent and empty but he could smell cooking. He was silent for some time and then said that it was difficult to speak. He said that he felt irritated and did not want to come, preferring to stay under the covers in bed. I felt frustrated and disappointed, and said that although he was saying he did not want to be here, I thought that he was actually preoccupied with me, but did not like me seeing this. He said that he preferred to be "five degrees off", out of the centre of my vision. I added that, then, he would not feel I would notice that he was looking at me because he believed that I did not want to be seen. I thought he was terrified of my response so preferred to be "five degrees off" to keep himself, and his observation of me, hidden.
>
> He agreed, and said that he was always "five degrees off".
>
> I said he feared that our eyes would meet because he believed that I couldn't bear knowing that I was being looked at directly by him, because

he would then know my feelings and would know, what he feared was true, that like his mother, I did not want to be with him.

This felt unbearable for him and he believed it was unbearable for me to know this and needed to be avoided.

Although pained, he was relieved. He said he felt that being with me was like being with his mother. He said that as a child he never felt that she was happy being his mother, or living with his father, and believed that she would eventually leave. When he returned from school he often thought that the house would be empty and that she would have left home and abandoned the family. At this point, I recalled that when he showed reluctance, like earlier in the session, it felt very unpleasant. I felt reluctant, it was difficult to concentrate, the atmosphere felt heavy, and sometimes I felt lulled towards sleep.

I believe that in the transference I was being drawn into an enclave based on a defensive collusion between Mr A and his mother. This provided a retreat from the painful reality of disappointment and rejection because he expected to be experienced by me, and originally by his mother, as an unwelcome intruder, particularly if he showed curiosity. My being curious felt like a relief that broke the spell, but then I was occupying the unwelcome third position as an observer who, like a father, threatened to disrupt the collusive relationship between mother and son. In his childhood, his father, whom he described as hard and punitive, occupied this unwelcome position and became a repository, through projection, of his hostile feelings, as well as his desires and curiosity. In essence, I think he located, in his father, a very restrictive and dangerous internal object, a superego figure, a "sinister eye" that he sometimes felt watched him and which he identified with when he took a distant observing position.

Mr A's superego figure reminds me of a restrictive superego figure that I have encountered in a child with Asperger's syndrome, which he represented in a drawing of a monster with many eyes. In Mr A, this figure was externalized, and because his natural curiosity was mixed with it, this restricted his life, limiting his capacity to make full use of his imagination and intellect. Through analysis, the strength of this figure and degree of his restriction reduced.

I think the origin of Mr A's difficulties lay in his relationship with his mother and his sensitivity to her emotional difficulties. I had the impression that she was a very narcissistic woman with not only difficulties in her relationship with her father, but with her psychic third position and its possible occupants. I learnt that his grandfather had left his grandmother following an affair when his mother was young and that this was a cause of considerable shame. He described his grandmother as a harsh woman who was very prudish about sexual matters. He described his mother maintaining a strong attachment to her father and that she felt this was viewed as an illicit affair in her mother's eyes. Thus, his mother maintained an oedipal illusion, as described by Britton (1998, p. 36) as a way of avoiding the pain of the oedipal situation, through a phantasy of replacing her mother in the parental couple. This pattern was repeated when my patient felt invited to join an exclusive couple with his mother from which his father was excluded. This pattern of mutual seduction, which there was a transference pressure to repeat in his relationship with me, was tantalizing and exciting, but ultimately disappointing. In this situation, Mr A felt invited not just to displace his father, but also to take the place in his mother's mind of her father. Thus, behind Mr A's oedipal illusion lay his mother's oedipal illusion. I suspect that behind the figure of Mr A's excluded father, occupying his psychic third position, lay the spectre of his maternal grandmother, who occupied his mother's psychic third position, who, excluded by his mother's relationship with her father, was felt to be a jealous and dangerous figure from whom this coupling, which felt like a shameful secret, must be kept obscure. This was a source of the superego figure that restricted my patient's curiosity, which had been transmitted from an earlier generation.

## *Discussion*

I have described two different patients, one of which has been diagnosed with autistic features. What they both have in common is an inhibition against being curious and using their minds, determined by their concern for the effects of their curiosity on their primary objects, that is, their mother's, and this is manifest in their behaviour in life and in the transference during psychoanalytic treatment. I think that for these patients, ultimately, this inhibition derives from their fear that their curiosity about their mothers will bring to light facts that their mothers will find too painful to bear and they equate being curious with inflicting pain. I would suggest that both patients feared that their curiosity about their mothers would reveal unacceptable facts, which they considered to be deficits, which would then risk exposing their mothers and, by reflection, themselves to guilt and shame.

In Sam's case, I suggest what could not be known was his mother's guilt and shame about his existence as her unwanted, handicapped son. In Mr A's case, the shameful and guilt inducing deficit, for his mother, was derived from her parents' relationship and the oedipal illusion she developed in response to this. I suggest this adversely affected her emotional availability to his father, and to him, which increased her guilt and shame and provoked the further enactment of her oedipal illusion in her collusive relationship with him.

These patients demonstrate how the development of curiosity can be inhibited through the interaction between a child's hypersensitive concern for his mother's feelings, an early depressive psychic atopia, and his mother's difficulty in tolerating her feelings about her child, where she finds it too painful to allow observation from a third position. I would suggest that, in these situations, oedipal illusions are used by the child and the mother as a defense against the emergence of the psychic third position and the painful feelings this threatens to reveal. This is clearly evident with Mr A, but I think was also operating with Sam. Oedipal illusion, according to Britton (1989, p. 94), is used to avoid the reality of the oedipal situation when the realization of a third position is believed to be catastrophic for the couple. Essentially, they avoid psychic reality through obscuring the link between the internal parental couple. I think that, for these patients, the presence of a third position threatened a catastrophe of guilt and shame for their mothers, and for themselves, at the hands of persecutory superego figures that could occupy an observing third position in their minds. Oedipal illusions were required by these patients, as children, to maintain their mother's illusions and, thus, her and their own psychic equilibrium, and this persisted into later life. The cost of this psychic retreat is the inhibition of curiosity and the loss of ego capacity to appreciate reality. I think this process is at the heart of autism, where it is at its most profound, and is the basis of difficulties in being curious and facing reality seen in a much wider group of people.

I think these ideas extend and develop some of Tustin's important ideas about autistic states, in particular her suggestion of a hypersensitive allergy to "not me" and her view of autism as a retreat from the problem of relatedness to others.

## Note

1. This case example was originally published in 2002 as "Learning disability as a refuge from knowledge" in *Psychoanalytic Psychotherapy, 16*(3): 215–226, © The Association of Psychoanalytic Psychotherapy in the NHS, reprinted by kind permission of Taylor & Francis Ltd, www.tandfonline.com on behalf of The Association for Psychoanalytic Psychotherapy in the NHS. It was also published in *Unexpected Gains: Psychotherapy with People with Learning Disabilities*, edited by David Simpson and Lynda Miller (published by Karnac in 2004), and is reprinted with kind permission of Karnac Books.

## References

Abraham, K. (1973). Restrictions and transformations of scopophilia in psychoneurotic; with remarks on analogous phenomena in folk psychology. In: *Selected Papers of Karl Abraham*, D. Bryan & A. Strachey (Trans.) (pp. 166–234). London: Hogarth.

Bion, W. R. (1962). *Learning from Experience*. London: Heinemann.

Bion, W. R. (1967). A theory of thinking. In: *Second Thoughts* (pp. 110–119). London: Heinemann.

Bion, W. R. (1977). *Seven Servants*. Northvale, NJ: Jason Aronson.

Britton, R. (1989). The missing link: parental sexuality in the Oedipus complex. In: J. Steiner (Ed.), *The Oedipus Complex Today* (pp. 83–101). London: Karnac.

Britton, R. (1998). *Belief and Imagination*. London: Routledge.

Fordham, M. (1976). *The Self and Autism*. London: Heinemann Medical.

Freud, S. (1909d). *Notes upon a Case of Obsessional Neurosis. S. E., 10*: 153–249. London: Hogarth.

Klein, M. (1975a). Early stages of Oedipus conflict. In: R. Money-Kyrle, B. Joseph, E. O'Shaughnessy, & H. Segal (Eds.), *The Writings of Melanie Klein, Vol. 1* (pp. 186–198). London: Hogarth.

Klein, M. (1975b). The importance of symbol-formation in the development of the ego. In: R. Money-Kyrle, B. Joseph, E. O'Shaughnessy, & H. Segal (Eds.), *The Writings of Melanie Klein, Vol. 1* (pp. 219–235). London: Hogarth.

Klein, M. (1975c). A contribution to the theory of intellectual inhibition. In: R. Money-Kyrle, B. Joseph, E. O'Shaughnessy, & H. Segal (Eds.), *The Writings of Melanie Klein, Vol. 1* (pp. 236–247). London: Hogarth.

Klein, M. (1975d). The Oedipus complex in the light of early anxieties. In: R. Money-Kyrle, B. Joseph, E. O'Shaughnessy, & H. Segal (Eds.), *The Writings of Melanie Klein, Vol. 1* (pp. 370–419). London: Hogarth.

Klein, S. (1980). Autistic phenomena in neurotic patients. *International Journal of Psychoanalysis, 61*: 395–402.

Simpson, D. (2004). Learning disability as a refuge from knowledge. In: D. Simpson & L. Miller (Eds.), *Unexpected Gains: Psychotherapy with People with Learning Disabilities* (pp. 69–97). London: Karnac.

Simpson, D. (2014). Some consequences of being the wrong child: effects of the intergenerational transmission of an ideal-ego. *British Journal of Psychotherapy, 30*: 181–196.

Stein, L. (1967). Introducing not-self. *Journal of Analytical Psychology, 12*(2): 97–113.

Tustin, F. (1981). *Autistic States in Children*. London: Routledge & Kegan Paul.

Tustin, F. (2009). The perpetuation of an error. *Attachment: New Directions in Psychotherapy and Relational Psychoanalysis, 3*: 89–106.

CHAPTER TEN

# Language used as an autistic object

*Lia Pistiner de Cortiñas*

> "It is sometimes said that animals do not talk because they lack the mental capacity", Wittgenstein once observed. "And this means: 'They do not think and this is why they do not talk'. But—they simply do not talk. Or to put it better: they do not use the language—if we accept the most primitive forms of language. Commanding, questioning, recounting, chatting, are as much a part of our natural history as walking, eating, drinking, playing"
>
> (Wittgenstein, 1922).

## *Introduction*

In this chapter, I want to put forward some ideas about disturbances of the symbolization process in autistic functioning, disturbances that can be observed and investigated in the development and use of verbal language. My interest in this topic has its roots in my clinical experience with autistic patients, whose development and use of verbal language was clearly disturbed. The difficulties of communication in autistic children stimulated my interest in trying to understand why these children do not learn to speak or why their use of verbal language is so impaired, since speaking seems so natural to human development. In autism, the arrest of mental growth and the zone of non-existence evolve towards a situation in which isolation, disconnection, the predominance of the proximal tactile senses prevail and autistic objects of sensation are used to avoid contact with any human relationship, thereby blocking the vital nutrients for emotional and cognitive development. Dwelling in this zone of non-existence—which can be conceived as a frozen desert—with its lack of interest in others has consequences that hinder the construction of both an internal space in which one may feel that one exists and is real, and an external space, where one recognizes the existence of other human beings. As a result, private communication of the self with the self and communication with others becomes difficult and sometimes impossible.

Psychoanalytic authors have described that the essence of autism is a severe disturbance in intersubjective personal engagement with others, and that what children with autism lack is not only a theory of the mind, but also a sense of an interest in other people. In a model of the mind that involves a two-person psychology, the mind contains not just the self with its particular qualities, orientations, and possible deficits, it also contains mental functions and relationships with others and with internal objects (Klein, 1959). The development of these mental functions—and verbal communication is one of them—requires a container–contained relationship (Bion, 1962) where normal projective identification—as a primitive form of communication that depends upon maternal reverie and alpha function—initiates a capacity to think and communicate. In autism, failures in this container–contained relationship—often following from an unfortunate combination of a depressed mother and an absent father—can be factors that interrupt this primitive communication. Instead of projective identification, one finds an adhesive identification that implies bi-dimensionality and lack of an internal space.

Bick (1968) suggested that a failure to introject a containing experience in early life might require an infant to find some other way (e.g., adhesive identifications) to hold him/herself together physically and psychically. She termed this a "second skin formation" and described it as a way in which dependence on the mother is replaced by pseudo-independence. She identified the inappropriate use of certain mental functions as one such mechanism. My conjecture is that, in autistic functioning, this second skin is what has been described as a shell in the service of encapsulation. In this chapter, I shall follow up on that conjecture by putting forward the hypothesis that verbalized language used as an autistic object—imitation and/or jargon—can also function as a second skin and defensive protection against the anxiety of the self's liquefying and spilling away.

Tustin (1990) showed that, in autism, the repetitive rituals and repetition of words have no symbolic meaning and are used instead to shut out meaning and life. In imitation, words are not used to convey meaning, but to maintain the illusion of no differentiation from the object. There is no "music" in imitative speech. On the contrary, to the listener, it sounds and feels quite mechanical.

In *Explorations in Autism*, Meltzer (1975) outlined a psychoanalytical theory of speech development inspired by the ideas of Langer, Wittgenstein, Cassirer, Chomsky, and others. His central thesis is that, in its genesis, language includes a song-and-dance level (the most primitive form of symbol formation) that uses projective identification to communicate emotional states of mind. He also differentiates meaningful from meaningless communications, the latter including imitation.

Many severely autistic children might have no language at all and, even worse, they might never have babbled playfully. Alternatively, as we will see with my patient Mariana, they learn to speak, but they do not use language to communicate emotions and mental states. The technical challenges that such patients present for the analyst are crucial: how can we reach a child with no language or with such an impaired use of language that it is essentially meaningless?

In *Dream Life*, Meltzer (1983) explores the concept of internal space conceiving it as the "Theater for generating meaning". The meaningful dialogue between internal objects and the self takes place in this internal space. In observing the young child's development of language, from the song-and-dance level of deep grammatical discourse of lalling and babbling to the lexical level of social communication, he then puts forward the hypothesis of a first step: a "Buccal theater for generating meaning" (Meltzer, 1986, p. 185). The latter is neither external nor internal. It is a kind of transitional space, with implications for both speech development and for character.

In Meltzer's view, lalling is the vocal aspect of a more general phase in cognitive development, in which the physical space of the mouth is used as the theater for phantasy and playing, a kind of midpoint between external play and internal dreaming. Lalling and babbling imply sounds that do not have a consensually agreed upon fixed meaning; rather, their meaning depends on their combination with other sounds. In normal development, the buccal theatre is followed by a dream theater for generating meaning. The latter implies a further step in the differentiation between internal and external and between what is "me" and what is "not me".

The evolution from the song and dance level of deep grammatical discourse to the lexical level of social communication, as described by Langer and Chomsky, is dependent on the move forward from a buccal theater to a dream theater for generating meaning. Although, at this later stage, the child develops an understanding of the conventional meaning of words, the tendency to employ the buccal theater continues throughout life in such activities as playing with words, in jokes, and all the devices of poetic diction. These later achievements fail to develop in autistic children.

One of the fundamental challenges for human beings, from early childhood and throughout development, is whether to avoid frustration or tolerate it, trying to change if possible—often in a container–contained relationship with an external object—the circumstances that are causing that frustration. For the infant, the solutions to the problem of frustration will heavily depend on the mother's reverie and alpha function (Bion, 1962). Introjection of the latter is a central factor needed to develop tools for containing mental pain and transforming it through thought and thinking.

Intolerance of frustration also implies intolerance of contact with reality, because frustration is inherent to life and living. Being aware of the world in which we live is an essential part of our contact with reality, and is essential for emotional growth. Thus, extreme denial of reality is a source of severe pathologies, such as psychosis and autism. If acting to change a frustrating reality—internal and/or external—is hindered because of one's mental state, hate is often directed against the mental functions on which awareness of reality depends. However, as we shall see, in autistic states the problem is not that of hatred and the failures in the development of verbal language are not the results of attacks. They are mostly linked with disconnection and isolation and the use of language as an autistic object.

## *The mental functions on which awareness of reality depends*

The development of symbolization depends upon having multiple vertices of observation (Bion, 1965) and these are essential for being in contact with reality—internal and external. Thinking and dreaming are forms of private communication of the self with the self. Speaking, that is, the ability to put thoughts into words, is a means of communicating with ourselves and with others.

Bion (1962) extended Freud's notion of dreaming, putting forward the idea that raw "facts" (beta elements) and reality do not have a meaning unless and until they are "dreamed"; that is, transformed by alpha function, into "thoughts", integrated into our view of ourselves and of the world. He argued that truth, "dreaming", and "meaning" provide the nourishment of the human mind. "Dream-thoughts" and models have the important functions of notation and registration of emotional experiences and are significant for the development of the function of attention. Attention, which, of course, depends upon contact with reality, must be available for the registration of emotional experiences and to enable sense impressions to be used for dreaming and making models. That is, attention must be available for meeting with new emotional experiences and also for discerning psychic reality.

The differentiation between psychotic, neurotic, or autistic functioning depends in part on whether or not it is possible to develop a contact barrier (Bion, 1962) between conscious and unconscious, so that there will be no confusion between thoughts, phantasies, and the "thing-in-itself". In the infant and the psychotic, this barrier has not yet been developed or else fails, and is replaced by a beta screen (Bion, 1962). When this happens, everything is conscious, but only as a rudimentary consciousness, which perceives, but is not aware of what it perceives.

In psychotic functioning there is a hypertrophy of projective identification with an excess of beta elements, "things in themselves", (Bion, 1962) that can only be used for evacuation and which do not allow for differentiation between the thing and the "no-thing". Evacuative projective identification without a suitable object that can contain and transform these identifications results in confusion between what is internal and what is external. An image, an idea, a word becomes a "no-thing" that can be used only for evacuation.

Thus, emotional impressions experienced as "things" (beta elements) cannot be assimilated.

In contrast, in autistic functioning, we find a different kind of problem: projective identification—as a primitive communication—stops and patients live in a world where emotions seem to have disappeared and are replaced by sensorial elements. These are mostly tactile, while the distal senses, sight and hearing, have been obliterated. Very often, autistic children seem to be deaf. What we see in this kind of functioning are self-generated sensations that are used for encapsulation and adhesive identifications that do not allow for authentic learning. What might seem to be "learning" is actually copying and imitation, a mimetic function that is a kind of second skin (Bick, 1968) and cannot be used to think or to speak with the intention of conveying a meaning. Thus, autistic children can endlessly repeat words as an experience of making physical sounds: "words" that are sounds with no meaning.

Another feature of autistic functioning, or the autistic part of the personality, is that subjectivity and self-awareness are missing. Echolalia and mimetic use of words replace true language used to communicate feelings and thoughts. Words have no meaning and the mimetic way they are used implies the failure of subjectivization and the creation of a potential space for thinking, dreaming, and playing. The creation of this potential space, thus, must become one of the aims of psychoanalytical treatment. Such a space is necessary if meaning is to be created and the patient will develop self-awareness and feel continuity-in-being instead of living in a world of "non existence".

Given the autistic patient's concrete use of words and his extreme isolation, is there some way to reach these patients or this part of their mind? Is psychoanalytical treatment of these patients possible? As we know, Tustin thought that some autistic children and also adults (not all) could be approached through psychoanalysis. I want to stress this point, because, in psychoanalysis, especially with adults, we usually depend on verbal language to formulate our interpretations and our constructions. With children, we have an additional resource: we can play, that is, we use a kind of action in the form of playing as a means of communication. This might also be possible with adults, although this is a more controversial matter.

### *Some further characteristics of autistic children and adults*

Autistic patients have been described as isolated and disconnected. Their means of communication are poor or non-existent. They avoid eye contact and avoid communicating through the usual channels of language, playing, drawing, etc. Some autistic children are echolalic, so their verbal productions seem very limited and bizarre. Sometimes, what may superficially appear to be "playing" is a repetitive activity that is so restricted it is difficult to call it play.

Autistic children have often been described as lacking empathy and imagination. As they lack self-awareness, it seems that they also lack an inner life, and it is difficult to think that they have phantasies. So, with these patients, an analytic treatment cannot rely upon interpretations or constructions based upon assumptions of a pre-existing, unconscious, symbolic meaning. A different approach is needed. The significant and very early arrest of their emotional and cognitive development implies that the treatment has to focus first on the development of mental functions that will allow the creation of a potential space and capacity for symbolization and upon learning to use verbal language for communication, instead of using it to generate physical sensations.

### *The representation of reality*

Freud's discovery of the unconscious also implied an epistemological vertex: the psychoanalytical perspective that ultimate reality is unknowable. The most we can do is to formulate analogical hypotheses that can help us deal with the world. From this perspective, cognitive and emotional development consists in the construction of more and more analogies that work adequately. Playing and language are privileged means of creating analogies or metaphors and are also useful for communication. A child's development and mental growth implies the development of an internal space where he may introject and assimilate the constructions of his family and culture. This process develops in the course of the different interactions that take place during caring activities between the infant and his first objects. The state of mind of these objects and of the infant during these interactions will prove essential for the construction of analogies. As a result of a combination of unfortunate circumstances, autistic children have remained fixated to sensations produced by raw stimulation, which probably stem from bodily processes and inborn and not yet transformed tropisms (Bion, 1992). We will see in the clinical material how Mariana "learned" to speak, but, for her, language was more an imitation than a means to communicate.

The behavior of autistic children becomes automatic and mechanical. Tustin (1986) realized that we can find similar problems in an isolated part of the minds of patients with normal or neurotic functioning, so she spoke of both autistic and non-autistic parts of the personality.[1] In my experience, perhaps because we now live in what might be called an "autistic culture", it is more frequent to see this autistic part of the personality in our current patients. Sociologists, when analyzing our western culture, speak of shopping malls, airports, and other public buildings as "no places". Also, changes in the structure of the family are significant. We have moved from a world of an extended family with grandparents, aunts, uncles, etc., to one made up of a small family with parents and children or, when divorced, just one parent.

### *The use of autistic sensation objects and its disastrous consequences*

When the normally developing infant finds his thumb and sucks it, this implied exploration of his own body indicates the beginning of self-awareness. These explorations can be associated with phantasies that enable the child to learn to wait, until satisfaction from the real breast arrives. To be able to wait favors the creation of a potential space where emotional links of the self with the self develop. This is not what happens with autistic children, in which sucking has been replaced by clinging to autistic objects that have the characteristic of being hard. The constant resort to autistic sensation objects—predominantly tactile—implies that these children will remain in a mental state of disconnection, in which they do not receive the nourishment they require to become emotionally attached to other human beings and that they will not develop the discipline required to wait, to think, and to speak with meaning.

By discipline, I also mean contact with reality, which is first acquired in breast-feeding via its rhythms. When the latter goes well, the infant learns from experience that the breast will arrive and slowly develops a sense of time. These developmental achievements depend upon awareness and acceptance of the existence of a now empty space where the breast was and is no more. They also imply differentiation, the creation of a space for self-awareness and the capacity to wait, all of which are necessary for the development of the use of language for communication.

Infants that develop autistic tendencies do not tend to explore their own bodies, or the vocalization of sounds they produce. Instead, they seem to be at the mercy of very primitive, innate patterns, which become stereotyped and do not change with experience. They suck their tongues, bite the inside of their cheeks and vocalize to stimulate sensations rather than communicate meanings. These actions are also thought to become enmeshed in atavistic elements and archaic phantasies (Tustin, 1986). They seem to feel threatened by predatory creatures or mouths, fear that they could be crushed like insects, or that they are struggling with other creatures in a desperate effort to survive. It is as if they felt enmeshed in a world of very primitive rivalry in which hard objects seem to function as extensions of nails and teeth.

The constant use of autistic objects, including using sounds as autistic objects, also ensures that the child has little opportunity to learn to tolerate frustration and communicate using sounds and, later on words, the latter implying and requiring tolerance of frustration. To speak in order to communicate (which implies the use of tongue and mouth for making words instead of sucking) requires accepting weaning and differentiation between mouth, tongue, and breast. Autistic children are unable to exercise other ways of dealing with frustration when the mother is absent or to play with sounds when she is present. When frustration does appear, these children are terrorized by tantrums and, in their terrors, they are afraid of a total destruction. A vicious circle is produced, because, to avoid these terrors, they cling even more to autistic objects, so they never have the opportunity to learn to deal with situations of frustration in a more adequate way, to develop thoughts and the capacity to think when the object is absent (Bion, 1962).

Winnicott (1958) showed the significance of transitional objects for the development of creativity and also as a kind of bridge or transition towards adaptation to reality. There is a difference between the transitional objects and playing with sounds and the use, including the imitative use of autistic objects of sensation. In normal development, the first transitional objects are a transition towards the development of contact with reality. In contrast, the autistic objects of sensation form a barrier that obstructs this process, because they are used for isolation and prevent the apprehension of realities that can be shared with other human beings and, later on, with the general culture. The persistence of tactile sensations and imitation blocks the projective–introjective process, which is the deep and primary root of learning (Bion, 1962). Because of the disconnection of these children, not only can nothing come in, but nothing can come out. This is a very significant issue, because it destroys the possibility of realistic projective identification (Bion, 1965) in a container–contained relationship of mutual benefit, which, in the relationship of mother–infant, is the source of the development of the function of thinking. Playing with sounds in an interaction with the mother and other human beings is essential for the development of a language that has also an emotional meaning.

The frustration produced by situations of disillusionment that have turned unbearable can lead to clinging to autistic objects instead of creating adequate situations of illusion (Winnicott, 1971). The use of autistic sensation objects can be associated with disturbances in the development of spontaneity and creativity. Pacifiers and blankets used in excess and for too long a time might be transformed into autistic objects and, when that happens, children do not learn to wait. This has catastrophic consequences, because, instead of a development leading towards dreams, phantasies, thoughts, and communication through speaking, the infant starts to manipulate autistic sensation objects (including sounds), which, being tangible and always present, allows the child to function in a very concrete manner. Such functioning is far from being qualified as mental. The autistic sensation objects to which the child has turned as a way of dealing with frustrations also hinder the development of memories, imagination, and thinking, which, in a process of development towards mental growth, make more tolerable the frustrations that are inevitable.

## *Verbal language and autistic functioning*

Echolalia is a manipulation of words and sounds as if they were tangible things. It is a way of transforming them into "me", almost as if they were a part of one's own body (Tustin, 1990). This use of sound by autistic children is similar to the use of the analyst's hand as a part of themselves. The echolalic noise is an autistic object, produced because the sensations it stimulates help to sustain the "illusion" of no separation, of no differentiation. The repetitions of echolalia sometimes are reinforced by adults who, without being aware of the problem, repeat what the child says as a way of trying to engage his attention. This leads to a vicious circle, of which, we, as analysts, must be aware. If we fall into this trap, we leave these children trapped in their pathology and without possibilities of developing authentic human relations, characterized by cooperation and dialogue.

I now present a clinical vignette to illustrate the use of language as an autistic object.

## *Mariana*

Mariana was an eight-year-old child with autistic functioning who did not speak until age three. When I first met her, she had already been seeing a psychiatrist, an educational psychologist, and a psychologist. These treatments helped her learn to speak, but her speech was—as I realized later in her analysis—more an imitation than a communication. Rather than using language to communicate ideas or feelings, her vocalization was more using her tongue and voice to create stimulating sensations and her imitative vocalizations contributed to an illusion of non-separation from the objects she mimicked. For example, she would take a toy phone, sit on the floor and speak, imitating her mother's voice. In this activity, I felt that she was not playing "as if" she was her mother, but creating a concrete feeling that she *was* her mother.

When Mariana started treatment at two times per week, she unaccountably would say, "I'm not lying." I did not have the impression that she was lying and only after a long time did I realize that, for her, imitation was "lying". It seemed that a non-autistic part of her personality knew when she was being authentic in her communication or when she was imitating, that is, being disconnected and just making sounds, *being* the mother. This imitation was not a projective identification, but only mimicry used to maintain the illusion of "non-separation", non-differentiation. As the treatment went on and I began to realize when she was using language as imitation rather than to convey meaning, we began to talk about and distinguish when she was being authentic and when she was just making sounds as if she was communicating. This, in a way, was a relief for her and she began to recognize and accept this difference with the declaration, "This is me."

Mariana is the first daughter of a still young couple and has a brother five years her junior. Both parents have a very high intellectual standard: the mother is a writer and the father is a lawyer. Mariana's mother seems always to be overwhelmed with anxiety, which she cannot contain. A symptom of this anxiety is that it is very difficult to end the interviews that I have from time to time with the parents, so it seems that mother also has a problem with tolerating separations. Mariana's father seems calmer, sometimes a little disconnected, but tries to contain his wife. From what they told me and I could observe in my interviews with them, I thought that this kind of relationship existed between the parents when Mariana was born and mother seemed overwhelmed by the baby. The mother has been in analysis for many years and, although she seems to be becoming less anxious, she still easily feels overwhelmed at times.

Mariana's mother was born prematurely, spent some time in intensive care separated from her own mother, and then later in childhood, when her mother became ill, was sent far away to be raised by two spinster aunts. I describe these circumstances of the mother because I think it adds a transgenerational component to the development of Mariana's autism.

When she began her treatment with me, Mariana's body was precociously developing and this frightened her parents, who were told by doctors that menarche was near. At night, she had frequent enuresis and would respond to her bed-wetting by awakening everyone in the house. Her parents felt overwhelmed and seemed tyrannized and helpless in the face of her behavior, unable to set limits or deal with her distress. In school, she was being passed from one grade to the next despite not having learned to read or write. For many years, her parents continued to ignore this fact. (One mark of success of the parental intervention in this treatment has been that, in the last year, they have transferred her to a new school in which she can repeat the work of the grades she had never mastered and so allow herself the opportunity for true development.) Prior to the analysis and parental intervention, mother's response to Mariana's learning difficulties was to spend all weekend "doing homework" and struggling with her in a futile effort to help her learn. This "doing homework together" only seemed to reinforce the illusion of "no separation".

Initially, I had several interviews with the parents and tried to convey the importance of setting limits in relation to the bed-wetting, homework struggles, and certain of Mariana's eating habits. I felt this was important, because accepting limits encouraged frustration tolerance, recognizing the "otherness" of others and maintaining contact with reality. I also underscored the importance of the active presence of the father, who had withdrawn into his work and came home very late at night. This initial parental work, which I believe can be especially important in working with autistic children, helped the parents begin to understand their own anxieties, allowed them to have some insight into their daughter's problems and to introduce changes in their parenting, becoming firmer and setting limits. In turn, those changes made it possible for Mariana to develop greater contact with reality.

With Mariana, I spoke about the contrast between her body, almost grown up, and her mental functioning, which was not only that of a child, but beset by difficulties in thinking and learning. Exploring how she felt about the changes in her body and her difficulties thinking and learning helped her to become aware of her emotional problems. These discussions were also a step forward in naming and exploring her feelings.

In her second year of analysis, the parents accepted my suggestion to increase the number of sessions to three times per week and stop the speech therapy and other treatments. Discussion of these changes with Mariana helped strengthen her non-autistic part and understand the distinctions between objects who could help and those who could not. Through all the years of these other treatments she seemed to have gained little insight and learned nothing at school. She is currently fourteen years old and ending primary school, where she feels better, although it remains very difficult for her to read, write, and, most of all, learn mathematics, because with mathematics she cannot use imitation. She has to think and establish relations between numbers and operations. She still does not have friends but now worries about that, so that one of her motivations to get better is that she wants to have friends and a boyfriend.

In the initial phases of treatment, when Mariana demonstrated a severe restriction in her capacity to read, write, or express and communicate in an authentic way and not through imitation, she began to develop an esthetic skill in her drawings and an interest in art. This contrasted with her difficulties with abstractions, writing, knowing the time, understanding dates, the calendar, etc. The striking difference between her skill in drawing and her difficulties in reading, writing, and speaking is noteworthy. Mariana seemed to have been able to develop a capacity for geometric–esthetic symbolization, but speaking and writing required a more abstract kind of symbolization, which implied the use of tongue and mouth for "disciplined" communicative, rather than sensorial, purposes.

Her drawings were a starting point in the development of a symbolization process. For example, she would draw two hearts, as if they were one, and inside she wrote both our names. I told her that the meaning of this drawing was that we were one heart, with no separation. Then, when we were discussing imitation and as she was beginning to become aware of it, she started making drawings of her face and her mouth and tongue. As her analysis evolved still further, an important indication of the beginning creation of a potential space and dawning awareness of her problems was a drawing she made of her "little brain" marked by black holes that she said represented her difficulties in thinking. The psychic space for differentiation and thinking was occupied by holes, which represented what she did not understand and her attempts to hide it. Later on, when she developed verbal representations of her mental functioning, she referred to her autistic mental states as like being in a dark box, while her more connected mental states were like being in a colored box. These metaphors reflected her condition: still in a box, that is, more aware of herself, but still isolated. Drawing and naming her mental states was a step in her development and use of words for communicating instead of using them as concrete sensations for imitation.

Currently, when Mariana speaks, she does not express emotions, but speaks with a peculiar quality of stiffness. She never cries and her smile is often stereotyped. She still sucks her tongue and her lips, a symptom that Tustin (1981a) described as stimulating sensations to keep up an "illusion" of having mother always present and available. She sincerely says she wants me to help her, but accepting this help implies going through emotional experiences of differentiation, "me"–"not me", which she still cannot tolerate. Often, when I can reach her with some interpretation which she understands, she stares at me in a way that is a kind of control and a way of not seeing me, annulling her understanding. The father told me that she also stared at him like this, as if erasing him, and that there were times when she did not speak to him as a way of ignoring him. Lately, she speaks about a phantasy of a magic cure, which she expresses by saying that she would like to be my daughter, because then she would not have the problems she has.

Given all of the denial and disregarding of her difficulties, in both Mariana and her parents, I started trying to show her what she really did not know. Her ignorance was disguised and hidden by a kind of over-adaptation, an appearance of adaptation based on her skill for imitation. I also helped her to become aware of her moments of disconnection through actively drawing her attention to them, showing her not only that she did not see me, but also asking her to look at me. For example, as soon as I opened the door, she used to run upstairs to the consulting room without saying hello. I interpreted this to her as a means of denying the fact that she had arrived for her session and that we were meeting again after having been separated. I took her hand so she would realize my presence and little by little she became more aware of my absence. Along with these actions, I interpreted the many ways in which she tried omnipotently to believe that I was an extension of a part of her.

A month before her fifteenth birthday, Mariana decided to stop wetting her bed and began to take care of herself during menstruation. She viewed these steps as a model of what she could achieve if she decided to change. Her parents also bought a new mattress and Mariana spoke of how the old one had an awful smell. This implied differentiation (old mattress/new mattress; smell/no smell) and a step forward in the capacity of becoming aware and of speaking as a way of communication and not an imitation, as enuresis had also been a means of no-separation, no-differentiation, and denial of the reality of her growing older.

Often, when Mariana said something that she seemed not to understand, I asked her what she meant. When she could not tell me,

I showed her how she was using words mindlessly and to imitate speech and this brought her relief, because, as she said, she started to feel that she did not have to pretend that she knew how to speak, or that she understood, and could start to tell the truth instead of lying. I told her that she was not lying, she was "pretending" to understand so nobody would be aware of her difficulties. I described to her this method of defense, and explained that this was why she could not learn and that she was trapped in a vicious circle. Her parents then helped by making her take singing lessons. This required her to use her voice to express emotions through song, something she did not do in a mechanical way but often with pleasure.

Our work has been a constant struggle. The non-autistic part of Mariana's personality wants to learn, the autistic part clings to ritualization and imitation. The autistic use of language is "favored" because it is very painful for her self-esteem to accept that imitating without understanding left "holes" in her mind and that in using her voice, her tongue, and lips to communicate, instead of using them to maintain the illusion of non separation, she is accepting being differentiated from her objects. On the other hand, she also understands that truth is a relief and an opportunity for authentic growth, which she feels that she needs as she is growing up and becoming a teenager and also is very much interested in boys and romance.

## *Some final comments*

The autistic use of language—copying and imitation—implies not speaking and not using words to think and communicate, but, rather, to produce sensations with the tongue and mouth, sensations that sustain the illusion of non-differentiation, no separation. This kind of speech provides sensations similar to those of sucking the tongue or biting the inside of the cheeks. Mariana could not accept the relief provided by symbolization. The children that evolve and go through their oedipal conflict arrive at a latency stage that enables them to learn to read and write. Autistic children seem to skip weaning—they maintain the illusion that mouth, tongue and breast are one—and they skip all the steps of growing up that imply weaning as a differentiation process. In my clinical experience, I could see that Mariana and the other autistic children that I have treated, instead of developing towards a latency stage, arrive at, or stay in, a mental state of non-existence. They seem, instead, to live in a kind of "nowhere land", as described in the song by the Beatles.

## *Note*

1. This division is analogous to that described by Bion (1957), who described a psychotic and non-psychotic part of the personality.

## *References*

Bick, E. (1968). The experience of the skin in early object relations. *International Journal of Psychoanalysis, 49*: 484–486.

Bion, W. R. (1957). Differentiation of the psychotic from the non psychotic personalities. In: *Second Thoughts* (pp. 43–64). London: Heinemann.

Bion, W. R. (1962). *Learning From Experience*. London: Heinemann.

Bion, W. R. (1965). *Transformations*. London: Heinemann.

Bion, W. R. (1992). *Cogitations*. London: Karnac.

Klein, M. (1959). Our adult world and its roots in infancy. In: *Envy and Gratitude, and Other Works 1946–1963*. London: Hogarth [reprinted in *The Writings of Melanie Klein*, London: Karnac, 1995].

Meltzer, D. (1975). *Explorations in Autism*. Strathtay, Perthshire: Clunie Press.

Meltzer, D. (1983). *Dream Life*. Strathtay, Perthshire: Clunie Press.

Meltzer, D. (1986). *Studies in Extended Metapsychology*. Strathtay, Perthshire: Clunie Press.

Tustin, F. (1981a). Autistic *States in Children*. London: Routledge & Kegan Paul.

Tustin, F. (1981b). Psychological birth and psychological catastrophe. In: J. Grotstein (Ed.), *Do I Dare Disturb The Universe: A Memorial to Wilfred R. Bion* (pp. 182–196). Beverly Hills: Caesura Press.

Tustin, F. (1986). *Autistic Barriers in Neurotic Patients*. London: Karnac.

Tustin, F. (1990). *The Protective Shell in Children and Adults*. London: Karnac.

Winnicott, D. W. (1958). Through paediatrics to psychoanalysis. In: *Collected Papers*. London: Karnac.

Winnicott, D. W. (1971). *Playing and Reality*. London: Tavistock.

Wittgenstein, L. (1922). *Tratactus–Logico Philosophicus*. Mineola, NY: Dover Publications.

CHAPTER ELEVEN

# The struggle to make the autistic child human

*Vincenzo Bonaminio*

## *Introduction: some remarks on the multi-factorial etiopathogenesis of autism*

Thirty years after Mahler and Tustin's pioneering work on a psychoanalytic approach to the treatment of autism, no one can maintain that this disorder is exclusively psychological in origin. The authors never openly made claims about the psychogenic origin of autism, although one may find vague references to this concept in their work; it is more likely they chose not to focus on this complex issue. This might also be explained by the fact that neuro-imaging, which has permitted new discoveries about the malfunctioning of the brain in newborns who later suffer from autistic spectrum diseases, had a long way to come. Mahler, Tustin, and their followers were mainly interested in understanding the autistic child's psychic functioning.

The impressive progress of contemporary neurobiological science, together with the possibilities offered by brain imaging, compel us to consider autism a fundamentally a multi-factorial neurobiological disorder.

However, the contemporary decline of the psychoanalytic approach and the attacks on it, have led to a focus on cognitive–behavioral therapy (CBT) as the treatment of choice, as though the dominating biological component of this illness must exclude any psychological implication whatsoever.

The aim of this chapter is to rediscover the many insights provided by a psychoanalytic approach, and to make the techniques of conditioned learning less robotic. In fact, from a psychoanalytic perspective, these techniques might well tend to reinforce the autistic defenses of the child.

## *The necessary human touch*

At the beginning of his revolutionary paper, "Fear of breakdown" (1974), Winnicott writes,

> It is my purpose here to state as simply as possible this which is new for me and which perhaps is new for others who work in psychotherapy. *Naturally if what I say has truth in it, this will already have been dealt with by the world's poets.* (p. 103, my italics)

Winnicott was well aware that when one attempts to understand the deepest layers of the mind, areas which consist of unconscious desires and phantasies, one encounters vulnerability, not only in the patient but also in the psychoanalyst who is courageous enough to venture here, being aware that in doing so he must cause the minimum harm possible.

Many of the authors who have approached primitive states of mind (Alvarez, 2012; Balint, 1969; Bion, 1962, 1967; Ferro, 2010; Grotstein, 2010; Levine, 2013; Ogden, 1989; Reiner, 2009, 2013; Tustin, 1981a,b,c, 1994; Winnicott, 1945, 1964, 1967; and others) have made frequent reference to poets. Contemporary psychoanalytic practitioners, like poets, are faced with the issue of the unrepresented, and how to represent it in a way that can be shared between two people, as Levine has suggested (2013).

Using metaphor, poets attempt to grasp the essence of the ineffable, and capture something of the experience and meaning of the germination of psychic life, which, being nascent, can be both joyful and painful. Sensitive to this idea, Winnicott took into consideration varying stages of germination, which relate to Tustin's (1981a) idea of the "infant premature state of *agony of consciousness* . . ." where the body is left alive but "dis-spirited", or "disembodied", to use Reiner's (2009) poetic term. These are useful terms to consider when making a diagnostic evaluation of pathology in the autistic spectrum.

Winnicott goes on to say,

> This very primitive kind of anxiety can only happen in states of extreme dependence and trust, that is, before there has been established a clear distinction between the I-AM central *me* and the repudiated world that is separate or external. When the disorder develops very early, there may indeed be almost nothing there to be defended, except just something of a self that carried the body's memory of anxiety that is completely beyond the infant's capacity to cope with. The mental mechanisms for coping have not yet become established. In many cases, however, this condition starts late, as when the child . . . is 12 or 13 months old. In such cases, it is to be presumed that there is a very great deal that is being defended in the fortress. (1967, pp. 220–221)

Winnicott conceived autism as an extreme defense against "primary depression" and "primitive agonies", a highly sophisticated organization characterized by "invulnerability": "The child carries around the (lost) memory of unthinkable anxiety, and the illness is a complex mental structure ensuring against the recurrence of the conditions of the unthinkable anxiety" (1967, pp. 221–222).

Almost saddened by what he was highlighting, Winnicott also noted that

> it seems necessary to add to this the concept of the mother's unconscious (repressed) hate of the child. *Parents naturally love and hate their babies in varying degrees.* This does not do damage. At all ages, and in earlier infancy especially, the effect of the repressed death wish towards the baby is harmful, and it is beyond the baby's capacity to deal with this . . . that is, to counteract the parents' unconscious wish (covered by reaction formations) that the child should be dead. (1967, pp. 221–222, my italics)

It is this controversial assertion, one that I have reluctantly concluded on the basis of my clinical experience sometimes appears to be relevant, that I wish to consider further.

I do think that Winnicott is being deliberately provocative when he asserts that the desire of the autistic child's mother is that "the child should be dead", but I think this assertion should be considered in terms of the parent's unconscious influence on the psychic life of the newborn and *vice versa*. Today, it is less shocking to us to consider that, to varying degrees and over varying periods of time, many parents might, consciously and unconsciously, wish that their child were dead, or otherwise, had never been born, etc., and these desires are no longer thought of as a specific agent in the etiology of autism. Questions as to whether such a desire can be considered a "normal" parental fantasy and whether it always has a pathological influence on the child's psyche are important but beyond the scope of this chapter. As I have noted in previous papers on autism (Bonaminio, 2005, 2010), what is important for me is that no one, other than Winnicott, has been courageous enough to make such an assertion. Contemporary studies on autism clarify—and I would agree with them on the basis of my clinical practice—that it is not a single disease. We speak of autistic *spectrum* diseases and consider it a multi-factorial disturbance where neurobiological, environmental, constitutional, and, perhaps, neuroendocrine factors are intertwined.

The real problem is that contemporary leadership of the cognitive–behavioral approach has completely dismissed and tried to discredit the psychoanalytic results of psychotherapy with autistic children. The psychoanalytic approach has never denied that a variety of causes stand at the basis of autism, but it is very evident that, among other factors, if one is able to see it, the unconscious attitude of the parents and the early caring environment might sometimes play a part in the reaction to, if not the genesis of, autism.

In regard to this particular constellation, I find particularly illuminating a further observation of Winnicott's, which anticipates some of his clinical thoughts:

> at the earlier stages that relate to the subject of autism, the baby can only show the distortion that results from his having been cared for by someone whose positive actions are all reaction formations; direct or spontaneous, free and adaptive movement would reveal the repressed/dissociated death wish. (1967, p. 222)

In other words, when these dynamics are set in motion, the mother cannot ever relate to the child in a spontaneous way, because she has to protect him from her desire that "the baby should be dead". Correspondingly, when this is the case, the child might be faced with an inauthentic mother, one who is "reactive" and "mechanical".[1]

In "The a-symbolic nature of autistic states" Tustin (1981b) insisted on the difficulty or impossibility of representation for the autistic child. During one of her lectures, when she suggested there was "no hope" for these patients, I asked if she was being excessively pessimistic. She replied that she had considered the issue extensively, and also consulted her husband, Arnold, whom she called the "logic mind" in their relationship, but had decided on this view because it seemed to highlight what lay behind the auto-sensual world of the autistic child, the fact that *there is nothing*.

> I have also used it essentially for therapeutic technique reasons, to stop the wild interpretations that analysts build on their counter-transference, mistakenly confusing them with something that belongs to the child and that maybe—they think—the child has projected into them, or that evokes something moving inside him. Shaking a stick for hours in front of his face has no meaning for the autistic child, no symbolic meaning, if not to keep him together, to protect him from dispersion; to make him hard and protected from internal and external invasion. It is a protective activity of the body-self; only a self-sensory activity. (1981c)

This is a hard concept to grasp, somewhat like when Winnicott almost unwillingly stated that the child who will become autistic is the target of the mother's unconscious hate. He believed that this unconscious hate is transgenerational, passes through her, and is "deposited" in the unconsciously hated child. A repressed, removed hatred, dissociated from the continuity of the child's being, becomes an object alien to the ego, which the child does not know how to manage. Therefore, this maternal hate, which is unrepresentable, unknown to the child, and, thus, impossible to deal with, comes about as a consequence of those anti-life defensive maneuvers between mother and child, and prevents the creation of a space where symbolic thinking can occur.

Whatever its origins, this is a flat space, where the "psyche is extended; knows nothing about it", wrote Freud (1941f, p. 299). It is the first psychic space, or, better, *corporeal* space, which must host the mother's hate.

We might wonder whether this bi-dimensional flat space is such because the mother's hate, or "motherly hate object", is elusive and, thus, not representable, or whether it is the opposite, that is, the flat space induces the non-representability of the mother's hate.[2] (Of necessity, I am compelled to use metaphors, as approximate as they may be, in order to describe a primitive state of experience, where "experience" is already a too sophisticated term.)

Let us hypothesize, as a purely theoretical "normative fiction" (Emden, 2014), that from this bi-dimensionality the child cannot inflate an object that lies inert, oppressing his mind in *statu nascendi*; that from this primitive primary space, the first auto-sensual, development-distorting sensations are born. In her revision of the theory of autism, Tustin (1994) is clear and explicit in considering pathological the mother–child fusion that is evident *ab initio* and distorts normal development. Through this, she abandoned her own hypothesis that considered the existence of normal autism a perpetuation of an error. Winnicott's statement, even if difficult to accept, may at times find significant support in clinical evidence, especially in cases where the mother or the parental couple is treated in parallel with the autistic child. Tustin's expression of the a-symbolic nature of autism is perhaps, at first glance, too trenchant. However, I believe it is a central concept because it is fundamental to understanding several of the concepts Tustin derives from it, such as the auto-sensual, self-centered experience of the autistic child. It is the theme of the ungraspable nature of autistic shapes.

The notion that the a-symbolic nature of autistic states is at the core of the child's cognitive, linguistic, and metaphorical inabilities is a challenge to the analyst. It implies that, in order to pull the autistic child away from his a-symbolic world towards proto-symbolic communication, he must employ the rudiments of what makes him human: symbolic communication. However, until the notion is crystallized within him that this child's mother wished he were dead, and until this is worked through in the transference with a new object, not even minimal change can be achieved, by which I mean a hint of proto-verbal, proto-symbolic communication.

On this issue, Tustin writes,

> The psychotic [autistic] child is drowned in an uncontrollable sea of waves of sensations which have not been held by adequate symbolization. Thus, it is important to be aware of the a-symbolic nature of such a child's functioning, so that our behavior and our interpretations will be appropriate to his state of being and so that we shall be alert to facilitate the stages in the development of symbolizing capacities

> and to correct those situations which handicap this development. To do this we need to be in touch with the peculiar nature of his states of awareness, which are basically auto-sensual. (1981b, p. 134)

## *From conceptual hypotheses to clinical evidence: the transgenerational factor*

While underlining Winnicott's pioneering hypothesis on autism, I do not intend to fully accept it. I wish to underline his courage in touching upon a very delicate theme, which, in clinical practice, and in the psychotherapy of autism, we frequently face. The unelaborated phantasies of preceding generations are transmitted from one generation to the next and, in the end, deposited in what will become the autistic child. In my view, this does not contradict a neurobiological view of the origins of autism, but adds a further perspective, which helps us understand the inner world of the autistic child.

Following this hypothesis, particularly the existence in the case I shall describe of the mother's phantasy that the child should have been dead, I will describe my dramatic experience with Ugo in his first year of therapy, a child who seemed to be in a shell, locked up in autistic armor, who developed within the five-year treatment some ability to communicate symbolically.

## *A fragment of the treatment of an autistic child, supervised by Ms Tustin*

During the time of Ugo's treatment, I took notes on Frances Tustin's supervision of the case, in the years she attended our department at the University of Rome as a Visiting Professor. Ugo was one of the many children I had the privilege to follow under Tustin's supervision,[3] and he was one of many cases who were considered by her more severely autistic than she was used to observing. In our research unit, we were working on a project which involved the observation of what would be named the autistic mother–child relationship. We were struck by the fact that these mothers were trapped in a sort of autistic loop, because of the collapse and depression induced by the fact of having an autistic child, while mothers with healthier children appeared more resilient, or at least, in Winnicott's term, "good enough". We came to understand that the healthier children, who were better able to satisfy their parents' wishes for loving, attached responses, were not hosting the mother's unconscious wish that the child should be dead.

We were struck by a significant difference in mothering, inadequate in the case of the autistic child. We understood that the child's pathology was not only his problem, originating from his non-responsiveness, which Bergman and Escalona (1949) called "unusual sensitivity in young children", but it was also evident that when the child could tentatively or weakly stretch out towards his mother, he or she had not found an adequate answer, due to the mother's depression or his temporary autistic encapsulation. (Today, I would wonder if this came about as a result of her unelaborated and unconscious death wish.) We had already started to understand that it was a non-human or a non-humanizing encounter which induced in the child a psychotic depression, a concept that Tustin ran into while considering some observations by Winnicott and Bibring not belonging to her more familiar Kleinian lexicon. In other terms, we had started to understand that the right approach to a psychoanalytic understanding of the autistic world was that it was not the single "refrigerator" mother's responsibility. Behind every pathology of an autistic child there is a story of suffering, depression, and a tragic non-encounter between mother and child. This goes beyond the neurological damage the child might have had, which, at the time, we could not diagnose because neuro-imaging was a relatively recent practice. None of us, in particular Ms Tustin, ever attributed responsibility for the autistic outcome to the parents or the mother alone; rather, she made an effort, as we were already doing, to provide help and support to a difficult mothering situation.

Ugo was a child locked up in his hard and unshakeable corporeal armor, which seemed impenetrable to every attempt at contact and which severely challenged the analyst's ability to hold and be aware of his countertransference. As therapy with Ugo proceeded, he slowly seemed to accept, in the safety of the infantile transference situation, a minimal interaction with the other, even though for months he remained locked in his autistic shell.

I will keep the biographical data to a minimum. Ugo is the son of two not particularly wealthy office clerks. He has a sister who is six years older. He seems to have been conceived in order to try to patch up a significant fracture in the parental relationship. His birth was preceded by an abortion that caused the mother to become depressed. Ugo was conceived to "replace" the dead child, but, in the mother's unconscious, I believe he represented the usurper, the one who should be dead. He was born, when the mother was thirty-nine, from a dystocic and premature labor.

As mentioned earlier, I wish to focus on the primitive agonies the child felt. I shall also try to show how he always conveyed a sense of being about to fall into emptiness, as if he were swaying while walking on the edge of a cliff. This was evident especially in his uncertain and robotic stance. He would often run in the room, capsizing furniture and crashing violently against objects, even against me. At first, I felt like an inanimate object, just like the other things in the room, and then gradually, even if warned by Ms Tustin against imposing my countertransference on the patient in order to give myself some consolation for the loneliness induced by his a-symbolic activity, I felt at times perceived as a live being.

With her invitation not to overuse the countertransference, to overlap our supposed intuition with the "crude" behavior of the child, Ms Tustin was suggesting that the autistic child lives in an auto-sensual, sometimes scary, sometimes self-centered and self-soothing world, made of autistic "shapes". Initially, it was hard to understand the meaning of these shapes, and what Ms Tustin meant, but my three-times-a-week interaction with Ugo somehow brought me closer to that understanding. Often, at home, outside of the therapeutic session, I would find myself repeating Ugo's gestures. I was at first scared, then curious, since these lonely events somehow seemed to be a way into his world.

During supervision, facing my desperation at not being able to understand the non-responsive Ugo, Tustin told me, "You think with your head, as if Ugo were a neurotic or psychotic child . . . try to feel it in your body. Can't you see he is making 'autistic auto-sensual shapes'?"

I was perplexed and asked, "See? How?"

Ms Tustin, who had very developed sensibility, surprised me by replying, "Push your back hard against the back of the chair where you are sitting. Push, push more. Then move forward again. Now focus on the strange sensations you are feeling in your back, sensations left by the strong pressure you exerted on the back support. You will feel something moving, as if your back was slowly recovering its shape. The autistic child, Ugo, feels inside him similar sensations, weak, strong, and he intentionally but unconsciously provokes them. This is 'making autistic auto sensual shapes'."

Bollas (1987), Bion (1970), and Smith (2012) suggested the analyst must be infected with the illness of his patient in order to understand him, but becoming ill with autistic-like behaviors is frightening. You have the feeling they will never leave you, even though you obscurely perceive that this form of "imitation", or experience of contamination, is a means of gaining access to his world. It is like starting on a rough course for which you do not know the destination, but are accompanied by the awareness of what I would call "auto-sensual mithridatism". Slowly, you inoculate yourself with the poison of a nameless dread, a primitive agony, and, since you are supposed to be stronger, you hope it will not contaminate you completely, but actually help you to learn to tolerate it.

At the end of the first year of analysis, after a separation from his mother for work reasons, there was an evident regression and a dark period where Ugo would spend the whole session curled up in a corner, emitting guttural sounds and staying totally and scarily motionless. I often had the sensation that he did not even recognize me, or that his perception of my body was hesitating, uncertain, discontinuous. After my patience and tolerance of his avoiding behavior, his excluding me, were almost totally consumed, I started to observe small variations of posture, sudden runs, desperate screams without an apparent meaning, movements of the arms and hands in space that would begin to give me an approximate idea of the total darkness in his a-symbolic interior life.

Another significant change that Ms Tustin had noticed was the gradual getting out of his corner and walking around the room. She would say, "You'll see that soon things will begin to change. You had the ability not to interfere." Some time later, during a supervision, I told Ms Tustin that, for the first time, I had a specific fantasy about his moving around the room. I said it cautiously because, from her teachings, I knew how careful she was to avoid overusing the countertransference, which, in her opinion, created a "second child" in the room that had nothing to do with the real one, a defensive formation of a lonely therapist. I told her I had pictured in my mind Ugo as the robot, R2D2 in Star Wars, with his rigid and sliding movements on wheels.

Ms Tustin replied, "OK, the time has come. Try to tell him, with your stomach, not with your head, that it seems to Vincenzo that 'you', Ugo, are always about to fall, as if on the edge of a cliff."

The time came when Ugo, in one session, seemed to swerve more abruptly than usual. I said, "Today Ugo was about to fall off the cliff . . . because he always walks on the edge, as far as possible from Vincenzo." To my great surprise—reported triumphantly to Ms Tustin—Ugo produced a guttural sound, which seemed to come from his deepest interior: "fall-pa-in. Ma-amma", a first sketch of speech.

I replied, "Ugo is afraid of pain, he is afraid to fall forever, to lose himself, to dissolve, but he walks like a puppet on the edge, to see if the sensations inside his stomach can keep him tied to the ground, to keep him from falling."

I thought the autistic shapes Ms Tustin had talked about had a self-protective value. It was as if, by clinging to these shapes, Ugo could feel attached, could hold on to himself, thus avoiding the fall into emptiness. When I reported to Ms Tustin this interpretation, she liked the idea of the auto-protective shapes. She had never thought about them in these terms, how they might attach him to the ground, but naturally she said that I had been too "mental" and that my interpretation should have been done with a sing-song voice, with the body and the belly.

She gave me an example. I will never forget of how brief this sing-song interpretation was: "You feel that you're falling down, but you also feel that inside of your body the sensations in your tummy keep you at bay."

From that point on, I tried to put my head aside and respond to Ugo only with physical sensations: "pain . . . Vincenzo sad . . . Vincenzo cries . . . pain to the leg . . . punch in the stomach", if he hit me involuntarily or on purpose. Finally, Ugo seemed to understand my language. He would come cautiously nearby and give me a stick, one of the ones he would wave obsessively in front of his eyes. Then he would want it back and scream; however, some kind of rough communication had been established. I was anxious that it could disappear anytime, and so it was. He went back for weeks into his corner. Ms Tustin observed that the child had felt my anxieties, like the ones in his mother's womb, and in some way had felt expelled, as in his dystocic and premature birth. Thrown away, Ugo had regressed. That moment of minimal contact, perhaps activated by my picturing him like the

Star Wars robot, always about to fall down the cliff and get lost, and re-live his primitive agonies, a fall that had happened already, was dissolved (Winnicott, 1964). My desperation was eased only by Ms Tustin's very supportive replies to the brief letters I wrote to her.

Suddenly, from this state of non-thought and inertia, in one session Ugo suddenly stood up and started running in circles, screaming. I had difficulty understanding his words, but then, when he repeated them, I grasped some sense, even if I had the clear sensation that for Ugo they were a-symbolic sounds, all coming from the stomach. In other words, they were beta elements (in Bion's meaning) that for me had some sense: "ma-amma, poo hole fall, pain, mama mean, Vinzo mean."

I told him that Ugo was terrified of falling endlessly in emptiness, of dissolving in a way that had already happened. But now, with Vincenzo, with whom he could vomit away all of the poo inside, he might feel better. He dived to the floor and kicked me to stop me getting closer. His mother, noticing the screams, knocked on the door and asked if she could come in. I told her to please wait for the end of the session. I felt I had to deal with this myself.

I sat beside him and, remembering the autistic shapes in the back, I started to caress his back. After a while Ugo calmed down, but the session was almost over. I was wet with sweat: my body, flesh and blood, had taken over the role of my mind. I helped him to stand. Spontaneously, he gave me his hand and said in a whiny voice "I-waan-waant . . . ma-amma . . ."

In this session, I felt that I had learned something through sharing an experience with Ugo, which related to his terror of falling into emptiness, nothing, a terror of non-being. It is, for me, the quintessence of the treatment of the autistic child and the reason that analytic therapy holds a relevant place in that treatment. It is the experience of sharing that makes humans relate to each other. For this reason, I believe our efforts in the therapy of autistic children should follow these lines, allowing for such experiences, so the autistic child can become a human being among other human beings.

## *Notes*

1. Perhaps these dynamics relate precisely to the designation, "refrigerator-mother", which Kanner (1943) refers to, and is considered by him a possible etiopathogenethic factor. I wonder if Kanner—who was not

an analyst but an illustrious child psychiatrist – had intuited exactly this vicious circle, which could be called *anti-life*: on one side a robotic and unspontaneous mother, locked up in the armor of her reaction formations; on the other a child who feels cared for only as part of a mechanical routine and is not touched by the libidinal sensuality of the mother, which is terrorized by her death wish towards him. Although of course even in these instances, it may be impossible to say which situation initiates the process and which the reaction.

2. I am aware that what I am talking about is very similar to, if not overlapping with, Meltzer and colleagues' (1975) conception of bi-dimensionality, but, for brevity's sake, I am compelled not to analyse differences and similarities.
3. In the days of Tustin's consultations at the University of Rome, most of us followed her theoretical and clinical lectures, many specifically prepared in relation to her activities with us. Many of these lectures can be found in the volume *Autistic States in Children* (1981a), where she testifies to, and describes, the intense mutual cultural exchange she had with our department.

## References

Alvarez, A. (2012). *The Thinking Heart: Three Levels of Psychoanalytic Therapy with Disturbed Children*. London: Routledge.

Balint, M. (1969). *The Basic Fault: Therapeutic Aspects of Regression*. London. Tavistock.

Bergman, A., & Escalona, S. (1949). Unusual sensitivity in young children. *Psychoanalytic Study of the Child, 3–4*: 333–352.

Bion, W. R. (1962). *Learning from Experience*. London: Heinemann.

Bion, W. R. (1970). *Attention and Interpretation*. London: Heinemann.

Bollas, C. (1987). *The Shadow of the Object*. London: Free Association Books

Bonaminio, V. (2005). "Il bambino che era caduto nel burrone". Catastrofe psicologica, depressione primaria, difesa maniacale e "riparazione in funzione della difesa materna organizzata contro la depressione". Richard e Piggle. Volume 13, numero 1 gennaio/aprile 2005, pp. 5–26.

Bonaminio, V. (2010). L'Installarsi della psiche nel corpo. Stati di integrazione, non-integrazione e l'identificazione primaria. In: Udire con gli occhi. Adriano Giannotti tra neuropsichiatria infantile e psicoanalisi (pp. 103–130). Vitebo: Sette Città.

Emden, C. (2014). *Nietzsche's Naturalism: Philosophy and the Life Sciences in the Nineteenth Century*. Cambridge: Cambridge University Press.

Ferro, A. (2010). Experiencing emotions, avoiding emotions: between Hercules and Puss-in-Boots. In: J. Van Buren & S. Alhanati (Eds.), *Primitive Mental States: A Psychoanalytic Exploration of the Origins of Meaning* (pp. 31–46). London: Routledge,

Freud, S. (1941f). Findings, ideas, problems. *S. E., 23*: 299–300. London: Hogarth.

Grotstein, J. (2010). Orphan of "O". The negative therapeutic reaction and the longing for the childhood which never was. In: J. Van Buren & S. Alhanati (Eds.), *Primitive Mental States: A Psychoanalytic Exploration of the Origins of Meaning* (pp. 8–30). London: Routledge.

Kanner, L. (1943). Autistic disturbances of affective contact. *Nervous Child, 2*: 217–250.

Levine, H. (2013). The colorless canvas: representation, therapeutic action and the creation of the mind. In: H. B. Levine, G. S. Reed, & D. Scarfone (Eds.), *Unrepresented States and the Construction of Meaning: Clinical and Theoretical Contributions* (pp. 42–71). London: Karnac.

Meltzer, D., Bremner, J., Hoxter, S., Weddell, D., & Wittenberg, I. (1975). *Exploration in Autism. A Psychoanalytic Study*. Strathtay, Perthshire: Clunie Press.

Ogden, T. (1989). *The Primitive Edge of Experience.* New York: Aronson.

Reiner, A. (2009). *The Quest for Conscience and the Birth of the Mind*. London: Karnac.

Reiner, A. (2013). Pre-verbal language in the treatment of a mother and infant: a clinical exploration. In: J. Van Buren & S. Alhanati (Eds.), *Primitive Mental States: A Psychoanalytic Exploration of the Origins of Meaning* (pp. 156–172). London: Routledge.

Smith, H. (2012). Personal communication.

Tustin, F. (1981a). *Autistic States in Children*. London: Routledge & Kegan Paul.

Tustin, F. (1981b). The a-symbolic nature of auro-sensous states. In: *Autistic States in Children* (pp. 123–134). London: Routledge & Kegan Paul.

Tustin, F. (1981c). Transcription of Tustin's replies during a talk at the Department of Child and Adolescent Psychiatry, Rome University, Spring 1981.

Tustin, F. (1994). The perpetuation of an error. *Journal of Child Psychotherapy, 20*: 3–23.

Winnicott, D. W. (1945). Primitive emotional development. In: *Through Paediatrics to Psychoanalysis* (pp. 11–33). London: Tavistock, 1958.

Winnicott, D. W. (1964). The importance of the setting in meeting regression in psychoanalysis. In: C. Winnicott, R. Shepherd, & M. Davis (Eds.), *Psychoanalytic Explorations* (pp. 96–102). London, Karnac, 1989.

Winnicott, D. W. (1967). The aetiology of infantile schizophrenia in terms of adaptive failure. In: R. Shepherd, J. Johns, H. Taylor Robinson (Eds.), *Thinking About Children* (pp. 218–226). London: Karnac, 1996.

Winnicott, D. W. (1974). Fear of breakdown. *International Review of Psychoanalysis, 1*: 103–107.

CHAPTER TWELVE

# Beckett's *Endgame*: the collapse of mental life

*Annie Reiner*

This chapter is an examination of primitive anxieties and defenses seen in the life and work of Samuel Beckett, in particular in his play, *Endgame* (1957). Considered to be among the most influential writers in modern literature, Beckett provides a unique experiential perspective on these primitive mental states that are also the purview of psychoanalysis. I will examine these states in relation to certain of Frances Tustin's ideas about being and not-being, and the sense of falling and dissolution of the personality, as well as to the ideas of Wilfred Bion, with whom Beckett had treatment during a mental breakdown at the age of twenty-seven. As Bion reminds us, these breakdowns are also break*throughs into* experiences of forgotten traumas, and we will see in Beckett's work how his personal descent into those primitive states contributed to his uncanny insight into the deepest levels of the mind.

"Birth was the death of him. Again" (Beckett, 1986d, p. 425). This opening line of one of Beckett's plays reflects the experience of falling into a state of endless hopelessness. The source of Beckett's personal understanding of despair can be seen in his life-long difficulties with a cold, demanding mother unable emotionally to hold her sensitive child, as well as a warm but meek, unambitious father upon whom

Beckett nonetheless relied to counteract the effects of his cold mother. These characteristics are consistent with the lack of faith in the facilitating environment that Tustin saw as the psychogenic causes of childhood autism. She described it as the conjunction of the particular child's nature along with a "temporary state of depression or under confidence in the mother" (Tustin, 1984, p. 285), and an absent or ineffectual father. Beckett was not autistic, but the developmental derailment of the child's self and mind by the absence of emotional connection gives rise to similar states of detachment and dissolution at different levels of functioning. Bion (1970) writes that the destruction of a sense of time and evacuation of emotion creates in the personality "a domain of non-existence" (p. 20). A confusion ensues between being and non-being, between birth (or life) and death—"Again"—as Beckett says in the quote above, for this death of the personality replays throughout life. It is often the basis of analytic work, not just for autistic children, but also for adult neurotic patients with an autistic enclave. Although it might be unconscious, the sense of falling is continuous and terrifying, and, as Tustin (1984) points out, the analyst must be aware of the "dreadful terror of annihilation" (p. 159), as well as the desire to undermine the analyst that hides beneath the passivity of the adult patient's autistic capsule.

In examining this rudimentary confusion between mental life and death, I distinguish two different but related experiences of falling. The first is a pathological fall into nothingness, due in part to being emotionally dropped and in part to the defenses against the pain of that experience. The individual is "dropped" by the lack of emotional containment of the object, but then his or her own defenses, meant as protection from pain, cause a further drop into nothingness, leaving the individual further lost. This second kind of fall, though also terrifying, can be revisited in the potentially healthy fall of a psychological birth.

Tustin (1990a) also describes this kind of secondary nullification of the self, and how difficult it is for the analyst not to be "rendered null and void" by patients' falls into non-existence. She writes, "This nullifying by autistic children plays as much a part in their sense of nothingness as does being cared for by a depressed mother who . . . could not be a lively, confident, playful presence" (p. 110). What I am describing as this second fall into nothingness is the analytic necessity of a fall from the pathological defensive structure and into life, a leap of faith into an opportunity for growth that must pass *through* the original nullifying fall. Bion's (1970) idea of "Faith" is linked to the belief that truth exists, in this case the hope that one may reclaim one's natural potential for a mind. It is a chance for a "do-over", as children say in playground games, daring to take a new leap into life with the faith that one's fall might this time find a softer landing into the "arms" of truth. It is not really, as we and our patients often think, into the arms of the analyst, who is just the container and messenger of truth. While it requires maternal aspects of reverie and emotional containment, the analyst's intention is not to be a "better mother" than the original primary object, but to be an analytic object.

The deadly defenses against attachment and emotional life are implicit in another of Beckett's plays in which he writes, "Peace, yes, I suppose, a kind of peace, and all that pain as if . . . never been" (1986c, p. 312). But, of course, the pain, though split off and projected, still exists. It cannot be processed mentally, however, and, as is painfully evident in *Endgame*, it results in a destruction of the mind. From this state of emotional deadness or non-being one must "fall" into life, a painful re-enactment of the original birth into an unsafe environment. These dual experiences of falling will be examined with reference to a detailed case presentation, as well as the literary perspectives of Beckett's work.

## *Beckett and Bion: a historical perspective*

I have been fascinated for years by Beckett's odd mix of pathos, philosophy, humor, and profound existential pain. I have devoured his plays, novels, and stories since I was sixteen, at which point I was even inspired, or presumptuous, enough to try to write a play *á la* Beckett. My spectacularly unsuccessful effort made me admire Beckett's genius even more. Thirteen years later, while reading a comprehensive biography about Beckett (Bair, 1978), I learned of his treatment with Bion at the Tavistock Clinic in the 1930s. For me, a very young therapist at the time, these convergent facts about my two reigning heroes surprised and delighted me. I had somehow connected these two brilliant men in my mind, perhaps not so surprising considering the fact that both were intrepid explorers of primitive mental life, with sly and wicked senses of humor.

Bion was then living in Los Angeles, and, in addition to having a clinical seminar with him for several months, I attended every lecture I could. I approached him after the next lecture and told him excitedly about my discovery about Beckett. He looked at me with his very warm, open, owl-ish eyes and said, "Yes . . . I don't believe I helped him very much." The humor in his comment derived from its simple honesty and humility, refreshing among analysts who often seemed intent on showing how much they knew. Bion, on the other hand, was determined to remind us how little he, and the rest of us, knew about the mind. As he often said, "We have barely scratched the surface." Still, I took Bion's assessment with a grain of salt, for, although he was young, not yet an analyst when he treated Beckett, it seemed to me that two creative geniuses in a room together in intimate conversation, three times a week for two years, could not help but significantly affect each other. It seemed especially likely when the geniuses in question were, as Bion's widow said, ". . . very much alike" (F. Bion, 2011).

I am clearly not the first to comment on the intensity of Bion's gaze. In fact, Beckett, whose eyes stared out from his own photographs with similar intensity, remarked on it, writing, ". . . [Bion] fasten[ed] on me his eyes like cinders with all their seeing" (Miller, 2013, p. 28). Implicit in his observation is a capacity, evident in both men, to go on observing despite the searing agony of their respective baptisms by fire. We know that both men, at various times in their lives, were left in the ashes of their primitive pain, and each tried valiantly to keep his eyes open—"not the blue," as Beckett (1964, p. 8) put it—to the painful realities of life.

There are also differences between them, of course, for, unlike Beckett, who places the time of his death at birth, Bion dates his mental death from the time of his horrifying experiences as a young tank commander in the First World War. He states clearly that he had died at the battle of Amiens, giving the date of his death as August 8, 1918 (Bion, 1982, p. 232). Life emerged from the ashes of mental death, however, and, having survived physically, Bion struggled to figure out "how those same dead bones gave birth to a mind" (Bion, 1991, p. 60). The fact that they did allowed generations of analysts to work at doing the same, as we see in Tustin's work.

In Tustin's opinion, *á propos* of this, the autistic child has too early suffered too much consciousness of separateness and reality before the development of any mechanism for holding or containment of experience. The child's "agony of consciousness" (Tustin, 1986) leads to the explosion of his experience, his objects, and his self, leaving the child in a world very much like the one we see in Beckett's *Endgame*.

The clinical details of Beckett's treatment are not well known, and might never be known, although information about his relationship to psychoanalysis and to Bion can be gleaned from his abundant correspondence. We do have details about his family history, and the painful and confusing symptoms during his breakdown. His first real sign of trouble came shortly after the death of his beloved father. While walking down the street, all of a sudden Beckett had the feeling (to quote his own later famous lines), "I can't go on. I'll go on" (Beckett, 1958, p. 179). He crawled to the next pub where he sat, perfectly still. He was soon bedridden with a mile-long list of symptoms (insomnia, panic attacks, constipation, inability to urinate, cysts, boils), all unresponsive to medical treatment. He unleashed torrents of anger toward his mother, with whose anxiety, coldness, and intrusiveness he was hopelessly enmeshed. These qualities were a perfect recipe for schizoid detachment in the sensitive child—a mother so cold he could not get near her and yet so demanding and intrusive that he could not escape her. It was then that his psychiatrist friend, Geoffrey Thompson, referred him to the Tavistock Clinic in London, where he began seeing Bion.

Not surprisingly, Beckett was resistant to treatment, but he was also very engaged in it. He sent Bion a Christmas card after he left treatment, and reported the response to Thompson, now a colleague of Bion's, saying, "Bion . . . does me the honour to remember me, deprecates my untimely departure, just when I was all set to become the *uomo universal*, and [he] looks forward to getting his hooks into me again" (letter from Thomas McGreevy, 22 December 1936: Miller, 2013, p. 73). This reference to a *uomo universal* alluded to Beckett's view of Bion as a mystic, which apparently Bion had often denied. Why this came up we do not know, but it is surprising in view of the fact that most people look upon that mystical aspect of Bion as pertaining to his late work. Perhaps Beckett had the insight to see an attribute in Bion that even now continues to escape some psychoanalysts.

## The Fall: the other side of Eden

Like all creativity, Beckett's plays are his waking dreams, his access to those confused, "crazy", brilliant aspects of one's mind which enlighten one to these states of mind. Beckett's disturbances reveal the fact that mental distress has the same source as creativity and wisdom, and underline the need to honor these disturbances as important communications from the depths. Like the analyst, Beckett's audiences can feel the terror, but also the profundity of experiences for which Beckett serves as ambassador. Although his plays disturb us, they also entertain us, again not unlike the analyst's interpretations, which disturb the patient but provide the relief of truth.

The two experiences of falling converge in the process of psychological birth, in the recreation in analysis of the experience of being dropped. That early terror is now, hopefully, experienced in the presence of a thoughtful object, able to contain the experience. The idea of containment, however, is more than empathy or saying reassuring things, for allowing the terror to overtake the mind provides the analyst the opportunity for a new awareness about the patient's experience to be seen and communicated to the patient. This includes the confusion about mental life and death which arose as the initial experience of falling gave way to defenses of splitting, fragmentation, or emotional anaesthesia, as feeling itself became confused with evil and pathology. These distinctions must be made clear to the patient in order to separate these "bad" feelings of terror from this potentially "good"—or useful—reliving of it.

Sensations of falling and dissolution which Tustin describes in autistic states can be seen to greater or lesser degrees at all levels of mental functioning. While neurotic patients might have more capacity to symbolize or dream these experiences, primitive fears exist across a broad spectrum of diagnoses, which affect different levels of mental and social functioning.

## Clinical vignette

One patient, "Angie", had several early traumas, including a premature birth in which both she and her mother had life-threatening problems. She not only spent weeks in an incubator separated from her ill mother, her mother was also in general unable to contain her own or her child's feelings. This sensitive infant was thrust into a nightmare of nothingness, a world without the gaze of a mother to give form and meaning to her first weeks of life. Angie continued falling into this nothingness for forty years, before and during some of her fourteen-year analysis. Inherently bright and capable, she developed to a very high level of functioning, although any changes or separations led either to ferocious anger or to that dizzying sense of falling. Birth, as Beckett said, was the death of her. Re-enactments of being dropped from her mother's body replayed the neuropsychological electrical tsunami that, over and over again, overwhelmed her mind. All she could do was anaesthetize herself, furious at me for invading the "protective" shell of her mental death, an encapsulation in a phantasied womb which seemed then her only hope for safety.

Despite Rank's (1929) idea of birth itself as a trauma, the normal transition of birth might more accurately be seen as a disturbance, painful and frightening, perhaps, but part of the normal "shocks that flesh is heir to" (Shakespeare, 1600, III.i. 62–63). It is less likely to bring on the kind of terror and mental death endured in autism, or by neurotic patients like Angie. If this natural transformation becomes *un*naturally traumatic, it is often due to other physical or emotional factors. While Angie had to contend with both, she nonetheless rallied the strength and courage to endure years of repetition of that first terrifying fall into mental death as she slowly came to understand the analytic process of her "fall" *into* life and mindfulness.

The difference between these two aspects of falling depends on whether or not anyone is mentally present to "catch" the infant emotionally. The emptiness of a child for whom "no mother" equaled "no self" was compounded by a family life of violence and abuse, where her earlier drop into nothingness, confusion, and rage was solidified. Nothingness became this infant's reality. This gave rise to a hatred of truth, and of reality itself, and to a protective shell that seemed impenetrable for the first eight years of analysis.

Tustin's (1990b) idea of the autistic shell as a defense against feelings of non-existence is reflected in the sense of nothingness permeating Beckett's work, the apocalyptic world of *Endgame* and the futile search for meaning in *Waiting for Godot* (1986a). It is helpful to see these states of mind represented, for like all artistic endeavors, it is a sort of dream played out in a way which allows our minds to dream the feelings as well. Beckett was, in fact, familiar with the analytic idea of retreat into an imagined womb, of which he learned at a lecture by Jung at the Tavistock in 1935 (Miller, 2013). Beckett was deeply affected by Jung's comment about a young girl patient whom he thought "had never fully been born", an idea Beckett associated with his own fearful retreats into bed. He found a way to depict this state of being buried alive in his play, *Happy Days* (1986b), in which the main character is buried up to her waist in dirt in Act I. In Act II, she is buried up to her neck, so things are clearly going in the wrong direction, a fitting representation of a sort of reverse birth, an emotional encryption or encapsulation. In another play, entitled, *Play* (Beckett, 1986c), the three characters are in giant urns, entombed, as it were, in dead wombs.

Before his breakdown, Beckett's scholarly essays and lectureship at Trinity College had him headed for an academic career. Many of his hapless and hopeless characters are filled with fragments of grand ideas and great thinkers, embodying the conflict between mindlessness and the remnants of an impressive, but now useless, ego. This is a self denuded of emotional connections to others, or within oneself, the collapsed world of autistic enclaves. It is certainly in line with Bion's idea that intellect cannot develop divorced from primitive emotional reality. Like Beckett, Bion had his own fight with this ungrounded intellect, of feeling imprisoned by reason, memories, and desires. Tying ideas up neatly and rationally was like pinning a dead butterfly to the wall, a version of thinking which did not reflect the chaos and paradox of mental experience. In *Memoir of The Future*, Bion (1991), like Beckett, turned to fiction to try to express the multi-dimensional reality of the mind, and the seemingly "unreasonable" level of reason that was the basis of thinking. The healthy fall into nothingness and the accompanying terror of losing one's mind reflects the dissolution of the groundless rationality of a false self. It is the necessary cracking of the hard shell of autistic states.

Some of this is reflected in the myth of the Fall in Genesis. The pain of processing the fear and uncertainty of birth, or psychological birth, is projected and felt as punishment from a purposefully cruel, God-like parent for transgressions the infant knows nothing about. However, the pain is, in fact, a natural part of development from the oneness of unconscious experience to an experience of separateness at the heart of thinking.

While Adam and Eve appear to have everything (the beauty and opulence of the Garden, and its spiritual treasures of Immortality (the

Tree of Life) and Morality (the Tree of Knowledge of Good and Evil)), the fruits of these trees are forbidden. Metaphorically, this is knowledge that is out of reach, that is, unconscious knowledge that is, therefore, of no use in thinking until it can be consciously experienced. Adam and Eve, as representatives of mankind in its infancy, are endowed with the *potential* for awareness, but have no way to access it. This would require a fall from this erstwhile paradise of an infant undifferentiated from the mother, still in the bliss of her womb-like mental protection. In order for that human potential for consciousness to be realized, one must do the painful work of individuation, which includes integrating the dual aspects of human "being"—good and evil, life and death. This esoteric knowledge, like the treatment of autism or other states of nothingness, involves a systematic breakdown of the false safety of the protective barrier, a journey from that womb-like oblivion of Adam and Eve to the uncertain and unending struggle for knowledge and truth in an infinite and constantly changing world.

## Endgame*: a model of nothingness*

Beckett's *Endgame* represents the dreaded fall into primitive experiences previously denied, but this potential for psychological birth feels like death. It is a descent into hopelessness, into an even darker place than, for instance, *Waiting for Godot*, written four years earlier. In *Godot* there is a dim sense of hope that someone or something is worth waiting for. In *Endgame*, as in severe autistic states, there is little hope of salvation. Outside of the rundown room in which the two hapless main characters are sequestered, the land and seas have dried up and all the people are dead. For Hamm and his servant, Clov, the apparent protection and "cure" of mental death and emotional numbness have substituted for all human feeling. It is an uneasy peace, for they are dependent on each other for everything. Hamm, practically blind, can no longer walk; Clov, who waits on him, cannot sit, and he serves as Hamm's eyes on to the devastation outside. While they need each other, it is within the circumspect relationship between master and slave, where roles, habits, and rituals take the place of needs and feelings. They get by, anaesthetized by their rituals, and helplessly observing the encroaching oblivion.

Hamm's parents, Nagg and Nell, are alive, but they are "stored" like useless objects in two trash cans on stage, popping up now and then to annoy Hamm. These fragments of "internal objects" litter Hamm's mind with the detritus of undigested childhood memories. Like Beckett's ambivalent attachment to his own mother, Hamm can neither make peace with them nor free himself of them. Not only do these parents exist in his mental garbage can, he also takes care to "screw down the lids". They do not stay down, of course, and this sort of splitting off of feelings leads us to the strange scenarios we create for ourselves to live in, like the one in *Endgame*, and in the clinical example I present below.

*Endgame* is filled with many enigmatic images that, like dreams, stimulate multiple conjectures and interpretations. At one point, Hamm mentions "Mother Pegg", with no explanation as to who she is. It is not Nell, his mother in the trash bin, for Mother Pegg is dead. It is said that she "died of darkness" because Hamm would not give her oil for her lamp, although, as it turns out, he did not have any oil to give. We are left wondering who this apparently important person was, one of many references in Beckett's writings by which even Beckett scholars are stumped. One makes reference to the story in the gospel of Matthew (25: 2–13), of ten young bridesmaids waiting for their "bridegroom" (Jesus) to come. Each waits through the night with a lamp, but a few "foolish" maidens have forgotten to bring oil, so they fall asleep in the dark and miss the groom. Metaphorically, these are the ones who were not ready for the spiritual enlightenment of a symbolic marriage to Christ. This seemed like a relevant observation, but, as Freud pointed out, symbols are over determined, and my own more earthly association was to two important "Peggys" in Beckett's early life. The first was Peggy Sinclair, his first love, a beloved cousin who died young, just before Beckett's father's death. The other was Peggy Guggenheim, the American heiress and gallerist with whom Beckett had a brief affair in his twenties. He was "in love with me for ten minutes", Guggenheim said, describing him as a "pure intellectual" who "couldn't make up his mind about anything" (Bair, 1978, p. 276). She nicknamed him "Oblomov" after the literary character who "did not have the willpower to get out of bed" (Bair, 1978, p. 276). These "Peggs" were his first loves, and, from a psychoanalytic perspective, the infant's first love is his mother, whose capacities for reverie and emotional containment facilitate the development of the child's mind.

We might then see Mother Pegg as a symbol of the capacities for mindfulness and thinking, the spiritual knowledge of "O". At a primitive level, this kind of authentic attachment to a good mother is the precursor to "love", and I would conjecture that it is this capacity which died of darkness as the traumatized infant (Hamm or Beckett) turned away in despair and disappointment. He had no "oil" to give her, no light or love, for she had not given any to *him*. Like the foolish bridesmaids, Beckett's mother seemed to have come to motherhood emotionally unprepared and unavailable to love. Without the "oil" to fuel her own emotional enlightenment, she could not help her infant to learn to love, to think, or to be. Although it is her job to provide the light and the love, the infant attempts to save the mother who has emotionally dropped him by idealizing her. This lie at the core of the personality is an abandonment of emotional truth that results in the death of the real, flawed mother in the mind, the death of truth and of the mind. Fairbairn (1952) called it the "moral defense" (p. 65), the infant's need to see himself as evil to preserve the goodness of that ideal mother in his mind. "It's better to be a sinner in a world ruled by God than to live in a world ruled by the devil" (Fairbairn, 1952, p. 65).

The encroaching wasteland of *Endgame* reflects this picture of the infant's inner world denuded of the possibility of attachment, truth, and love. We get more insight into it in the story Hamm tells of his visit with a madman in the asylum, who thinks it is the end of the world. He sits in the corner, but Hamm drags him to the window and says, "Look! There! All that rising corn . . . the sails of the herring fleet! All that loveliness!" (Beckett, 1957, p. 44). But the madman, bereft, quickly returns to his corner, and Hamm explains, "All he had seen was ashes" (Beckett, 1957, p. 44). His only reality was an internal world stripped of life and meaning. The roots of this inner deadness are evident in Hamm's relationship to his parents, as described by his father, Nagg.

"Whom did you call when you were a tiny boy, and were frightened, in the dark? Your mother? No. Me. We let you cry. Then we moved you out of earshot, so that we might sleep in peace" (Beckett, 1957, p. 56).

Beckett's unwavering view of the truth renders this child's nightmare darkly comedic, but, of course, there is nothing funny in not being received, seen, or heard by parents who are emotionally absent or asleep. The precocious awareness of separation from the safety of oneness with the parent thrusts the child into a world without meaning that

Tustin (1981) called an "agony of consciousness" (p. 169), not yet mentally equipped to process his reality. The result might be the kind of post-apocalyptic inner world depicted in *Endgame.* It is, in a sense, an ongoing, but unconscious, re-enactment of that first "fall" from safe holding, also re-enacted in the transference. The following clinical example illustrates the development of such a world and something of how to work with it in practice.

## *Clinical example: "Betsy"*

"Betsy's" "fall" began at birth. A nurse at the hospital, not knowing the infant was to be adopted, brought Betsy to her mother to nurse, and, when the mistake was discovered, Betsy was taken away. This bright, intuitive, successful woman in her forties was adopted by a young couple, soon to be divorced, after spending four months in a series of foster homes. She struggles with violent feelings of abandonment, which she can sometimes feel, but from which she is often so emotionally disconnected that she cannot feel anything. She is outgoing and frequently garrulous, and I sometimes have to stop her to point out that she does not actually seem to be talking to me. After many years in analysis, she can experience this emotional absence or presence without the rage my interpretations had previously elicited.

When she finally arrived at her adoptive parents' home, she had severe diaper rash and never cried. In her later choices of unavailable men, she is often thrust back into this traumatic abandonment by her birth mother, a trauma compounded by the emotional abandonment by her clinically depressed adoptive mother, and the actual abandonment by her adoptive father, who disappeared after the divorce when Betsy was three. As we came to see, her relationships with men who abandoned her also reflected her deep abandonment of her own emotional self, deadening herself as Tustin described (see above, p. 3).

The session prior to this one felt so entirely dead that I found myself unable to breathe, as if there were no life, no air in the room at all. I commented on her sounding as if she felt dead. She sank down into the couch, and into despair, then said, "I don't know what to do." She was somewhat familiar with this feeling of utter detachment from herself, but this time the sense of death was so powerful that I, too, felt at a loss as to how to help her.

In this (the next session) we saw the nightmare beneath this deadness. "I woke up at 3 a.m. feeling scared and alone," Betsy said, ". . . wondering how can I survive in this world all alone?" After going back to sleep she had this "weird science fiction dream".

> I was some kind of machine, maybe I was an alien, I don't know. I was being examined by an authority of this machine world, like a State or medical group. He looked over my body from the toes up, and then I was to have an MRI to examine the inside, to see how I was doing, if I could be sent back into circulation or needed a new body before being sent back out. When he got to my breasts I said I'd had a breast reduction. "I know," he said, "I saw it on the last exam." I wasn't aware of having been there before so I was confused. I didn't know if I was the only alien, or part of a society of machines.

"The examiner looked human," she said, "but maybe he was a machine, too. I was like a puppet in someone else's world . . . it was eerie . . . sinister." We had seen similar worlds represented in Betsy's dreams before. One involved what she had called "a manufactured world", a gray stark sterile metropolis created by another controlling group. She had spoken often of a recurring childhood nightmare of "the evil doctor" who was trying to kill her. I had often represented the evil doctor in her treatment, but, ultimately, the evil doctor was an internal (superego) object promising to help cure her of unbearable feelings of terror by killing them off. The cost of this temporary relief was her own emotional deadness, and a terrifying inability to assess whether the "helpful" methods of this doctor were good or evil, killing her or bringing her to life.

She iterated her confusion in the dream, of not remembering she had already seen this machine doctor. "It made me wonder what was real," she said. My thoughts went to her one meeting with her birth mother, an event she was consciously unable to remember. I said that I thought her breast reduction stood for that one experience of nursing, followed by a breast so drastically "reduced" that it was gone forever. This imago was a dead mother, with whom she was now completely identified. The despair and confusion of this loss has unconsciously dominated Betsy's life and kept her alienated from her infant feelings of loss and terror. I added that she might have experienced her subsequent bottle feeds as lifeless machines, to which she replied, ". . . and all the people giving them . . . Everything in my family has a formula, a structure for how to act, how to learn . . . everything . . . never any space in that structure for anything new or surprising." There was no room, I said, for *her*, a child suffering the effects of an unthinkable loss she could not remember.

Her series of abandonments contributed to the sense of falling into nothingness, which Betsy attempted to stop by turning into a machine. This "cure" instituted a fall into deadness which was in a way more deadly than the original trauma, for she was, as Tustin (1990a) described, ". . . a 'nothing' surrounded by 'nothingness'" (p. 111). These traumas supplant the truth in the mind and become solidified as reality. While I had often interpreted the traumatic loss of her mother, and a few times this loss of the breast, I sensed more access here to the machine-like deadness that took over. In the effort to find safety, her humanness had exploded into the eerie feeling of being an alien in a strange world, much like the one in *Endgame*.

I agreed that the rigid "structure" of her adoptive family's emotional detachment must have exacerbated her feelings of being a machine, lending support to the deadness in her mind. Betsy was not psychotic, but there were pockets of an encapsulated self with a very hard shell. Hard autistic objects are replaced here by the hardness of this aspect of the patient's own personality, a personality dominated by rigid ego functions of reason and intellect lacking access to more soft-edged aspects of feeling and a capacity to dream. Without a hospitable container for that dreaming function of the mind, Betsy was filled with the remnants of frozen feelings, and her parents, like Hamm's, were just the "litter" of unrecognizable feelings to a mind unable to dream. Betsy had experienced that frightening deadness in the last session. Paradoxically, in other words, she could feel the feeling of no feeling. Paradoxically, by becoming the deadness, she had experienced life, a moment of truth that could then be symbolized in the dream. Revisiting that deadness is at the heart of Tustin's idea of psychological birth, developing the capacity to dream the feelings of her buried self. Having had them witnessed and experienced by me made her able to be a witness to her own experience, a consciousness of self able now to be contained in her mind rather than dropping her into an endless darkness.

This capacity to dream is an essential prerequisite to the capacity to think, which includes the capacity for language. Beckett's relationship to language is interesting from this perspective.

In his novel, *Murphy*, Beckett wrote, "In the beginning was the pun," and in *Endgame* there are layers of puns. The names "Hamm", and "Clov" relate to animals—the cloven hoof or the spice used in ham—and the lack of emotional connection in these characters does render them less than human. There are more Biblical references here, for "Ham", as Noah's son, is also a fitting symbol for the flood of unthinkable emotions which can wipe out the whole world of the infant's mind as its contents overwhelm its container. Also, at the beginning of the play, Hamm is covered by a sheet, and a linen cloth covers his face. It has been suggested that this is a reference to the story of Lazarus where the dead are wrapped in linen, with a napkin covering the head anointed with spices and oil, adding another layer to the over determined symbol of "Clov". The ability to generate such diverse feelings and conjectures speaks to Beckett's instinctual openness to unconscious thought processes, which he stimulates in his audience. It speaks to his genius, if we consider Bion's (1970) description of genius as the ability to use one's psychotic [or primitive] thought processes, "in a manner adequate to promote growth or life (which is synonymous with growth)" (p. 63).

His ability to plumb the depths of his unconscious might be a remnant of Beckett's treatment with Bion, and his writings are a kind of analytic enterprise which includes the ability to inhabit or receive that level of inherent metaphysical, mystical knowledge which Bion associated with O. Beckett's characters are striving for essential existential truths, for a connection to a real sense of mental existence. Their tragedy is knowing that they have the potential for this level of human "being", but, lacking the equipment to realize this potential, they end up in that half human–half animal, or even half inanimate, state. This unmet potential is also the source of the humor and playfulness in Beckett's works, as hope and possibility collide with hopelessness, which is always either good for a laugh or a good cry. Beckett's humor walks the line between the two.

Since human beings can only aspire to ultimate consciousness, our limited hopes might be the best we can hope for. It is a sober perspective on mental integration as something that exists only in our attempts at intermittent consciousness. Bion was always reminding his audiences of the limits of our knowledge, and Beckett's genius, like his humor, lies in this same capacity to tolerate and express these flawed attempts to realize our human potential. As Bion (1970) pointed out, if we have minds at all, they are *in the process of becoming*, constantly compromised by our obstructions to this constant process of mental change and growth.

Like any good analyst, Beckett is a kind of mental tomb raider, descending to buried depths of the mind. Of course, he is not a psychoanalyst, but, like analysis, the Arts help us in ways we might not know, and do not necessarily need to know. Doing his work with the eye of the writer/infant/philosopher, Beckett transforms primitive despair and terror into something that enlightens the mind to think about those hidden depths.

We might say that if one is to develop an authentic, vital mind capable of thought and creativity, one must be possessed of some degree of intermittent genius, at least according to Bion's (1970) definition of "genius" described above (p. 18). The genius was also described as the "exceptional person" or "mystic" (p. 64). Lacking the capacity to access and contain one's primitive experiences, which is the basis of the capacity to think, what develops instead is mental illness, as aspects of the mind are deadened and overtaken by forces against life and growth. The rigid defenses against emotional contact, the psychic retreats, autistic and schizoid states, thought disorders, obsessions, compulsions, which we see in our patients and ourselves, are beautifully demonstrated in *Endgame*. Hamm's obsessive need to have his chair placed "exactly in the center" of the room, for instance, belies his desperate belief in the lie that this action will allay his terror. But, like most obsessions, it masks the primitive terror of not knowing how to find that enigmatic existential center of his self. Capable of access to those primitive feelings, the "genius" or "exceptional person" does not have to rely on actions to deny truth, for it is able to be contained in a *mental* "action", leading to life, rather than death, of the mind.

## *Summary and conclusions*

In any creative enterprise, it is contact with the child within that leads one to the source of creativity and genius. Picasso once said that it took him four years to paint like Raphael, but a lifetime to paint like a child. Similarly, when Beckett was asked why he wrote in French, he replied,"*Parce qu'en francaise c'est plus facile d'ecrire sans style.*"

("Because in French it is easier to write without style"). Without a style imposed by the ego, by external standards of good and bad, one is not *trying* to write in any particular way, one is simply writing or painting in much the way a small child does, an instinctual expression of "being". Like all great artists, Beckett attempted to find the child, the fresh untainted self beyond the one who had fallen into mental death in the unsatisfactory early relationship with his mother. Paradoxically, one begins this resurrection in that breakdown of, or breakthrough to, the painful confusion of unformed baby feelings, otherwise so scrupulously avoided. It is a search for something essential in the mind, that which Bion called O. For Beckett, writing in French seemed to be an effort to find his real "mother tongue" before the divorce from his mother and his self. Tustin, too, was looking for that child, able to connect, buried somewhere deep beyond the seeming impenetrability of autistic defenses, and, like Bion, she stressed primitive, sensory, and pre-verbal experiences as crucial precursors to the development of these higher aspects of thinking.

The struggle in *Endgame* between states of mental life and death are central to analytic work with patients. In each session, the analyst must make the subtle distinction between these forces that either facilitate or obstruct the patient's emotional contact, both with the analyst and with himself. Within what is often the nullification of non-being, the analyst must also recognize the sometimes subtle signs of life. We see it in Hamm's rare plea to Clov at the possibility of their separating—"Touch me, kiss me"—or in Clov's yearning, "I want to sing!", or simply in their determination, in the face of unbeatable odds, to figure out what the hell is happening to them. It is this great human gift of curiosity that impels us in the direction of truth, often elusive but not yet abandoned. Like these lost, pitiable characters, we often have to rely on the tiniest traces of hope and light to lead us—temporarily—out of the darkness.

I have given some thought to the direction of Beckett's work over the years, whether his literary grappling with these issues of mental life and death helped him to succeed in his own psychological struggle. There is certainly no guarantee of this. In fact, in some later plays, there seemed to be a steady slide *away* from feeling and further toward stasis and death. It is hard to assess whether his increasingly spare words and imagery is evidence of succumbing to that mental wasteland or a brave attempt to find and embrace whatever genuine, authentic reality remained in the wreckage of his mind. His increasingly spare images were often like visual poems, making them like dreams direct from his inner life, and so might have represented, as in analysis, a fall into the death of the self in order to reconnect with the life.

We are in a better position to access Beckett's role as an artist in society, for he has helped us, his audience, in our own struggles for truth. One goes to a Beckett play to have an experience of those dead spots in the mind which are so clearly delineated psychoanalytically by Tustin's work on autism—the sense of nothingness, terror, and despair—and the awareness which might help restore life to the mind. Beckett's plays are not exactly entertaining or fun, but they do provide an opportunity for an emotional experience of those pre-verbal "dreams" Tustin sought to illuminate in her patients. In his ability to contain the depths of these experiences along the autistic spectrum, Beckett also provides us evidence of his genius, a beneficial use of psychotic mechanisms to promote growth, health, and life. Schopenhauer gave another enlightening description of genius, saying, "Talent hits the target no one else can hit. Genius hits the target that no one else can see." Mental life in general cannot be seen, and the mental life of the infant or fetus lies further beyond representation, which is why we are so grateful for artists like Beckett, able to create forms for the formless through waking dreams such as these.

## *References*


Bair, D. (1978). *Samuel Beckett: A Biography*. New York: Harcourt Brace, Jovanovich.

Beckett, S. (1938). *Murphy*. New York, Grove Press, 1957.

Beckett, S. (1957). Endgame. In: *Endgame and Act Without Words*. New York: Grove Press, 1958.

Beckett, S. (1958). *The Unnameable*. New York: Grove Press.

Beckett, S. (1964). *How It Is*. New York: Grove Press.

Beckett, S. (1986a). *Waiting for Godot*. In: *The Complete Dramatic Works* (pp. 7–88). London: Faber and Faber, 1953.

Beckett, S. (1986b). *Happy Days*. In: *The Complete Dramatic Works* (pp. 135–168). London: Faber and Faber, 1961.

Beckett, S. (1986c). Play. In: *The Complete Dramatic Works* (pp. 305–320). London, Boston: Faber and Faber, 1962.

Beckett, S. (1986d). *A Piece of Monologue*. In: *The Complete Dramatic Works* (pp. 423–429). London: Faber and Faber, 1979.
Bion, F. (2011). Private communication.
Bion, W. R. (1970). *Attention And Interpretation*. London: Karnac.
Bion, W. R. (1978). Private communication.
Bion, W. R. (1982). *The Long Weekend*, F. Bion (Ed.). Abingdon: Fleetwood.
Bion, W. R. (1991). *Memoir of the Future*. London: Karnac.
Fairbairn, W. R. D. (1952). *An Object Relations Theory of the Personality*. New York: Basic Books.
Miller, I. S. (2013). *Beckett and Bion: The (Im)patient Voice in Psychotherapy and Literature*. London: Karnac.
Mitrani, J. (2001). Private communication.
Rank, O. (1929). *The Trauma of Birth*. New York: Dover Press, 1993.
Shakespeare, W. (1600). *Hamlet*. New York: Signet Classics, 1963.
Tustin, F. (1981). Psychological birth and psychological catastrophe. In: *Autistic Shapes in Children* (pp. 96–110). London: Routledge.
Tustin, F. (1984). Autistic shapes. *International Journal of Psychoanalysis, 11*(3): 279–290.
Tustin, F. (1986). *Autistic Barriers in Neurotic Patients*. London: Tavistock.
Tustin, F. (1988). The 'black hole': a significant element in autism. *Free Associations, 1*: 35–50.
Tustin, F. (1990a). The autistic capsule in neurotic adult patients. In: *The Protective Shell in Children and Adults* (pp. 97–121). London: Karnac.
Tustin, F. (1990b). What autism is and what autism is not. In: *The Protective Shell in Children and Adults* (pp. 1–32). London: Karnac.

*CHAPTER THIRTEEN*

# The autistic object, ethology, and neuroscience: a way to a Copernican revolution in the understanding of autistic spectrum disorders (ASD)?

*Paulo Duarte Guimarães Filho*

One of the interests manifested by the organizers of the 7th International Conference on the Work of Frances Tustin was on papers focusing on how Tustin's ideas (and their subsequent development by others (Tustin, 1980, 1984, 1986, 1992)) intersect with current biological and neuropsychological thinking. This chapter shows how Tustin's concept of the autistic object, which we consider one of her most fertile contributions in the clinical field, also has correlations in the neurobiological area which favor the recognition of how psychological factors participate in the determination of some forms of ASD. The symptoms of ASD are well defined, but there is a great variation in the manner and intensity in which they appear, from which arises the notion of a spectrum of disorders. An important piece of information is that recent studies have shown an increase in the atypical cases of ASD, or those that in *DSM-IV* are labelled as NOS (Not Otherwise Specified) (Fombonne, 2007; Towbin, 2005). In contrast, advances in neurosciences have led to the identification of brain abnormalities in several of these patients (an informative example is the work by Courchesne et al., 2005). Likewise, genetic studies demonstrate the participation of a genetic component in several of these cases (Rutter, 2005). This has led to the widely accepted view that ASD would have a predominantly neurologic and genetic etiology. While the presence of these kinds of alterations in many ASD cases is clear, and despite the fact that empirical evidence is already available demonstrating that genetic vulnerability might be less important than environmental factors (e.g., Hallmayer et al., 2011), it must be noted that the existence of neurological and genetic components tend to lead to a lack of acknowledgment, and appropriate investigation, of the role that psychological experiences could have as causal or contributing factors to ASD.

To examine how Tustin's concept of the autistic object in particular may serve as one of the bases for changes in the prevailing system of conceptions about ASD, we must start by examining the proximity of the autistic object with ethological observations of animals who do not have any contact with others from the same species during a specific period in the beginning of life ("critical period") and establish a bizarre and intense connection to certain objects or stimuli, in lieu of recognizing the members of their species. Here, there are already similarities with what Tustin identified as the autistic object, but before addressing more about that, we must say that the observation referred to above involves the phenomenon known as "imprinting". Such phenomenon consists in a period, at the beginning of life, which has been denominated sensitive or critical, during which an adequate contact with other beings of the same species is necessary so that they can be recognized as fellow creatures and develop an appropriate relationship with them. We can have a very concrete notion of this phenomenon by recalling its discovery by Lorenz (1970). He verified that young geese without contact with other geese after birth, and having only contact with him, came to relate to Lorenz as if he were a goose, at the same time not recognizing real geese as such. More important, with regard to ASD and showing great resemblance with Tustin's autistic object, is that if the young geese were left in a cage with only a piece of wood, instead of having contact with other geese or with Lorenz, they came to treat that piece of wood as another goose, again failing to recognize real geese as such (Lorenz, 1970). Situations of this type were subsequently widely reproduced with other animal species and different stimuli (Sluckin, 1964).

The parallel between these manifestations and those found in autistic patients is remarkable and could be acknowledged taking into account Tustin's concept of the autistic object. This fact has led us to develop a hypothesis regarding the participation of a distortion of imprinting in determining autistic states (Guimarães Filho, 1990, 1991, 1996, 2008). In the present work, we suggest some changes to this hypothesis, so as to include it in a broader proposal of ASD as disorders of the social brain, as we will discuss below. It should also be explained that the relationships of the distortion of imprinting with the autistic object does not configure as a permanence of the same original object, but as a much more varied and complex phenomenon that can only be better accompanied through clinical situations, as was studied in the above mentioned papers (Guimarães Filho, 1990, 1991, 1996, 2008).

Regarding that hypothesis, it should be said that it is not just complete deprivation of contact that can lead to a disconnection of the autistic type, but that early difficulties in interpersonal relationships can also favour the substitution of personal ties by other concrete stimuli, or those that have been called, in other study contexts, as "non-social objects" (Muratori & Maestro, 2007), similar to what happens in the distortion of imprinting in animals. Although it is very difficult to verify, with a degree of certainty, that a substitution of this nature has been determinant in a specific case of autistic detachment, there is an area of research that provides important data in this respect. These studies have been carried out on films made by relatives of children who later present autistic symptoms. In one such study, Muratori and Maestro (2007) examined not only social attention, as is usual in this kind of research, but also what they called non-social attention. They considered two observations to be of great importance, made during the first year of life, as follows:

> The first consists of the decrease, during the second semester of life, in differences between children later diagnosed with autism and typical children as far as attention to social stimuli are concerned. The other finding consists of the increase in behaviors regarding attention to non-social stimuli, which is present in both groups but is more evident in infants with autism, so that by the end of the first year these children are significantly more attracted by objects compared to typical children, whose social attention always remain at a higher level. (p. 57)

As we have just observed, the emergence in the psychoanalytical area of the concept of the autistic object by Tustin (1980) allowed visualization of the similarity between these and the distortion of the imprinting in animals. We already have here a very clear indication of how the structural and functional development of the brain depends on appropriate psychological experiences. Along with these observations, there are also other clinical observations in human beings and experimental situations in animals in which psychological or environmental factors would have led to autistic manifestation, therefore not supporting the hypothesis that autistic manifestations are limited to neurologic or genetic determination. In these clinical situations and animal experiments, the participants had little or almost no contact with other members of the same species in the beginning of life, and, after this initial period, displayed manifestations similar to those found in autism. The main reason for choosing these examples is that they show, in a well-defined manner, relationships between psychological or environmental factors followed by manifestations with autistic characteristics. Thus, examining situations where one can see a clear nexus between psychological factors and manifestations with autistic characteristics help us to see, as mentioned above, that genetic and neurological factors might not be exclusively responsible for ASD. Considering these elements, we suggest that these manifestations can be more consistently understood if they are seen as disturbances of what has been called the "social brain"—the functional and structural cerebral systems that play a significant role in establishing and developing interpersonal relationships (Johnson et al., 2005). The importance of this is that the social brain is not only an anatomical structure, but also a functional one; the anatomical structure only develops appropriately if a basic psychological relationship exists during a certain period at the beginning of life (Schore, 1994; Tucker, 1992), as already seen in regard to imprinting. Also mentioned is the importance of the "critical" or "sensitive" period (Rauschecker & Marler, 1987; Schore, 1994). Based on these data, which had their meaning clarified from the concept of autistic object by Tustin, we can suggest a kind of Copernican revolution in this area if, instead of placing genetic–neurological autism in the centre of a system, we put the notion of a social brain and the different kinds of disturbances that can affect it during the critical phase when it is being structured. Such a change would make it easier to understand how different factors, not only genetics, epigenetics, and other organic pathologies, but also psychological experiences, especially significant deprivation, or trauma, could lead to manifestations with autistic characteristics (Kraemer, 1985; Reid, 1999; Rutter et al., 1999).

For proper knowledge of some data that provide grounds for this hypothesis, we also present studies on children from Romanian orphanages adopted in the UK with a high degree of autistic manifestations; alongside that, we examine data on the syndrome of monkeys raised in isolation which also developed autistiform symptoms.

## *Study of Romanian children*

We have a very significant example suggesting that psychological factors are linked to the high occurrence of autistic manifestations in 116 children from Romanian orphanages adopted by British families. When these children arrived in the UK, Rutter and colleagues (1999) verified that eleven of them presented symptoms of an autistic nature that were indistinguishable from typical autism. Two years later, another evaluation revealed that two of these children still had symptoms compatible with typical autism, while another seven had experienced improvements that do not usually happen in typical cases and were designated by the authors as "autistic-like". These seven children continued to have some symptoms, mainly inadequate social contact, while one of them came to improve from the autistic disorder in an unusual manner, as described in the paper.

The division between typical autism and "autistic-like" established by the authors in these cases is valid as long it is understood as a possible classification based on a certain scientific hypothesis about ASD, as was considered at the beginning of this chapter. This hypothesis places genetic and neurological-based autism at the centre of a system, hence the "typical" designation. In this sense, the evolution observed among the Romanian children would have an unspecific character, hence the term "autistic-like". The alternative hypothesis we are proposing in this chapter is that the system of social brain disturbances be considered whereby there would be no typical or "autistic-like" autism, but different causes of ASD provoking alterations in the social brain and leading to clinical entities with some differences among them. According to this hypothesis, bearing in mind that it still needs to be much more investigated, the manifestations of the Romanian children would not be considered unspecific, but as a modality within the ASD, one that indicates the participation of psychological factors in its determination.

A psychological view helps to highlight the role of environmental factors as possible determinants of these cases and the recognition of their specificity, as seen above. It can also contribute by, for example, highlighting the relevance of investigating structural cerebral alterations among children coming from the Romanian orphanages. In one of these studies, carried out by Mehta and colleagues (2009), fourteen children were submitted to magnetic resonance imaging to examine the amygdala, hippocampus, and corpus callosum, and significant morphological alterations were found. In this case, a psychological view helps to identify important data that have not been included in the research. As we mentioned, the Rutter and colleagues' (1999) study found a group of eleven children, of the total of 116, with manifestations more characteristically autistic, of which seven were designated "autistic-like" and two as typically autistic. This is a small group and, therefore, cannot lead to conclusive data, but an investigation of this specific group with magnetic resonance, or other techniques, would be very important in order to verify the hypothesis suggested in this chapter, that psychological deprivation experienced by children can lead not only to manifestations with autistic characteristics, but could also cause alterations in social brain structures. If this hypothesis were confirmed, there would also be the possibility of comparing the nature of the alterations that could be found in this group with those that are already being described in cases of autism in the literature, such as the aforementioned informative example by Courchesne and colleagues (2005).

## *Syndrome of monkeys raised in isolation*

A series of experiments have been conducted on monkeys kept in complete isolation from other monkeys for prolonged periods soon after birth (Harlow et al., 1965; Sackett, 1972; Sackett et al., 1976). As a result, a series of disturbances were observed, when the isolation was interrupted, including self-orality, huddling, self-clasping, stereotypies, and social interaction impairment (Sackett, 1972). The parallel between these manifestations and autism is so significant that some authors have already pointed out the similarity (Kandel, 2006; Sackett et al., 1976; Winslow, 2005) and it is worth citing Kandel (2006), a Nobel laureate in medicine, regarding Harlow's work with these animals:

> He found that when newborn monkeys were isolated for six months to one year and then returned to the company of other monkeys, they were physically healthy but behaviorally devastated. They crouched in a corner of their cages and rocked back and forth, *like severely disturbed or autistic children*. They did not interact with other monkeys, nor did they fight, play or show any sexual interest. Isolation of an older animal for a comparable period was innocuous. Thus, in monkeys, as in humans, there is a critical period for social development. (p. 373, my italics)

Despite recognizing the parallels, as mentioned above, the autistiform manifestations of the isolated monkeys did not lead to research focused on cerebral alterations in these isolated monkeys to compare them with those alterations found in ASD. It is likely that this scientific gap also relates to a notion of autism as a predominantly genetic–neurological condition. Thus, evidence in a concrete situation, such as that of monkeys raised in isolation, indicative of a psychological or environmental determination of manifestations with autistic characteristics, has not been recognized and investigated. A significant example of this was a proposal made by Kraemer (1985). This author started with relatively simple, well-known observations in the medical area, on alterations in cerebral structures caused by early sight deprivation (Garey et al., 1979; Hubel, 1978). With these in mind, Kraemer (1985) suggested that the early deprivation of social relationships in monkeys (the kind of "social blindness" to which they were submitted) could provoke similar alterations in the cerebral structures linked to these functions, which could be a privileged research route for what would come to be known as the social brain. We did not find references in literature that Kraemer's proposal was realized. This could be due to the interruption of the study of isolated monkeys for ethical reasons. Yet, it is also very significant that it has not been thought, regarding Kraemer's suggestion, that alongside the mapping of the social brain, the study of the cerebral alterations of monkeys raised in isolation could also lead to the discovery of cerebral alterations associated with the autistiform manifestations found in these animals. This comprises what could be considered a true animal model of ASD, in cases provoked by environmental circumstances and, to repeat, it is entirely surprising that investigations in this direction have not been carried out.

Despite the fact that Kraemer's (1985) proposal has not been realized, we can obtain valuable information from other kinds of work, considering what happens in the brains of monkeys raised in isolation, which can be compared to those alterations found among autistic patients. However, such studies are also very few in number. The most significant I could find was conducted by Sánchez and colleagues (1998), who studied the brains of these animals using magnetic resonance, correlated with an evaluation of their cognitive functions. Alterations in the medial and posterior corpus callosum were found, as were positive correlations with the results of cognitive function tests carried out on these animals. The authors cited papers referring to similar alterations in the corpus callosum of autistic children (Piven et al., 1997), but did not consider these correlations in a broader way. We were also unable to find references to subsequent investigations along the same line. This led to Sánchez and co-writers (2001) only citing briefly the previous paper (Sánchez et al.,1998) in their study of the effects of early adverse experiences on the brains of monkeys and rodents, with no apparent interest in an investigation of the possible relationships between the autistiform manifestations of those animals and ASD. This is similar to what happened with Martin and colleagues (1991), in a publication presented as the first part of an immuno-histochemical study of the sub-cortical regions of monkeys raised in isolation, indicating that a second part, examining the cortical regions, would follow. Again, I was unable to find it in the literature.

It is not difficult to recognize the importance of, and motive for, highlighting a comparative study, especially between the anatomo-pathological alterations found in autistic patients, mainly using recently developed techniques (Courchesne et al., 2005), and what happens in the brains of monkeys raised in isolation. This comparison could add something important to the parallels that are present in the clinical area. The point of relevance is that the "social blindness" experienced by the monkeys could have led to profound alterations in their brain structures. The suspension of studies on monkeys in isolation has made this information virtually impossible to obtain. However, due to its importance, it is worthwhile inquiring whether anatomo-pathological samples of the brains of these animals are still accessible, and, if so, whether they can be studied using the new techniques mentioned above (Courchesne et al., 2005).

There is one more aspect to this issue that should be mentioned. Because of the ethical objections to the study of monkeys raised in isolation, investigations are once again being undertaken on the cerebral alterations of animals raised, not in isolation, but having periods of contact only with other young monkeys. One of these is the paper by Winslow (2005). Although he recognizes the parallels between the manifestations shown by isolated monkeys and the autistic symptoms, and especially those referred to by Rutter et al. (1999) regarding the Romanian children, his paper was published after the suspension of research of monkeys raised in absolute isolation, so that he did not make a deeper study of the relationship with these cases. In fact, his investigation is restricted to what happens with the neuropeptides that are mobilized during affective–social experiences in monkeys that live only with other young monkeys in the beginning of their lives. Another work, by Spinelli and colleagues (2009), was also conducted with monkeys under the same kind of partial isolation. It is very significant that equally in these animals cerebral alterations were found on the structural and functional levels. However, a differentiation must be made that was not duly considered in these studies: the monkeys raised early only with other young monkeys gave indications of having especially traumatic experiences due to not having their needs suitably attended by older monkeys. In fact, their symptoms are more of the post-traumatic type, not with the autistic characteristics that were seen in monkeys that had been subjected to total isolation.

## *Some considerations and two clinical examples*

The lost opportunities of increasing our knowledge about autism, as described above, have been associated with very concrete opposition to the psychoanalytic treatment of ASD patients. Unfortunately, this combines with a lack of information on how is the psychoanalytic work in this area and of the advances that have been achieved in it. Because of this situation, I consider it important to present two clinical fragments that give concrete examples of the value of psychoanalysis for such patients, and that can also illustrate, in a more vivid manner, some of the issues presented in this chapter. I chose two patients at the opposite ends of the so-called autistic spectrum. The first could correspond to a case of "Autistic post-traumatic developmental disorder" (APTDD), as proposed by Reid (1999). It also makes very clear the participation of psychological factors in the determination of the clinical diagnosis and can serve to consider issues in respect of this. The other case comprises typical autism, allowing us to follow some of the contributions made using the psychoanalytic approach and the rewards they can bring.

## *André*

The first child was seen by my colleague, Janete Mizerkowski Torres, a pediatrician and psychoanalyst, who authorized the publication of this material. I followed her psychoanalytical work with this patient for some time and it was also presented at the "Grupo de Estudos e Investigação dos Transtornos Globais do Desenvolvimento" (Pervasive Developmental Disorder Research and Study Group) we coordinated at the Brazilian Psychoanalytic Society of São Paulo (SBPSP). André, the patient, began treatment at the age of two and a half. According to the parents, and to films the analyst came to watch, André was developing well until the age of one and a half, beginning to say "daddy" and "mummy" and maintaining adequate affective contact. Due to health problems, he underwent a surgical procedure soon after birth and was subjected to examinations every six months. He was afraid of these exams, but, at the age of one and a half, his reaction was very intense, with severe anxiety and disorganization, actually preventing the exam from being carried out. After this, he developed manifestations of intense terror from contact with people in general, accepting only the parents and normally clinging to the mother, as well as stopping his speech development and spending a lot of time watching films on television. There is one interesting fact, which is that, even during the initial period, where he showed no signs of disturbances, he very much liked holding certain objects and this intensified markedly after the traumatic experience at the age of one and a half.

I shall refer only briefly to some events in the analysis. It took a few weeks for the analyst gradually to try to make contact with André, who remained in the safety of the mother's lap. The analyst would bring toys and place them near him, telling the patient what she was doing and carefully inviting the child to interact, until he also began slowly to accept the contact. One point of interest in terms of what is being seen in this paper is that this approximation took place with intermittent phases of André withdrawing and, at times, holding some wooden pieces from the toy box. The toy box also contained wooden toys featuring faces and, as the patient got closer to the analyst, accepting her more, his holding of the wooden items continued, but with the toys that featured faces. I shall refrain from a detailed look at what could be considered regarding this change and, although it seems quite clear that this child did not have a predominant link with an autistic object, there are indications that he would go in that direction at times, without, however, becoming fixated on such objects. The possibility of having a link with the analyst as a person in whom he found a holding function certainly contributed to what Muratori and Maestro (2007) termed as ties with "social objects" prevailing over the "non-social" ones. This brief analytic experience serves in particular to provide clear demonstrations that we are not faced with an exclusively "neurological disease" with a fundamentally organic course, and to show how this course can have something to do with the nature of psychological experiences. Even with the other child, diagnosed with typical autism, we will see events in the same direction.

Continuing with André, there was another event that could contribute to further our understanding. While still at the initial stages of contact with the analyst, when he would only utter inarticulate and incomprehensible sounds, one of his first games, which was repeated often, was to take a small toy horse and move to the edge of the table, and then let it fall, saying "help . . . help . . .". The mother explained that André often watched a film in which a cowboy would fall off a cliff with his horse, crying for help. Here, it is interesting to consider how a child who had yet to develop language as a system of signs capable of conceptually representing experiences seems to have an apprehension at only the iconic level: that is, he could probably make a connection between the elements of similarity represented by the cowboy's fall and cry for help with his traumatic experiences of the medical exams without having somebody to appeal to, but now he could have the analyst as someone to whom he could communicate his anguish. In summary, we can think that the traumatic experiences André lived through have provoked disturbances, including at the level of his social brain. All this affected his emotional and communicative relationships, even causing moments of withdrawal to an autistic object, albeit not to a very intense degree. These not very intense aspects of his symptoms certainly contributed to his being able to use the analyst's holding and to have progress, as shown in these small fragments, which were subsequently expanded in the course of his analysis.

## *K*

The other clinical fragment is of a child with very typical autistic symptoms and, as with the case of André, the intent is not to present all the case, but only some elements that have related to other points raised before. I began the treatment of K at the age of two and a half. His parents' account was that he developed well over the first six months, establishing visual contact, smiling, and starting to babble "papa" and "mama". When K was four months, the mother's parents fell ill and came to live with the family, which meant that, as they did not have a maid, she was left with little time to care for K, who would be left in a playpen to entertain himself with some toys and child magazines. The father worked and cared for K when at home. At around six months, they began to notice that he would no longer establish contact, did not continue verbalizing, and would spend most of his time handling toys, or building blocks, or watching films and looking at magazines. When going out, the blocks had to be brought along to calm K down. Some months ago, he began going to a nursery and, on his first day, K showed interest in a slide, but did not react when the mother left. At the nursery, K had more interest in objects and did not interact with other children. The patient came with the entire family for the initial interview and did not establish eye contact with me or with the relatives who came with him. Most of the time his activities had autistic characteristics, such as laying small toy animals or wooden blocks in lines, often repeating these arrangements or wandering around the room.

We can think that K is at a different end of the autistic spectrum compared to André, and our interest is in seeing some facets of these two distinct situations. Regarding the anamnestic data, it is not possible to distinguish if the patient had a primordial organic disturbance, or if the human contact limitations, around four months, could have favoured a link with predominantly non-social objects, as described by Muratori and Maestro (2007). It is very interesting to consider that, if it had been either alternative, the clinical signs that appeared were in the sense of there having been an impairment in K's social brain. This hypothesis can be made due to the fact that his bizarre and repetitive attachment was with concrete autistic objects, instead of people. I will not go into detail on how the psychoanalytic work went with this patient, but only state that I sought to detect the small interests showed by K, trying to explore them and guide the parents, who also participated in the sessions, in this same direction,. How this took place can be exemplified by an occasion in which K used a small wooden cylinder to make a drinking gesture. This was verbalized to the patient, a real glass of water was brought for him, with commentaries about all this. In subsequent sessions, I returned to using the wooden cylinder to represent drinking water, also offering it to the parents and myself, which he understood and went along with. In a situation like this, it is possible to verify that, despite K having clear signs of severe autistic disabilities and probable impairment in social brain structures, it did not imply the non-preservation of functioning of some of its areas or that they could have some degree of recovery, probably with the participation of cerebral plasticity. The recognition of these elements helped in choosing a suitable psychotherapeutic approach for the patient and for the parents' participation in the treatment. In this direction it was very important to use the points of interest that sometimes arose in K and seek to explore them, as was the case with the water.

One of these interests, gradually developed, was that I began to draw simple animals that were objects of K's attention, such as the "woof-woof" and the "tweet-tweet". Gradually we increased this activity, with the father's participation in the sessions and later at home. The father began to draw faces for K to complete, for example, drawing the eyes. In one of the sessions, the father tried with one of these drawings, but K refused, saying "woopeck", which the father explained was a woodpecker from a magazine that K really liked and would ask the father to draw. As we talked, K drew one of these "woopecks", in a simplistic fashion, but which was nevertheless recognizable. At the same time, the father showed me the drawing he was making of the woodpecker, which surprised me due to its esthetic strokes and led me to think how this factor probably participated in K's mobilization. It can be seen that the fundamental point of all this is how these focal interests, especially with autistic and non-social objects, opened up bridges for personal links, with me and the father, playing a role in this the use of representative and communicative instruments, such as the drawn image and naming of objects of interest: "woof-woof", "tweet-tweet", "woopeck", etc. In pointing out these events, it should be noted that, especially during this stage, these were moments where K's functioning was still very limited and he continued predominantly with autistic characteristics, although gradually he was making other achievements.

The presentation of these clinical fragments is intended simply as a limited complement to the central point of this work: the contributions that can be obtained from articulation of a psychological view, associated with those of neuroscience and ethology. What these cases may also demonstrate is that attending in treatment to the social brain and the psychological components of its development might lead to evidence of some degree of improvement of the autistic condition. In concluding this presentation, it must be stressed that, perhaps, the main contribution of Tustin's autistic object to a psychoanalytical view, articulated with those of neuroscience and ethology, is to throw a light on the psychological elements that participate as one of the complex factors present in the variety of ASD and that have been under some kind of shadow, produced by genetic–neurological buildings. One of the most fundamental consequences of this clarification has been seeing ASD as disturbances of social brain functioning, due to different causes and taking place at distinct levels of impairment. The development of this notion, this Copernican revolution, opens up space to consider whether this new system, with the social brain at its centre, could be considered more appropriate for the understanding of, and approach to, the variety of ASD.

## *References*

Courchesne, E., Redcay, E., Morgan, J. T., & Kennedy, D. P. (2005). Autism at the beginning: microstructural and growth abnormalities underlying the cognitive and behavioral phenotype of autism. *Development and Psychopathology, 17*: 572–597.

Fombonne, E. (2007). Epidemiology of pervasive developmental disorders. In: J. M. Pérez, P. M. González, M. L. Comi, & C. Nieto (Eds.), *New Developments in Autism: The Future Is Today* (pp. 14–32). London: Jessica Kingsley.

Garey, L. J., Blakemore, C., & Vital-Durand, F. (1979). Visual deprivation in monkeys: its effects and reversal. *Progress in Brain Research, 51*: 445–456.

Guimarães Filho, P. D. (1990). A hypothesis about the determining process of autistic states. *International Journal of Psychoanalysis, 71*: 393–402.

Guimarães Filho, P. D. (1991). Developments of a hypothesis about autism and its application to a clinical case. Presented to the 37th IPA Congress, Buenos Aires.

Guimarães Filho, P. D. (1996). On autistic object: new ideas and some of its theoretical and clinical implications. Panel of II Latin American Psychoanalytical Congress of Children and Adolescents, São Paulo, Brazil.

Guimarães Filho, P. D. (2008). Psychological and neurological research of autistic spectrum disorders: challenging issues. Presented to IPA Joseph Sandler Conference, Frankfurt.

Hallmayer, J., Cleveland, S., Torres, A., Phillips, J., Cohen, B., Torigoe, T., Miller, J., Fedele, A., Collins, J., Smith, K., Lotspeich, L., Croen, L. A., Ozonoff, S., Lajonchere, C., Grether, J. K., & Risch, N. (2011). Genetic heritability and shared environmental factors among twin pairs with autism. *Archives of General Psychiatry, 68*(11): 1095–1102. doi: 10.1001/archgenpsychiatry.2011.76

Harlow, H. F., Dodsworth, R. O., & Harlow, M. K. (1965). Total isolation in monkeys. *Proceedings of the National Academy of Science, 54*: 90–97.

Hubel, D. H. (1978). Effects of deprivation on the early visual cortex of cat and monkey. *Harvey Lectures, 72*: 1–51.

Johnson, M. H., Griffin, R., Csibra, G., Halit, H., Farroni, T., De Haan, M., Tucker, L. A., Baron-Cohen, S., & Richards, J. (2005). The emergence of the social brain network: evidence from typical and atypical development. *Development and Psychopathology, 17*: 599–619.

Kandel, E. R. (2006). *In Search of Memory: The Emergence of a New Science of Mind*. New York: W. W. Norton.

Kraemer, G. W. (1985). Effects of differences in early social experience on primate neurobiological–behavioral development. In: M. Reite & T. Field (Eds.), *The Psychobiology of Attachment and Separation* (pp. 135–161). Orlando, FL: Academic Press.

Lorenz, K. (1970). *Studies in Animal and Human Behavior*. Cambridge, MA: Harvard University Press.

Martin, L. J., Spicer, D. M., Lewis, M. H., Gluck, J. P., & Cork, L. C. (1991). Social deprivation of infant rhesus monkeys alters the chemoarchitecture of the brain: I. subcortical regions. *Journal of Neuroscience, 11*(11): 3344–3358.

Mehta, M. A., Golembo, N. I., Nosarti, C., Colvert, E., Mota, A., William, S. C., Rutter, M., & Sonuga-Barke, E. J. (2009). Amygdala, hippocampal and corpus callosum size following severe early institutional deprivation: the English and Romanian adoptees study pilot. *Journal of Child Psychology and Psychiatry, 50*(8): 943–951.

Muratori, F., & Maestro, S. (2007). Early signs of autism in the first year of life. In: S. Acquarone (Ed.), *Signs of Autism in Infants: Recognition and Early Intervention* (pp. 46–62). London: Karnac.

Piven, J., Bailey, J., Bonnie, J. R., & Arndt, S. (1997). An MRI study of corpus callosum in autism. *American Journal of Psychiatry, 154*: 1051–1056.

Rauschecker, J. P., & Marler, P. (1987). Cortical plasticity and imprinting: behavioral and physiological contrasts and parallels. In: J. P. Rauschecker & P. Marler (Eds.), *Imprinting and Cortical Plasticity: Comparative Aspects of Sensitive Periods* (pp. 349–356). New York: Wiley.

Reid, S. (1999). Autism and trauma: autistic post-traumatic developmental disorder. In: A. Alvarez & S. Reid (Eds.), *Autism and Personality* (pp. 93–109). London: Routledge.

Rutter, M. (2005). Genetic influences and autism. In: F. R. Volkmar, R. Paul, A. Klin, & D. Cohen (Eds.), *Handbook of Autism and Pervasive Developmental Disorders* (pp. 425–452). Hoboken, NJ: Wiley.

Rutter, M., Andersen-Wood, L., Beckett, C., Bredenkampf, D., Castle, J., Groothues, C., Kreppner, J., Keaveney, L., Lord, C., O'Connor, T. G., & ERA Study Team (1999). Quasi-autistic patterns following severe early global privation. *Journal of Child Psychology and Psychiatry, 40*(4): 537–549.

Sackett, G. P. (1972). Isolation rearing in monkeys: diffuse and specific effects on later behavior. In: *Colloques Internationaux du C. N. R. S., 198. Models Animaux du Comportement Humain* (pp. 61–110). Paris: Ed. Du Centre Nationale De La Recherche Scientifique.

Sackett, G. P., Holm, R. A., & Ruppenthal, G. C. (1976). Social isolation rearing: species differences in behavior of macaque monkeys. *Developmental Psychology, 12*(4): 283–288.

Sánchez, M. M., Hearn, F. H., Do, D., Rilling, J. K., & Herndon, J. G. (1998). Differential rearing affects corpus callosum size and cognitive function of rhesus monkeys. *Brain Research, 812*: 38–49.

Sánchez, M. M., Ladd, C. O., & Plotsky, P. M. (2001). Early adverse experience as a developmental risk factor for later psychopathology: evidence from rodent and primates models. *Development and Psychopathology, 13*: 419–449.

Schore, A. N. (1994). *Affect Regulation and the Origin of the Self.* Hillsdale, NJ: Lawrence Erlbaum.

Sluckin, W. (1964). *Imprinting and Early Learning*. London: Methuen.

Spinelli, S., Chefer, S., Suomi, S. J., Higley, J. D., Barr, C. S., & Stei, E. (2009). Early-life stress induces long-term morphologic changes in primate brain. *Archives of General Psychiatry, 66*(6): 658–665.

Towbin, K. E. (2005). Pervasive developmental disorder not otherwise specified. In: F. R. Volkmar, R. Paul, A. Klin, & D. Cohen (Eds.), *Handbook of Autism and Pervasive Developmental Disorders* (pp. 165–200). Hoboken, NJ: Wiley.

Tucker, D. M. (1992). Developing emotions and neural networks. In: M. R. Gunnar & C. A. Nelson (Eds.), *Minnesota Symposium on Child Psychology* (pp. 75–128). Hillsdale, NJ: Lawrence Erlbaum.

Tustin, F. (1980). Autistic objects. *International Review of Psychoanalysis, 7*: 27–39.

Tustin, F. (1984). Autistic shapes. *International Review of Psychoanalysis, 11*: 279–289.

Tustin, F. (1986). *Autistic Barriers in Neurotic Patients*. London: Karnac.

Tustin, F. (1992). *Autistic States in Children*. London: Routledge.

Winslow, J. T. (2005). Neuropeptides and non-human primate social deficits associated with pathogenic rearing experience. *International Journal of Developmental Neuroscience, 23*: 245–251.

# INDEX

For Product Safety Concerns and Information please contact our EU representative GPSR@taylorandfrancis.com
Taylor & Francis Verlag GmbH, Kaufingerstraße 24, 80331 München, Germany

www.ingramcontent.com/pod-product-compliance
Ingram Content Group UK Ltd.
Pitfield, Milton Keynes, MK11 3LW, UK
UKHW022205190926
475702UK00003B/211
* 9 7 8 0 3 6 7 3 2 4 3 4 6 *